(DIS)FIGURATIONS

PHRONESIS

A series from Verso edited by
Ernesto Laclau and Chantal Mouffe

Since 1989, when the first Phronesis book was published, many events of fundamental importance to the series have taken place. Some of them initially brought the hope that great possibilities were opening up for the extension and deepening of democracy, one of the main points of focus in our reflections. Disenchantment, however, came quickly and what we witnessed instead was the reinforcement and generalization of the neoliberal hegemony. Today, the left-wing project is in an even deeper crisis than it was ten years ago. An increasing number of social-democratic parties, under the pretence of 'modernizing' themselves, are discarding their Left identity. According to the advocates of the 'third way', and with the advent of globalization, the time has come to abandon the old dogmas of Left and Right and promote a new entrepreneurial spirit at all levels of society.

Phronesis's objective is to establish a dialogue among all those who assert the need to redefine the Left/Right distinction—which constitutes the crucial dynamic of modern democracy—instead of relinquishing it. Our original concern, which was to bring together left-wing politics and the theoretical developments around the critique of essentialism, is more pertinent than ever. Indeed, we still believe that the most important trends in contemporary theory—deconstruction, psychoanalysis, the philosophy of language as initiated by the later Wittgenstein and post-Heideggerian hermeneutics—are the necessary conditions for understanding the widening of social struggles characteristic of the present stage of democratic politics, and for formulating a new vision for the Left in terms of radical and plural democracy.

(DIS)FIGURATIONS
DISCOURSE/CRITIQUE/ETHICS

IAN ANGUS

VERSO
London • New York

First published by Verso 2000
© Ian Angus 2000
All rights reserved

The moral rights of the author have been asserted

Verso
UK: 6 Meard Street, London W1V 3HR
US: 180 Varick Street, New York, NY 10014–4606

Verso is the imprint of New Left Books

ISBN 1–85984–759–5
ISBN 1–85984–277–1 (pbk)

British Library Cataloguing in Publication Data
A catalogue record for this book is available from the British Library

Library of Congress Cataloging-in-Publication Data
A catalog record for this book is available from the Library of Congress

Typeset by M Rules in 11pt Garamond
Printed by Biddles Ltd, Guildford and King's Lynn

for Viviana

CONTENTS

Acknowledgements   ix

Preface   xi

1   Disfiguring   1

2   Constitutive Paradox   28

3   The Rebound to Contingency   51

4   Epochal Criticism   92

5   Reconstructing Democracy in the Media Environment   129

6   Ethics at the End of Philosophy   154

7   Beyond Gnoseology   184

8   Critique of General Rhetoric   214

9   The Epoch of Disembodied Signs   256

Index   265

ACKNOWLEDGEMENTS

I would like to thank the following journals and publishers for permission to use revised selections from material previously published in an earlier form: *Argumentation; Continuum: Australian Journal of Media and Culture; The Critical Turn: Rhetoric and Philosophy in Postmodern Discourse* (Southern Illinois University Press, 1993); *Ethnicity in a Technological Age* (Canadian Institute of Ukrainian Studies, 1988); *After Postmodernism: Reconstructing Ideology Critique* (Sage, 1994); *Viewing, Reading, Listening: Audiences and Cultural Reception* (Westview Press, 1994); *Communication Yearbook 15* (Sage, 1992).

PREFACE

The following reflexions engage a complex of issues in contemporary social and political philosophy that have arisen, or taken on new urgency, with the shift toward discourse as the central metaphor for social life. This shift has enabled new formulations of the project of modernity and its limitations. The concept of critique, the self-constitution of the critic, ethical legitimation of critique, the project of radical democracy: all, I argue, depend upon the discovery of a still-point, an opening, by philosophy. It is the social vocation of philosophy to insinuate this opening into the apertures where enlightenments may occur. Such insinuations require a preliminary dis-figuring, or pulling apart, of figures that have emerged from articulated connexions but have congealed into common sense.

The argument of the text draws on the whole tradition of phenomenology in dialogue with the political concerns of the Frankfurt School, post-Marxism and radical democracy. It attempts to sustain two different tasks: a Heideggerian sense of the institution of historical epochs and a Gramscian justification of interventions in the construction of common sense within a given epoch. The space of classical modern philosophy was defined by a continuous passage from common sense to epoch through the unfolding of the concept which was given its classic formation in Hegel's philosophy as the *Aufhebung*. The postmodern condition is the loss of this passage and a consequent tendency for these two tasks to be collapsed in one direction or the other. Debates about postmodernity have thus tended to be polarized between either totality or plurality. This description avoids such a counterposing and consequently discovers a new open space for theoretical discourse.

This new space is explored through the constitution of social relations within the sites of inscription that are inherent in language use. Such a focus on social constitution can be generalized from language itself, as a consequence of its metaphorical status, and applied to all forms of expression and communication. Communication, in this sense, is of the order of a primal scene that originates a complex of social relations. Philosophy provides the opening that can turn the general rhetoric unloosed by this plurality of discourses into an ethical opening to the other upon which the responsibility of critique depends.

1

DISFIGURING

Bringing one's own situation and time to thought in a manner that
engenders criticism of the social formation as a whole is a difficult
enough project, but to undertake this task of ideology-critique at
a historical moment which understands itself—in however mediated, insufficient or exaggerated a manner—as the end of a
historical epoch and, perhaps, as the beginning of something new
poses even more fundamental tasks. These tasks refer not only to
the social formation which is the object of knowledge, critique and
action, but also enfold the standpoint, criteria and activity of critical theory itself. Such reflexive issues are characteristic of a period
which struggles to understand itself as a transition and, in so
doing, must define what has become past in order to project a
future. Our time is in the process of becoming aware of such a historical break from the epoch of "modernity," in its complex
relation to "capitalism," which stems from the late Renaissance.
The postmodern condition, in this sense, is neither an "ism" which
one might adopt or refuse (as the term has often been used in artistic movements), nor simply a new set of circumstances to take into
account. Rather, it is a historical shift in the human condition
which enfolds both thought and being. It can be neither accepted

nor refused, but is the situation from which we must take up anew the tasks of philosophy and social critique.

Awareness of this new situation entered the history of thought with the nineteenth-century break from philosophy indicated by the names Marx and Nietzsche. Corresponding breaks in the history of Being are more difficult to name and are beyond the present possibility of explication. Nevertheless, it may be said that the First World War is one major index of such a break: The European self-nominated carriers of modernity and civilization found themselves in an internal fundamental conflict which could not be attributed to an extra-European conflict with "uncivilized" people, thereby initiating a profound crisis concerning the meaning of civilization. This internal crisis was experienced earlier in thought though it was, probably for this reason, tied up with proposed solutions that cannot be straightforwardly proposed as solutions after the historical break—Marx's proletariat and Nietzsche's superman seem to fall prey to the very situation they are used to analyse. Due to the centrality of philosophy to the Western tradition of thought, the nineteenth-century break with philosophy is an unprecedented break for this tradition. It is not only a rupture *in* the history of philosophy, but more fundamentally a rupture *with* the history of philosophy. It is a turning-outside of philosophy, though enabled from within philosophy by the concept of critique, that requires thinking the entire history of the West as a situated unity—a possibility that emerges only when the concept of universality forged by philosophy becomes experienced as "not yet universal enough" which prompts claims concerning the "end of philosophy." Through this break with philosophy a certain closure of the philosophical tradition is defined while simultaneously a certain opening to its outside emerges. To put it another way, the term "civilization" had been used for centuries as a mark for the self-nomination of European superiority. When this term becomes internally problematic within European thought, such that it can no longer be used as club and becomes a microscope for self-interrogation, a new relation with the Europe's other becomes possible, but this is by no means to suggest that this new relation is immediately and unproblematically established.

In so far as the philosophical tradition has been oriented around knowledge, its closure can be articulated through the discovery of a necessary limitation in the representation of experience. This is not a limitation of extent, as if there were something or some domain of experience that could be necessarily impervious to scientific representation. Rather, it is a limitation that is produced by the presuppositions of representation itself. In representing the world, it is arrayed in front of a (scientific) subject as an objective domain that can be determined through rigorous procedures. This means that the scientific subject and the changes that knowledge induces in a wider awareness cannot themselves appear within the field of representation. These changes are based on the prior transformation performed on the world in the process of arraying—what we might call the work of transforming praxis into objectivity, or the activity of becoming-science—that cannot appear within representation. In short, the process and consequences of arraying are invisible within a conception of philosophy and human science confined to the legitimation of representation. In so far as the philosophical tradition has been determined through various epochs of arraying the world in front of a knowing subject—that is, as a gnoseological tradition—the end of philosophy turns thought toward a conception of culture focused on both the pre-objective, practical engagements of everyday life and the plurality of forms of awareness that are articulated in artistic, religious, etc. (as well as scientific) manifestations of practical life.

The attempt to bring our present situation to thought thus devolves upon a concern with culture in the sense of a form of life (Wittgenstein) with a characteristic style (Husserl), including its diversity and the intersection of its diverse forms. The main approach to elucidating this concept of culture has been the shift to regarding language, rather than knowledge, as the leading problem for philosophy and the human sciences. This has generally been called the linguistic turn, or the discursive turn. For the moment, the differences between these formulations of the discursive turn are less important than the problem on which they converge—how to think "culture"?—and the issue that they seek to address—the problematic status of universality within a new appreciation of diversity. Within this context, I wish to confront the question of whether social critique has any theoretical legitimation or practical task in the postmodern condition of the human sciences. To this purpose, I will suggest that there is an unavoidable danger in the linguistic–discursive turn that would undermine any strong conception of social critique. My argument claims that, to the contrary, rather than rendering social critique anachronistic, the postmodern condition further universalizes its scope, though there are considerable reformulations required as a consequence.

The move toward a discursive and cultural theory of the human sciences and of the social formation itself has, at least in the first place, made things very difficult for social critique. Discourse theory begins by viewing language as primarily an activity which constructs the social world, rather than as a representation of the world.[1] It tends to present a given discourse as enfolding and constituting the very states of affairs which it purports to merely describe and, furthermore, to present the plurality of discourses as untotalizable. Thus, it seems to follow that in the human sciences there can be no critique, or legitimation, of a discourse that does not propose criteria that are internal to a given discourse—and, thereby, have no more legitimate basis than any other set of criteria. The advantage of a pluralistic recognition of the heterogeneity of human cultures seems to cut the ground out from under the project of elaborating systemic critiques of dominant cultural practices. The danger is that capitalism, militarism, Eurocentrism, and so forth, seem to be "just other sets of cultural practices." This danger is endemic to the linguistic turn and cannot be simply pinned on any intellectual tendency. However, it seems particularly evident in "social constructionist" social science, hermeneutic human sciences, and in the philosophy and social theory deriving from Wittgenstein. Kenneth Gergen, for example, has phrased the issue of the predominant approach of social constructionism in contemporary social science in this way:

Constructionism offers no foundational rules and in this sense is relativistic. However, this does not mean that "anything goes." Because of the inherent dependency of knowledge systems on communities of shared intelligibility, scientific activity will always be governed in large measure by normative rules. However, constructionism does invite the practitioners to view these rules as historically and culturally situated—thus subject to critique and transformation.[2]

The belated recognition of the enfolding of knowledge by culture as described here seems to entail that social critique is attenuated to specific criticisms recognized as legitimate within the norms of a given construction of rule-governed activity. Similarly, hermeneutic philosophy has argued that, since every argument takes place against the background of a tradition that can never be entirely taken up into the argument and expressed thematically, or propositionally, critique must be reduced to a moment of the continuation of a tradition. Hans-Georg Gadamer argued in this way in his debate with Jürgen Habermas.[3] Even if the hermeneutic task is understood widely as "discourse about as-yet-incommensurable discourses," such discourse about unfamiliarity confines the possibility of criticism within the practices of an already established community of interpretation. This hermeneutic argument for attenuation of the Enlightenment claims to total criticism has been phrased by Richard Rorty in the following way:

> The group in question may itself shift from the one point of view to the other (thus "objectivizing" their past selves through a process of "reflection" and making new sentences true of their present selves). But this is not a mysterious process which demands a new understanding of human knowledge. It is the commonplace fact that people may develop doubts about what they are doing, and thereupon begin to discourse in ways incommensurable with those they used previously.[4]

What is at issue here is the extent to which confrontation with unfamiliarity can be reduced to a moment in the self-understanding of a cultural group. In a similar manner, Wittgenstein's pragmatic redefinition of understanding as "knowing how to go on" elides the question of when not to go on any further or, more exactly, how the boundaries of a given language game are encountered and described.[5] While the critique of representation entails a rejection of a sovereign, pure, a-cultural, transcendental subject on which social criticism could be based, the danger is that this tends to lead in turn to a confinement of criticism within an established order—whether this order is conceptualized in terms of a socially constructed reality, a tradition, or a language game. It is this confinement and attenuation of criticism which is the necessary danger brought forth by the discursive turn in philosophy and the human sciences. It stems from the reflexive issue that must arise when an extra-social, onto-theological foundation for society is rejected and thus the issue of the origins and legitimation of a given discourse seems to become an entirely internal matter. This is a danger that cannot be simply refuted, but must be productively negotiated in some manner. The present reformulation of the task of social critique proposes such a productive negotiation by investigating the reflexive capacity of language as situated in a medium of communication. Through its medium, discourse is embodied in a "siting" in which it inscribes, and therefore alters, the world. Through extending to the horizon of historical formations, social critique can be understood as a push toward further universalization, rather than a retreat from universal claims. The closure of "the West," visible at the postmodern moment, aims at what Edmund Husserl called "the universal critique of all life and all life-goals, all cultural products and systems that have already arisen out of the life of man."[6]

The classic formulation of the critique of ideology is based on the metaphor of base and superstructure elaborated by Marx in the Preface to his *Contribution to the Critique of Political Economy*, published in 1859. In an oft-quoted formulation Marx claimed that

In the social production of their life, men enter into definite relations that are indispensable and independent of their will, relations of production which correspond to a definite stage of development of their material productive forces. The sum total of these relations of production constitutes the economic structure of society, the real foundation, on which rises a legal and political superstructure and to which correspond definite forms of social consciousness. The mode of production of material life conditions the social, political and intellectual life process in general. It is not the consciousness of men that determines their being, but, on the contrary, their social being that determines their consciousness.[7]

The critique of ideology centres on the *relation between* social being and social consciousness, on the nature of the "correspondence" between them. Ideology-critique thus seems to be committed to a model oriented toward the accuracy of representation of social being in social consciousness. Its critical focus would come into play by showing that the form of consciousness does not accurately, or sufficiently, represent the social relations operative in material production. The move to discourse theory in the human sciences apparently undercuts this approach altogether. It is clear enough that superstructural forms of consciousness—which, for Marx, meant primarily law, politics, religion, aesthetics and philosophy—are forms of discourse. But, is the real foundation of "social being" in the mode of production also to be understood as discourse? The predominant Marxist answer has been "no," or "not entirely," for the following reasons. If social being were understood to be entirely discourse, the critique of ideology would become a comparison between two different discourses, say religion and political economy. To argue that religion is an ideology on this basis would be to presume the fundamentalness of the discourse concerning political economy and, moreover, the truth of a specific (presumably Marxist) version of that discourse. Without this, the obvious incompatability between the discourses of religion and political economy would prove no more than that they are different discourses—which would certainly not be theoretically strong enough to earn the name of "critique of ideology." This option routes the relation between base and superstructure toward the legitimation, presumably in "scientific" terms, of a specific theory of political economy and its foundational character with regard to the whole of social being. In short, if one regards social being as entirely discourse, the critique of ideology can only be legitimated through a representational theory of science centred on social being. The consequence is that "social being" in Marx's usage splits into social being "itself" and the scientific representation of social being. However the Marxist theorist attempts to close this gap, after the discursive turn in the human sciences it will become increasingly impossible. Thus, we seem to be faced with an alternative between a naive realism and a naive scientism.

If one regards, as is much more predominant within Marxist theory, social being as not, or not entirely, discourse, then one reaches the same pass much more quickly. If it is the materiality of social being in the process of social production that exceeds discourse, then the critique of ideology is referred primarily toward this materiality. The question of how this materiality is known in such a manner, i.e. discursively, such that it can be compared with superstructural discourses must re-emerge at this point, again raising the unsatisfactory alternative of realism or scientism. In short, the two subtler alternatives, that social being is entirely or not entirely discourse, do not avoid the problems of the most crude formulation of the base–superstructure metaphor: that the superstructure is discourse, the base is materiality, and that the critique of ideology consists in the comparing of discursive representations with material realities. This version, centred on the base–superstructure metaphor, has always been predominant in the popular versions of Marxism. Its fundamental problem is, of course, that representations cannot be compared with "realities," but only with other representations—even if they are claimed to be true representations. Any attempt in this direction will route the philosophical foundation of the critique of ideology toward a theory of science—which seeks an epistemological legitimation of a privileged discourse in order to demonstrate that all other discourses do not meet its standard. The origin of Marxist scientism is thus the interpretation of material reality as non-discursive.

In marked contrast to this privileging of epistemology, the turn toward discourse in the human sciences becomes really radical when epistemology is shown, or argued, to be discursively constituted and legitimated. Without a prior discourse—which was traditionally philosophy, understood as epistemology—which would legitimate the representation of representations in a theory of scientific representation, one is left only with the comparison between various representations. There seems to be no point at which such comparisons can be hooked into "reality," material or otherwise. At this juncture, it seems to be necessary to abandon all reference to both "ideology" and "critique" in so far as both terms apparently require a no-longer justifiable reference to a non-discursive reality. Thus, the discursive turn leaves us in the first place with a simple plurality of discourses, some of which incorporate scientific claims. After the turn to discourse in the human sciences, there apparently can be no "scientific" discourse about the plurality of discourses—a representation of representation, meta-discourse, or epistemology regulating the entirety of discourses—which could root the comparison between different discourses in a "reality" (scientifically represented) subtending all of them. It is this denial that constitutes the postmodern aspect of contemporary philosophical discourse.

The general point here is that the base–superstructure posing of the critique of ideology runs aground on the problems of the theory of representation after the turn toward discourse in the human sciences. One may conclude that if one can speak meaningfully of the critique of ideology today, it cannot be on the basis of any formulation that begins from the base–superstructure metaphor in this manner. Marxism (though not all Marxist schools) has continued to be articulated around the base–superstructure metaphor even though this posing was actually surpassed in his work due to an encounter with similar difficulties. Let me just emphasize one aspect of the classic statement that remains completely overlooked in the dominant reading. After asserting, in a manner that is itself highly arguable, that the transformations of economic conditions can be "determined with the precision of natural science," Marx distinguishes from this the transformations in ideological forms in which humans "*become conscious* of this conflict and fight it out."[8] The German term for "become conscious" is "*bewusst werden*" and, interestingly, is used in all cases when Marx raises this issue, indicating that it is a neglected phrasing which may have, or imply, a conceptual status in his work. Thus, I want to suggest that it is not the base–superstructure distinction itself that is most important in this classic statement, but the formulation of the critique of ideology that Marx is able to suggest on the basis of this metaphysical distinction between consciousness and being. From this point of view, the apparently key terms "ideology" and "material reality" are not fundamental at all. They merely sketch initial distinctions, providing a general topology in order to pose the real issue, which is: How does this relationship emerge into consciousness? Or, alternatively stated, from within the discursive turn in philosophy and the human sciences, what is the discursive expression of the relationship between thought and being? My answer is that it is the medium of communication which incorporates the materiality of discourse. The issue here is how this conception can design a new basis for social critique.

The fundamental problem which the critique of ideology seeks to address is thus compressed in the idea of "becoming conscious." How is it that the conditions of social being become conscious in the course of social history? How can various forms of this *process of the becoming-conscious of practical involvements* be distinguished, related, and some preferred over others? How can some forms be declared ideological, and from what "standpoint"? When phrased in this manner, the issue is not fundamentally one of the legitimation of representation because the critique of ideology is not routed primarily toward a theory of science. Rather, it is a question of forms of consciousness as necessary *aspects of* practical involvements. In this sense, consciousness is the *manifestation* of practice, not its representation. Ideology consists in the reduction of manifestations to representation, that is, their structuring as supposedly self-referring systems with an independent history divorced from their origin and effectivity within embodied human praxis. With the formulation of the idea of "becoming-conscious" Marx broke with the philosophical tradition. The error of that tradition could thus be concisely phrased as the presentation of the products of the process of becoming-conscious as if they were independent, forming a self-enclosed sphere, and could thus be related directly as the self-development of the Idea—whereas they could actually only be related through the process of their manifestation in the history of praxis. This is a step back from concern with the validity of ideas and arguments within the philosophical tradition to the formulation of the conditions of occlusion under which the tradition can appear to be a unity. It is a reflexive step, which is (in a certain sense) a continuation of the tradition, though through a radical break with the tradition.

This nineteenth-century break is also apparent in the work of Nietzsche who, interestingly, also formulates it with the notion of "becoming-conscious," "*bewusst werden.*"

> Man, like every living being, thinks continually without knowing it; the thinking that rises to *consciousness* is only the smallest part of all this—the most superficial and worst part—for only this conscious thinking *takes the form of words, which is to say signs of communication*, and this fact uncovers the origin of consciousness. . . . Consequently, given the best will in the world to understand ourselves as individually as possible, "to know ourselves," each of us will always succeed in becoming conscious only of what is not individual but "average."[9]

With the loss of the independence of knowing the philosophical tradition undergoes a closure. Because of the unavoidable fact that this closure could only be formulated in terms provided by the philosophical tradition, it could always be misunderstood as a

IAN ANGUS

repetition of a traditional mode of critique—a sovereign transcendental subject representing the world in its true reality and
criticizing various cultural forms for their failure to fully embody
it. Or, alternatively, it could always be misunderstood as a simple
rejection of the universal claims embedded in the philosophical
tradition—Marx could be seen as simply a propagandist for the
proletariat, rather than as the theorist of the proletariat as the universal class; Nietzsche could be seen as the propagandist for the will
of the individual and his perspective, rather than as the theorist
who recognized the ineluctable interweaving of human and world
and, furthermore, that the possibility of his own radical critique
rested on Plato and Christianity.[10] To the simplistic Marxism of
the base–superstructure formulation, we may add a vulgar
Nietzscheanism of the unrestrained exercise of pure will. But such
polemical assertions of mere particularity against the universal
claims embedded in philosophy are simply symptoms in which the
critique of ideology brought forward by the nineteenth-century
break is turned back within the metaphysical closure to produce
new ideologies. If the postmodern cultural turn is understood
properly, against the background of the nineteenth-century break
with philosophy, it becomes clear that the polemical assertion of
particular interests against universality presupposes precisely the
opposition between particular and universal that reinstitutes the
philosophical tradition. A genuine break requires a rethinking of
the mutual implication of particular and universal through the
reflexive manifestation of praxis. It is this route that was opened up
by Marx and Nietzsche.

It is characteristic of the nineteenth-century break to have connected specific critiques of the current state of social institutions to
a critique of the historical epoch as a whole. Marx's concept of

14

capitalism and Nietzsche's concept of degeneracy provided just this linkage between the particular and the universal. Freud should really be added to Marx and Nietzsche to complete this account of the nineteenth-century break. One difference is that psychoanalysis was articulated against a positivist notion of science deriving from philosophy rather than against philosophy itself. But there follows the same dual phenomenon of a positivist reduction to interests simultaneously alongside a radical questioning of the possibility of self-knowledge—i.e. a vulgar versus a reflexive Freudianism. In this moment of the break, the passage from particular to universal was held together by the retrospective relation to philosophy that was simultaneously criticized. Classical Marxism, for example, was not faced with the problem of reform or revolution as an alternative; rather, their continuity was assumed. The issue was posed as an either–or only after the First World War. But as heirs to this break, we experience the either–or as fundamental: Either systemic change or intrasystemic, rules-bound tinkering; either restricted or epochal critique. The central issues thus can be located as problems of the "loss of linkage"—it is very difficult nowadays to "connect" a theory of the social formation as a whole with particular interventions, theory with agency, universal with particular. Thus, we tend to lurch back and forth from one emphasis to another. It is a key philosophical issue of our time how to think this relationship.

The argument presented in this book will attempt to sustain two different tasks: a Heideggerian sense of the institution of historical epochs and a Gramscian justification of interventions in the construction of common sense within a given epoch. The space of classical modern philosophy was defined through the connection between these tasks. It was articulated as a continuous transition, or passage, from common sense to epoch through the unfolding of the concept. This passage was given its classic formation in Hegel's philosophy as the *Aufhebung* which bound together particular and universal, beginning and end, form and content, near and far. The postmodern condition is the loss of this passage and a consequent tendency for these two tasks to be collapsed in one direction or the other: Either the necessity of political intervention tends to block out the task of circumscribing the limits of the historical formation as such—which used to be done through the notion of "totality" of Hegelian descent—or the description of the historical epoch tends to absorb political options to the point where they become indistinguishable. Thus, it is as much postmodern common sense that there "is" no totality, or that totality necessarily becomes totalitarian, as it is that political interventions are without limit, that "reality" is endlessly mutable. Debates about postmodernity have tended to be polarized between either the defence of totality—as a mode of production for Marxist critics—or the defence of plurality—which cuts off discussion of the homogenizing forces in contemporary society. The present description of the postmodern condition as a loss of passage avoids this counterposing of the two tasks and allows each its legitimacy. Consequently, it discovers a new and radically open space that used to be concealed by the ease of passage. The following chapters investigate this space in order to construct a philosophy that gives due weight to both political intervention and historical circumscription.

The discursive turn in philosophy and the human sciences not only allows a description of central issues of our historical formation, but is itself a central characteristic of the epoch. A focus on language-in-use sharpens the point that human society is constructed through meaning and is never simply an object either for its members or for an interpreter and critic. However, to regard language as meaning poses the further question of the relation between meaning and the more "material" dimensions of work, love and power that constitute a social formation. Critics have often erroneously assumed that the discursive turn in philosophy and the human sciences turns away from these issues altogether, whereas it rather uses language as a metaphor for the investigation of society and does not reduce society to the spoken or written word. Criticisms of this sort operate with a distinction between discursive and extra- or non-discursive in order to articulate their criticism, when that distinction is precisely what is rejected when language in use is taken as metaphorical. This terminology indicates the presupposition made by such critics is that material resources are conceptually distinct from language, which implies that language is taken in the straightforward sense of spoken (or written) words as opposed to non-linguistic things like punches in the face or social labour. That the criticisms are theoretically naive from the viewpoint of discourse theory I take as self-evident, and I do not propose to rehearse or enter these debates here, or to defend discourse theory from its critics. My present concern is quite different. Let me just state that the thrust of the criticisms points to a crucial issue, even though it is articulated in a language that does not appreciate what is has been accomplished by the discursive turn. When language is taken as metaphorical for philosophy and the human sciences outright, it must certainly be legitimate at some point to ask whether there is not something left out in this move.[11] The standpoint adopted in this book is to accept the discursive turn, at least in its general outline, as a beginning point for contemporary philosophy and human science but to look for an expression of the limits of the metaphor from within the formulations available after the discursive turn. A theory of the materiality of expressive forms can overcome the discursive/extra-discursive dualism, which even appears in many articulations of the discursive stance.[12] The materiality, or solidity, of certain aspects of the social formation needs to be captured by a theory formulated from within the discursive turn. The present argument claims that the constitution of social relations within the sites of inscription that are inherent in language use, rather than pre-existing or subtending discourse, is the core of this materiality. Such a focus on social constitution can be generalized from language itself, as a consequence of its metaphorical status, and applied to all forms of expression and communication. This is a communication theory of society, but communication understood in a special way as the constitution of social relations by the *medium* of communication. Communication, in this sense, is of the order of a primal scene that originates a complex of social relations. Thus understood, "materiality" does not have to be added to a discursive theory; the primal scenes instituted by communicative forms encompass material relations. The argument is that the Heideggerian and Gramscian tasks are held together by the social relations instituted and confirmed by media of communication.

One may see this argument as a revaluation and radicalization of the phatic component of communication, which was described by Roman Jakobson as the function of keeping the channel of communication open and thus confirming the relationship between addresser and addressee.[13] Redundancy in language makes this phatic function most clear since the maintenance of relationship becomes an end in itself. This phatic function is enfolded within the content-orientation of normal usage. While Jakobson's phatic component is not itself content, it is established through discourse oriented to content, or meaning. Redundancy is defined as such precisely on the grounds of its content adding nothing to prior content. Its function is thus not oriented to content but to the form of the relationship. The present argument proposes a rediscovery of the function of establishing and confirming social relationships throughout a plurality of media of communication. The primal scenes of communication open and confirm social relationships whose redundancy can be defined precisely by their pervasiveness. The apogee of this rediscovery is apparent in the phenomenon of silence. By silence I do not refer to a silence within discourse, a refraining-from-speaking, which would be in principle similar to speech, nor to activities performed without speaking but which, on the metaphor of discourse, would be understood as meaningful on the model of speech acts. I refer to a speech that designs its own end, a speech that prepares to stop in order to invite the other to begin. This is the origin of the ethical demand, as opposed to the conventional claims of duties and responsibilities within a language game already underway.

The original ethical demand emerges where the babble of competing speeches stops. Society, understood as a process of generalized persuasion, operates through a reciprocal cannibalism of discourses. This general agonistics must encounter a still point for the ethical demand to arise. This is the traditional social function of philosophy, which I reformulate but maintain. Silence is the entry of philosophy into discourse and the entry of the ethical demand into convention. On this point, the current argument is at odds with the main tendency of the discursive turn in philosophy and the human sciences which tends to enfold the philosophical call within the conventions of a language game, the text of tradition, the system of discourse, or in any case some

overarching conception of language. It maintains that there is an
indissoluble difference between the demands of reflexion and the
claims of convention. This difference can only be properly formulated and understood if it is pushed to its extreme rather than
being mediated or downplayed. To this extent, the transcendental–phenomenological reduction discovered by Husserl is essential
to the demand of philosophy for radical reflexion.

Philosophy has been congenitally suspicious of common sense.
In the *Republic*, Plato separated knowledge from opinion to
"define in his discourse and distinguish and abstract from all other
things the aspect or idea of the good" so as to be able to "gaze on
that which sheds light on all . . . [and] use it as a pattern for the
right ordering of the state and the citizens themselves."[14]
Philosophy turns one away from opinion toward knowledge of the
good, which only appears indistinctly in ordinary life, and thus
philosophers should be kings. This original form of the separation
between knowledge and common sense defined philosophy as
outside and above opinion. Its key metaphor was thus emerging
from a cave, and dialectic was the method of awaking and arising from darkness to light. Modern philosophy faced a different
problem. The abstraction from opinion was completed and had
already formed an esoteric tradition of knowledge distinct from
common sense. In the *Phenomenology of Spirit*, Hegel asserted that

in modern times, however, the individual finds the abstract
form ready-made. Hence the task nowadays consists not so
much in purging the individual of an immediate, sensuous
mode of apprehension . . . but rather in just the opposite, in
freeing determinate thoughts from their fixity, so as to give
actuality to the universal, and to impart to it spiritual life.[15]

Philosophy had thus to come back to ground to infuse common sense with knowledge. The image for this completion of the task of philosophy is thus a circle.[16] Whereas ancient philosophy had to construct abstractions from ordinary experience in order to articulate concepts, modern philosophy has attempted to bring abstractions back to earth. The common assumption that makes this a continuous tradition is that knowledge can ground ethics in order to reorganize opinion and common sense, first as an obligation to rule by those few who have ascended and, second, as an infusion of institutions by reason. The suggestion by Marx and Nietzsche that philosophy has come to an end pertains to this gnoseological tradition in which unfolding practical life could be contained within the self-development of the Idea.

One begins on a new foot when Husserl defines the orientation of knowledge as knowledge *of* opinion, or the lifeworld as the object of science.[17] While much of Husserl's concern lay with how the lifeworld functions as the unacknowledged presupposition of logic and knowledge, a more radical shift occurs when one is oriented to the question of knowledge of the lifeworld itself. It sets up a new relation between theory and praxis that is hinted at but rarely developed within the phenomenological tradition. The notion that knowledge and opinion have distinct objects, characteristic of gnoseology, is undone. The metaphor for thought becomes the horizon. Thought can neither pass over its practical concerns directly toward the horizon, for the horizon only appears as the background of a theme, nor reduce itself to a theme itself, which always takes its meaning from the horizons in which it stands. (Many today quickly say "context" in order to turn away from investigating the issue.) There is thus a continuous back-and-forth movement between theme and horizon in which knowledge is a continual striving but never an acquisition. This does not reject knowledge as too context-bound to sustain any claim to universalization, but it does release the practical domain from any direct subordination to knowledge (on the ancient model) or any application of pre-existing knowledge (on the classical modern model, whether in Hegelian or technocratic form). Such a releasing of the practical, while also making it the main theme of knowledge, devolves upon a new emphasis on the here and now in which action occurs. Levinas discovers an essential moment of such action when he says, in one of the most beautiful phrases in all philosophy, that the origin of all ethics is in the moment when one meets another at a door and steps back to say, "After you."[18] Philosophy is the accounting for oneself that opens the door for another. When one thinks of knowledge as a product, it can of course be opposed to opinion. But when one traces back knowledge to the ethic of striving to know for oneself, it becomes a horizonal presence in which one can never escape one's embeddedness in practical life. Radical reflection and common sense both repel each other and inform each other. They release each other for the demands specific to each. In a constitutively paradoxical sense, they are both opposites and intimates but are not reducible to a dialectical mediation. This is what is expressed by the transcendental reduction. I have tried to convey this notion through the title of the book, which refers to the undoing of congealed articulated connexions, or figures, by radical reflexion and thereby to the main activity of theory.

The text thus proceeds by pulling apart, or dis-figuring, figures that have emerged from articulated connexions but have congealed into common sense in order to redesign them for a renovated philosophy relevant to the project of social critique. It takes up several key themes for a contemporary critical theory of society: the constitutively paradoxical standpoint of the critical subject; the relation between common sense and the epochal horizon, the possibility of democracy in the postmodern media environment, and the social vocation of philosophy as the recognition of an ethical imperative. The project of radical democracy is dependent on this ethical imperative for both its theoretical rigour and practical energy. Thus, despite many qualifications, I assert the continued relevance of philosophy to social critique and enlightened practical action.

The main theory expressed in these chapters consists in a three-fold stratification of socio-historical experience expressed through the metaphor of language—a said, the saying and a site—and corresponding to certain "disciplines" of thought and practice. In its most obvious sense, language presents a "said," a content or meaning, which is not much investigated here because it is the main focus of most concern with language. Here we "see past" the phenomenon of language itself, as it were, by virtue of being oriented toward what is *said* about something else. It is the something else that is represented that is of concern in this case. This can not be eliminated from discourse, as *representation* itself cannot, though an exclusive focus on this component tends to obscure the activity of discourse and thereby encourage an outright rejection of the discursive metaphor for social action. If I may use the metaphor of a meeting, the said is the content of the speaking at the meeting; it is what is talked about. But a meeting requires a meeting-place that must be both built and maintained. *Poetry* pertains to the *instituting* of a society and is the construction of a *site* of discourse—the primal scene of communication. *Rhetoric* pertains to the ceremonial *confirmation* of the institution through the *saying*. Thus, poetry corresponds to the building of the meeting-place and rhetoric to its maintenance. These three levels are involved in every speech act, they are not separate activities but rather distinct facets of language use—though certainly a given social action may emphasize one of these over others. Poetry, rhetoric, representation: society is constructed from these three—the institution of a historical epoch, the confirmation of its common sense, the representation of matters pre-understood.

This threefold edifice, left to itself, consists in a generalized war between discourses. It has only such ethics as are always-already-legitimated within a given discourse. The field of discourse, composed of competing discourses, yields a general agonistics—a war of each against all. An ethical moment that can transform the field of discourse as a whole can only emerge from a speech that cannot be entirely contained within the discourse from which it emerges—a speech which produces, by its own explicit design, not more speech, but silence. Such silence is the introduction of radical reflexion, the transcendental reduction of the presupposition of the world, that reverses the agonistics into an ethics. A perspective purely immanent to society cannot ground an ethics that is more than conventional behaviour. To this extent, philosophy is constituted by its gaze toward the horizon, which issues in glimpses outside the socio-historical formation. It is not part of the threefold edifice, but pertains to its description, meaning and transformation through ethical insight. Philosophy is primarily doing, not talking-about.

NOTES

1. This point has been made by many contemporary writers using different vocabularies. See in this connection, Charles Taylor, *The Malaise of Modernity* (Toronto: Anansi, 1991) p. 33 and *Multiculturalism and "The Politics of Recognition"* (Princeton: Princeton University Press, 1992) pp. 32–4; Richard

Rorty, *Contingency, Irony, and Solidarity* (Cambridge: Cambridge University Press, 1989) pp. 10–16, 41, 75; Ernesto Laclau and Chantal Mouffe suggest that as a consequence of this point the term "representation" could be replaced with the concept of articulation in *Hegemony and Socialist Strategy* (London: Verso, 1985) pp. 58, 65.

2. Kenneth Gergen, "The Social Constructionist Movement in Modern Psychology" in *American Psychologist*, Vol. 40, No. 3, 1985 p. 173. See also Rom Harre, "An Outline of the Social Constructionist Viewpoint" in Rom Harre (ed.) *The Social Construction of Emotions* (New York: Basil Blackwell, 1986) and John Durham Peters and Eric W. Rothenbuhler, "The Reality of Construction" in Herbert W. Simons (ed.) *Rhetoric in the Human Sciences* (London: Sage, 1989). The perspective known generally as social constructionism is usually traced back to Peter L. Berger and Thomas Luckmann, *The Social Construction of Reality* (New York: Doubleday, 1967). It is less well recognized that it can be followed back further through Alfred Schütz to Edmund Husserl. This longer lineage would tend to suggest that the recognition that "reality" is "socially constructed" requires another standpoint from which the observation can be made. Husserl called this standpoint the "transcendental ego." This would also go some distance toward showing why, if reality is socially constructed, it is not normally perceived as being so by those involved in the "reality" in question. Everyday activity seems to presume, in contrast, the "externality" of reality. This is still key to the analysis in Berger and Luckmann (cf. pp. 1–2) but has disappeared in contemporary social constructionist literature.

3. Jürgen Habermas, "Review of Gadamer's *Truth and Method*" in *Understanding and Social Inquiry*, ed. Fred R. Dallmayr and Thomas A. McCarthy (Notre Dame: University of Notre Dame Press, 1977).

4. Richard Rorty, *Philosophy and the Mirror of Nature* (Princeton: Princeton University Press, 1979) p. 386, cf. pp. 343, 353.

5. Ludwig Wittgenstein, *Philosophical Investigations*, trans. G. E. M. Anscombe (New York: Macmillan, 1989) p. 61e, number 154.

6. Edmund Husserl, "Philosophy and the Crisis of European Humanity," Appendix 1 of *The Crisis of European Sciences and Transcendental Phenomenology*, trans. David Carr (Evanston: Northwestern University Press, 1970) p. 283.

7. Preface to "*A Contribution to the Critique of Political Economy*" in *The Marx-Engels Reader*, ed. Robert C. Tucker (New York: Norton, 1978) pp. 4–5.

8. Ibid.

9. Friedrich Nietzsche, *The Gay Science*, trans. Walter Kaufmann (New York: Random House, 1974) pp. 298–9; Book 5, aphorism 354, emphasis in original,

paragraph separation omitted. Throughout this aphorism the German text uses various conjugations of " *bewusst werden.* "

10. Ibid., p. 286; Book 5, aphorism 346 and p. 280; Book 5, aphorism 344.

11. Ernesto Laclau and Chantal Mouffe respond to Norman Geras' criticisms, for example, by restating their use of Wittgenstein's conception of a language game. Wittgenstein considers the case of a builder's assistant who, when asked to bring materials, brings things called blocks, pillars, slabs and beams. He comments that the words one uses to provoke these actions can be called "a complete primitive language," thus suggesting that the blocks themselves, however, are not a part of the language even though any actual building will involve language. Laclau and Mouffe suggest, following this line of thought, that putting bricks on the wall is extra-linguistic and bringing bricks at the command of another is linguistic. The totality of both acts, both of which are clearly necessary for the wall to be built, they call discourse, which they understand to be prior to the linguistic/extra-linguistic distinction. This distinction, then, refers to language in the ordinary sense in which language can be opposed to something other than speech, whereas discourse refers to meaningful activity (based on the metaphor of meaning drawn from language) that is prior to whether speaking occurs or not. In other words, building the wall, even if new blocks are not brought by an assistant who is commanded by words (but rather performed in silence by a single worker), is still a discursive action. This response clearly deals with the criticism through outlining a conception of language as constitutive of social action rather than merely a representation of it. What it does not do, however, is allow a place for questioning the limits of the metaphor of discourse, i.e. the question whether something is lost in characterizing the activity of building a wall as discourse. Is the heaviness of the blocks, for example, adequately captured by the term "discourse"? Should it be? In the formulation of the discursive conception of meaningful activity, the question of whether a certain reduction of social life may be implied is often occluded. But this is a genuine issue, one which can only be held up to investigation if the metaphorical aspect of the discursive turn is emphasized. This metaphorical dimension occurs in any social theory, however, and pertains to its capacity for universalization. It cannot, of course, be avoided (whatever one's model of theory) by a direct appeal to "reality." See Ernesto Laclau and Chantal Mouffe, "Post-Marxism without Apologies" in Ernesto Laclau, *New Reflections on the Revolution of Our Time* (London and New York: Verso, 1990) p. 100; and Ludwig Wittgenstein, *Philosophical Investigations,* trans. G. E. M. Anscombe (New York: Macmillan, 1989) part 1, number 2.

12. Stuart Hall, for example, refers to a distinction between the discursive

and the extra-discursive, without implying any distinction of levels between
(extra-) linguistic and discursive as do Laclau and Mouffe. He thus enters into the
intractable problem of how one can speak meaningfully about the extra-discursive, a question that is not resolvable in these terms. See, for example, Stuart Hall,
"The Toad in the Garden: Thatcherism Among the Theorists" in *Marxism and
the Interpretation of Culture*, ed. Cary Nelson and Lawrence Grossberg (Urbana
and Chicago: University of Illinois Press, 1988) pp. 51–2; "Encoding/Decoding"
in *Culture, Media, Language*, ed. S. Hall *et al.* (London: Hutchison, 1980)
pp. 131–2; and "On Postmodernism and Articulation: An Interview with Stuart
Hall," ed. Lawrence Grossberg, *Journal of Communication Inquiry*, Vol. 10, No. 2,
Summer 1986, pp. 56–7.

13. Roman Jakobson, "Closing Statement: Linguistics and Poetics" in *Style in
Language*, ed. Thomas A. Sebeok (New York: The Technology Press of MIT and
John Wiley and Sons, 1960).

14. Plato, *Republic*, trans. Paul Shorey in *The Collected Dialogues of Plato*, ed.
Edith Hamilton and Huntington Cairns (New York: Pantheon, 1966) pp. 766,
771; 534b–c, 540a.

15. G. W. F. Hegel, *Phenomenology of Spirit*, trans. A. V. Miller (Oxford:
Oxford University Press, 1979) pp. 19–20.

16. Ibid., pp. 10, 20.

17. Edmund Husserl, *The Crisis of the European Sciences and Transcendental
Phenomenology*, trans. David Carr (Evanston: Northwestern University Press,
1970) pp. 123–41.

18. Emmanuel Levinas, *Ethics and Infinity: Conversations with Philippe Nemo*,
trans. Richard Cohen (Pittsburgh: Dusquesne University Press, 1985) p. 89.

2

CONSTITUTIVE PARADOX

The industrialization of culture in the twentieth century has proposed both a new object of study and a new situation for philosophy. Moreover, in so far as a critical relation to its situation is constitutive of philosophy, the critique of industrialized society and culture demanded from contemporary philosophy reciprocally demands a revised conception of philosophy. I will develop an argument for the constitutively paradoxical character of contemporary social and cultural critique due to its necessity to reflexively constitute critical subjectivity within its own critical practice.

We may use the terms "common sense" and the "epochal horizon" to designate the complex of issues that arise with the postmodern loss of linkage between the two extremes that were called "immediacy" and "totality" by Hegel. Analysis of, and intervention in, common sense becomes central when the powerful classes and institutions come to pervade the processes of everyday action and opinion-formation. The proletariat, and the other forces of opposition, are no longer "outside the gates," as it were—or, in Marx's phrase, "in, but not of, civil society"— but thoroughly imbued with a common sense that perceives the system and its inequalities and exploitations as natural and thus inevitable. To the extent that potentially oppositional forces are imbued with the common sense that reproduces the social system, radical politics becomes a politics of hegemony. In the age of mass media, this development can perhaps still go a little further, but its direction and consequences are quite visible to us now.

As a consequence of this emphasis on the critique of common sense, attention has been turned away from the question of the social formation as a whole. It is even the case that many "post-modern" writers reject the possibility of theorizing totality at all. However, without some such conception, the critique of common sense must necessarily lapse into an internal reformism—it becomes incapable of contributing to a project of *systemic trans-formation.* But when one pushes the notion of politics past the relational differences within a given social system toward the character of the social system itself, one necessarily encounters the question of the *institution of the social.* This use of the term "institution" derives from Edmund Husserl's concept of *Urstiftung,* or sometimes simply *Stiftung,* which is normally trans-lated into English as "instituting," "primal instituting" or "establishment" and which refers to the setting-into-play of a primal scene that founds a scientific or philosophical tradition— that is to say, a distinct formation of temporality. It was developed by Maurice Merleau-Ponty to refer to social institutions. He also suggested that it could provide the basis for a theory of culture. Claude Lefort has connected this to the concept of "regime" in political philosophy and described it as a "shaping" which implies both "giving meaning to social relations" and "staging them."[1] Conceiving of this shaping requires that politics be understood in a more fundamental sense as the theologico-political institution of society. Such an instituting of society leads us to recognize various historical forms, or regimes, in which it has been manifested. In Lefort's words,

> what philosophical thought strives to preserve is the experience of a difference which goes beyond differences of opinion (and the recognition of the relativity of points of view which this implies); the experience of a difference which is not at the disposal of human beings, whose advent does not take place *within* human history, and which cannot be abolished therein; the experience of a difference which relates human beings to their humanity, and which means that their humanity cannot be self-contained, that it cannot set its own limits, and that it cannot absorb its origins and ends into those limits. Every religion *states* in its own way that human society can only open onto itself by being held in an opening it did not create.[2]

To speak of the epochal horizon within which the politics of common sense operates, we must speak of the shaping of regimes. And, ultimately, we must speak of the opening toward different regimes itself. This shaping of a regime cannot be a "totality" in any traditional sense, but is an instituting of form, a setting of the determinations of an epoch, to which the politics of common sense must be linked if it is to be a critique of the system as a whole. The necessary danger of the attenuation of critique in the postmodern world stems from the rejection of totality when understood traditionally as the universal synthesis of particular determinations. The uncovering of the notion of "shaping"— which the rejection of the notion(s) of totality from the prior philosophical tradition enables—is often immediately covered up by interpreting it as a rediscovery of a similar notion of totality (and either rejecting or accepting it as such).

The institution of the consumer-capitalist regime continuously pressures the politics of difference toward differences established within this regime. Only by speaking in some way of the epochal horizon can politics be drawn toward a difference in shaping—which may open the possibility of systemic transformation. George Grant has argued that differences within the regime survive only on condition of their non-essentiality:

> What is essential about North American society is not its pluralism but its monism. We are the inheritors of the European beliefs of the last centuries that the best society would be built by the overcoming of chance through the knowledge reached by the "objective" sciences. Power in that society is incarnate in the public and private corporations which organize the pursuit of that overcoming of chance. The rhetoric of pluralist liberalism was an extra tacked onto the monolithic certainty about the public good.[3]

While the contemporary talk about "difference" cannot be reduced to such internal differences, it is none the less essential to track from the differences settled within the instituted regime toward difference from the regime, otherwise all that can be accomplished is a rebalancing of some elements of common sense that do not implicate the horizon of the epoch. To put the point more concretely, difference will be routed toward the surface pluralism of consumer-capitalist society rather than the non-foundational pluralism required by post-capitalist radical democracy. Here it is a question of the "passage" between, or mutal imbrication of, common sense and the epochal horizon, but we must resist the Hegelian temptation to resolve them in a dialectic that would characterize this passage as an internal development, which implies a purely logical space.

The turn in the perspective of the Frankfurt School announced in the introduction to the *Dialectic of Enlightenment* is exemplary in demonstrating a shift from a restricted conception of ideology–critique within the common sense of an epoch toward a totalizing critique of the epoch. Referring to their prior work, Horkheimer and Adorno suggested that they had previously "still trusted too much in the modern consciousness" and consequently "still thought that in regard to scientific activity our contribution could be restricted to the criticism or extension of specialist axioms." In abandoning this perspective, they were forced to diagnose how and why "myth is already enlightenment; and enlightenment reverts to mythology."[4] This formulation is indebted to the influence of Nietzsche, after whom the achievements of reason cannot be simply counterposed to superstition since cruelty and unconsciousness are shown to be constitutive features of the genealogy of reason. The totalizing of ideology-critique inaugurates a critique of reason that seems to cut the ground out from under itself. If criticism is focused on what we may call the "extent of application" of specialist axioms, it is concerned to show in a given case whether a scientific proposition is being unwarrantedly extended into social life so as to limit or occlude possibilities for greater freedom and happiness. To take a key example, science oriented toward technical control tends to present social life as completely determined and therefore as inacapable of conscious transformation. The ideology of science and technology, understood through a restricted critique, becomes ideological when it is extended beyond its legitimate, delimited sphere and is taken to apply to the determination of the society as a whole. There are other situations when specialized scientific propositions are interpreted too narrowly because of prevailing forms of power. It is then the function of restricted critique to extend their implications for the realization of freedom and happiness toward the social totality. The Frankfurt School's utilization of psychoanalysis is a case in point, but we may also include the discoveries of the science of ecology in this context. When their implications for the organization of the social totality are taken into account, we are able to determine more precisely the interests of powerful blocks that limit the possibilities of widespread freedom and happiness. Through this procedure of "criticism or extension," restricted critique is focused on the *contribution of specific knowledges and practices*—what we would nowadays call discourses—to a general enlightenment of the social whole, but the social whole itself is never theorized as such. The activity of critique is understood as a contribution to a historically changing totality which can never itself be the object of positive knowledge or action. Restricted ideology-critique is concerned to clear away obstacles to the achievement of a better society, but the process of its realization can only be the product of the action of associated individuals discovering their freedom and can thus not be determined in any positive fashion—though it is a Hegelian confidence in the direction of history as increasing freedom that gives this apparently empty totality its inexplicit determinateness.

With the totalization of critical activity, it is precisely this theorization of the social totality that becomes paradoxical. The totality cannot be theorized as an unwarranted, ideological extension of a specialized science—the inadequacies of which were already shown at the previous stage—but while it cannot be a positive knowledge, neither can the totality be left as an empty space whose historical direction was assumed to be benign (as it was by the Frankfurt School at the stage of restricted critique). Most important, the discourse about the social totality must incorporate an understanding of the motive for turning from restricted to totalizing critique: The fact that previous elements of enlightenment—such as science, technology, industrialization, competition, and so forth—have themselves become ideologies reinforcing new forms of domination. If the elements of enlightenment can themselves become new forms of domination, the theorizing of the social totality cannot fix on definite elements, whose future roles may reverse completely—in the way that the Marxist critique of "bourgeois individualism" became an apology for state repression in communist societies, for example. Moreover, elements previously designated as myth can also be seen to have produced possibilities of reason and happiness. The dialectic of myth and enlightenment, since it can no longer oppose reason to irrationality, seems to fall into a contradiction, as Horkheimer and Adorno clearly recognized:

> The dilemma that faced us in our work proved to be the first phenomenon for investigation: the self-destruction of the Enlightenment. We are wholly convinced—and therein lies our *petitio principii*—that social freedom is inseparable from enlightened thought. Nevertheless, we believe that we have just as clearly recognized that the notion of this very way of thinking, no less than the actual historic forms—the social institutions—with which it is interwoven, already contains the seed of the reversal universally apparent today.[5]

Restricted ideology-critique is oriented to contradictions within a historical epoch, whereas totalizing critique is oriented toward the historical epoch as a whole.

The key question now becomes: From what standpoint can such a totalizing critique be performed? It could be from completely outside the historical epoch, from a superhistorical location, though this location would itself need some justification, presumably from an onto-theological discourse. But in this case it would not really be a critique of this specific historical epoch because the distinction between historical and superhistorical existence then tends to override any distinctions between historical epochs. In short, from a theological standpoint the real distinction is between eternal and historical life, thus the critique is of historical life in general not of the specifics of a given historical epoch. In this connection, it is worth recalling that the Frankfurt School recognized that ideology-critique is a transformation dependent on the philosophical tradition from which it stems and, in the late period of Max Horkheimer, also recognized that, for the popular consciousness, religion is an important carrier of "suprahistorical" values.[6] For this reason, the critique of a historical epoch must be, at least in part, from inside that epoch, but then its own location must be subject to the critique itself. Totalizing critique is thus necessarily in a difficult position with regards to its own possibility. Whereas restricted critique could oppose reason to domination within a given social order, and therefore speak of "contradictions," for totalizing critique reason is given form within the historical epoch as a whole, and thus cannot be effectively opposed to domination in social institutions (though this does not mean that all forms of reason are simply apologetic, or ideological in the sense developed by restricted critique). At this point, everything depends on whether this reflexive problem is properly called a "*petitio principii*" (Horkheimer and Adorno), a "contradiction" (Habermas), or a "constitutive paradox" (as I will argue).

In *The Philosophical Discourse of Modernity*, Jürgen Habermas used the concept of a "performative contradiction" in order to explain the dead-end into which Horkheimer and Adorno turned in *Dialectic of Enlightenment*—and which, he argued, is also characteristic of poststructuralists such as Lyotard, Derrida and Foucault—due to their Nietzschean conception of critique which "tears down the barrier between validity and power" since

> as instrumental, reason assimilated itself to power and thereby relinquished its critical force—that is the *final* disclosure of ideology critique applied to itself. To be sure, this description of the self-destruction of the critical capacity is paradoxical, because in the moment of description it still has to make use of the critique that has been declared dead.[7]

Habermas has defined a performative contradiction formally as "when a constative speech act *k(p)* rests on noncontingent presuppositions whose propositional content contradicts the asserted proposition *p*."[8] In general, a performative contradiction refers to a situation in which the content of an utterance contradicts the presuppositions on which the utterance itself rests. In keeping with the communicative turn away from subject-centred reason that characterizes Habermas's work, the charge of performative contradiction undermines the claims of those who, as Martin Jay has expressed it, "employ methods of argumentation that tacitly entail intersubjective validity testing to defend a position that denies communicative rationality its legitimacy."[9] Performative contradiction is thus not a matter of self-contradiction—of making two statements that contradict one another—it is a matter of a statement made in an intersubjective context, which consequently relies on conventions of intersubjective understanding, but which denies these conventions in its explicit utterance. Thus, a performative contradiction arises when claims made at the level of manifest deny the very possibility of a reflexive justification of themselves.

The problem raised by the Nietzschean turning of the *Dialectic of Enlightenment* is that the independent legitimation of the standpoint of social critique is undermined once the analysis of the culture industry claims that contemporary culture is a self-confirming totality without contradiction. Where could the critic stand in order to criticize this totality? Adorno retreated to the damaged subject whose experience is articulated in avant-garde art which accepts the communicative isolation of the critic and thereby runs the danger that cultural criticism appears merely eccentric. Others might return to a transcendent concept of philosophical criticism. In contrast to these immanent and transcendent options, Habermas has claimed that social and cultural criticism is legitimated neither by philosophy nor avant-garde art but by the ability of actors to reflexively thematize and discuss the communicative conventions which their statements presuppose or imply. Unlike both Adorno and Derrida, whom Habermas describes as "decoding the normal case from the point of view of the limit cases," he is interested in the "variations of context that change meaning [which] cannot in principle be arrested or controlled, because contexts cannot be exhausted, that is, they cannot be theoretically mastered once and for all."[10] When an assumption from the context becomes problematic, Habermas argues, the consequent reflexive argumentation presupposes idealizing pre-suppositions that transcend any particular language game and which can ground a definition of normal usage as against limit case. A necessary aspect of this turn is that the intersubjective horizon of communicative action cannot be thematized as a totality. When the presupposed background of everyday life has become problematic as a consequence of conflict and disagreement, certain themes can be made explicit and enter into a process of discursive argumentation which has certain reciprocity conditions, as Habermas argues.[11] But, since the background of everyday life cannot be thematized as a whole, critique is limited to specific aspects of everyday life that have become problematic and must reject the universal turn that it took under the influence of Nietzsche.[12] That is, he claims that the self-cancelling character of totalizing critique can be avoided if one returns to a more limited conception in which specific validity claims are reflexively legitimated through intersubjective agreement. While totalizing criticism regards limit cases as especially interesting because they provide clues to the closure of a social and cultural formation, limited criticism has lost any interest in what may be outside the social formation itself. It is a more domestic animal.

In Habermas's view the totalizing critique of reason is *necessarily* caught in a performative contradiction because of its self-referring character.[13] This performative contradiction he also calls a paradox, but is apparently not interested in the difference between these two characterizations.[14] I think that the characterization of self-referential criticism as paradoxical is preferable and that, in addition, it can legitimate the practice of totalizing criticism that Habermas wants to discard. Social critique becomes self-referential because its legitimation can no longer—as it was in the first generation of the Frankfurt School—be separated from the critical practice itself. What this means is that the philosophical legitimation of social critique and the practice of social critique have collapsed together. They cannot be separated into two hierarchical levels of critical practice, on the one hand, and reflexive legitimation, on the other.

A statement of social critique and its reflexive justification have collapsed into a single utterance. Any critique that claims relevance to the whole field of contemporary society and culture constitutes the subject who is enabled to utter the critique in the same speech act as the critique itself. This situation is, I think, definitional for the theoretical space of social critique as we currently experience it and accounts for the self-referential, self-constituting character of contemporary criticism as well as the impossibility of locating the subject of criticism in a social group already constituted prior to the critique. The meta-narratives—to use Lyotard's term—of philosophy and art have lost their overarching status as legitimations of the practice of social critique. Of course this does not mean that either philosophy or art has become irrelevant to critical practice. It means, rather, that their relevance has to be won again in each case of cultural intervention which implies a "philosophy of the act," to use Bakhtin's phrase, which begins from neither the subject's being nor its thought, but from the primary doing that is rooted in the body's self-movement, or "I can."[15] The reflexive level of legitimation cannot be separated from the act of critical intervention itself. This collapse of meta-narrative into narrative, of legitimation into practice, thus means that the subject of social critique enunciates its own reflexive legitimation. In other words, it is not only a collapse of meta-narrative into narrative, but also an explosion of narrative into meta-narrative—

and therefore an inability to stabilize this reflexive relationship by a definitive hierarchization of levels. The act is not a decisionistic prior to all thought, but co-extensive with justification, though neither can thought be an absolute prior to action—which would remove the indeterminateness from action and make it a simple consequence of thought.

The concept of paradox refers to such situations as this in which statement and meta-statement are mutually referring. The classical case of the Cretan who said "all Cretans are liars" illustrates this. If *I* say, "all Cretans are liars," I am simply right or wrong—if we consider the statement epistemologically—and prejudiced, mean-spirited or whatever—if we consider the statement rhetorically. Only because the Cretan's statement is self-referring does a paradox arise and, notice, that as a result the questions of both truth and persuasion, epistemology and rhetoric, are radically transformed because of this self-reference. It becomes undecidable whether the Cretan is right or wrong, since the paradox is that if he is right he is wrong and vice versa. It is no longer to the point what rhetorical persuasion the speaker intends, but it is crucial that a speech act of this paradoxical sort inhabits its standpoint in a different manner than other speech acts. Epistemologically, the question of the truth or falsity of this statement is pushed to a higher level that implies the undecidability of the concept of truth itself in relation to this statement. Rhetorically, the *ethos* of the speaking subject in the utterance functions to undermine the identity, or self-identity, of the speaker but also to constitute a new problematic identity at a higher level at which it is undecidable whether the speaker is, or remains, a Cretan or not. Indeed, the distinction between epistemology and rhetoric is itself undermined—the truth claim is undecidable because the identity of the speaker is self-referential.

A self-referring, self-constructing, rhetoric renders the utterance's truth undecidable.

But our contemporary situation is even more complex than this classic case of paradox would indicate. In the classic case, only if it is *already known* that the speaker is a Cretan does a paradox emerge—so that the undecidability of the paradoxical statement nevertheless presupposes an initial certainty concerning the identity of the speaker which the paradox then functions to undermine. What if the statement were made neither by me, nor by someone we already know to be a Cretan, but by a stranger of unknown origin, or by one among us who has changed in a manner which we cannot yet discern? Then the statement might be a straightforward claim to knowledge (if it refers to someone distinct from the speaker) or it might be a paradox (if self-referring) and—until we determine the identity of the speaker—it is undecidable which. In other words, it is undecidable whether the statement is undecidable or not.

What I mean to suggest by the notion that the independence of legitimation and intervention in social critique have collapsed together is that statement and meta-statement, claim and validity, are imbricated in any cultural intervention and that this is the case because social critique itself constructs the identity of the critic—which can therefore not be assumed as known prior to the critical statement itself. This situation has been produced by the dissolution of traditional philosophical legitimations for social critique by industrial culture. Classical paradox is trumped, as it were, by the undecidability of undecidability itself.

If we say that the identity of the speaker is constituted in the utterance, then it cannot be known definitively who speaks. It remains unclear whether the speaker is a Cretan, as it were. Since

IAN ANGUS

the utterance constructs the speaker, the spoken is anterior to the speaker. The speaker is spoken and the speaking comes from nowhere. This speaking from nowhere—utterance without location—can issue in a knowledge claim if the identity constructed is not the identity of which the social critique speaks. In other words, if the critic's identity is external to the criticism in the style of the early criticism of the first generation of the Frankfurt School or of Habermas, then social critique makes a claim to knowledge of the other. But if the self-identity of the speaker is constructed in the criticism then a paradox of undecidability emerges. Both of these options emerge from nowhere—a speaking without location. In one case, we get knowledge claims. In the other, we get a rhetoric of self-construction. If we can say that contemporary industrial culture is such as to problematize the speaking subject, that we cannot know the speaker's identity anterior to the speech, then the speech from nowhere—where it is undecidable whether the claim is undecidable—is constitutive of contemporary social identities.

If the classic liar's paradox can be called a paradox of reflection, contemporary paradox may be called a paradox of constitution—of constitutive, not reflexive, undecidability. The state of contemporary culture is thus a general rhetoric in which every utterance vies with every other as intervention, criticism and legitimation in order to constitute speaking voices. This is the theoretical space of contemporary social critique. The only kind of privilege there might be in this context is for an utterance that draws attention to its own self-constituting character. Rather than hiding its own self-constituting activity, it would thematize the undecidability of its own identity.

The notion of performative contradiction attempts to separate validity claims and their reflexive legitimation into distinct

42

discursive realms. In other words, it assumes, with the epistemo-logical orientation of the modern philosophical tradition, that a discourse about discourse—which would address reflexive ques-tions of validity, legitimation and critique—can be carried on as distinct from the rhetoric of cultural interventions. Alternatively put, that the universality of ethical–cultural discourse can be elab-orated apart from specific ethical–cultural interventions themselves. This is the source of the formalism of Habermas's dis-course ethics. Similarly, it supposes that cultural interventions—while they may have assumptions or implications relevant to reflexive legitimation—are not themselves contributions to such a reflexive discourse. The first generation of the Frankfurt School, in a manner renewed by Habermas's concept of performative con-tradiction, carried over this separation from the philosophical tradition which it criticized. In contrast, I have argued that the col-lapse of the separation between cultural intervention and reflexive legitimation imbricates philosophy and industrial culture in a novel manner such that social critique becomes a kind of "news from nowhere."

In order to clarify what I mean by "nowhere" I would like to recall Niklas Luhmann's claim that social institutions "deparadox-icalize" issues of reflexive self-reference.[16] It is perfectly logical to ask, for example, whether legal institutions really produce justice, whether educational institutions really educate students, whether religious institutions really produce the love of God. But while such reflexive questions are philosophically meaningful, Luhmann claims that they have no place within the institution itself. In order to function, the legal system *assumes* that it produces justice; universities simply *assume* they they produce educated students, and so on. In other words, a social institution transforms the philosophically meaningful reflexive question that can be asked about it into a tautology: justice just *is* legality for all practical purposes, a university degree just *is* education. It is a fundamental presupposition of the functioning of a social institution to render irrelevant, without institutional location, reflexive questions concerning the larger meaning and functioning of itself.

The concept of constitutive paradox that I am asserting here requires a deeper concept of the relation between location and social critique. It suggests that the very relation between location inside or outside is constituted by an undecidable, anonymous utterance. It is thus not possible to simply assign criticism to a non-institutional non-space as Luhmann does. Curiously, this view that social critique has no institutional location is a conception shared by both many radical critics who regard institutional legitimations as merely ideological reflexes and those conservatives who would expugn radical criticism from institutions. My analysis suggests that institutions themselves emerge from the same constitutive paradox as social critique. The question whether universities really produce educated students can thus not be rendered definitively external to the university because the very notion of inside versus outside the university is constitutively undecidable. Institutions are not merely tautological; their claims to higher truth—that universities *really* teach knowledge, that the legal system *really* produces justice—are a necessary aspect of their functioning because the boundary between a given institution and its cultural environment is constituted by the news from nowhere. An apparently enlightened cynicism with regard to institutional legitimations fails to understand both the necessity of such legitimations to their functioning and the opening to social critique that they offer. Institutional identity is as much at issue, no less unsettled, than the identity of the critic. They derive from the two directions into which the news from nowhere splits: The decidability of a knowledge claim when it is oriented to an other, the undecidability of a self-constituting identity when it is self-referring. Contemporary constitutive paradox is not just of undecidability, but of the undecidability of undecidability, and produces the simultaneous options of knowledge and paradox.

The theoretical space of contemporary social critique came into being with the unravelling of the suture between philosophy and social critique. The interest in universality and enlightenment can no longer be inserted into social critique through a reliance on a separate philosophical justification. Consequently, it risks succumbing to institutional closures, on the one hand, or merely self-promoting agonistic cultural practices—relativism—on the other. I have argued that in the present situation social critique necessarily occupies a theoretical space characterized by the constitutively paradoxical, self-referring character of utterances in a way that imbricates intervention, evaluation and critique. The difficulty of social critique today, the near impossibility of finding a place to stand from which to begin criticism—which is attendant upon its self-constituting character—is exactly that which makes it an important social task. It seems to be an activity without institutional location, but this outside is constituted in the same moment as the apparent location that an institution provides. The construction of the identity of the speaker through the utterance itself proposes and produces identities which are not contained by existing institutions precisely because institutions delay, but never definitively expel, the paradox from which they emerge.

Contemporary social critique is neither internal nor external to institutions, or—perhaps better—is both internal and external to institutions—because the constitutive paradox gives rise to an undecidable border between inside and outside. The option inside gives rise to institutional legitimations. The option outside gives rise to social critique. But these two options are simultaneous; one cannot displace the other. In a sense, the university—or justice, or the sacred—is everywhere, which is why it must ask the question whether it really educates and what is education. Utterances in this theoretical space are characterized by constitutive paradox because they find no justification outside themselves. Constituting both location and non-location, they can criticize the normal practices sustained by institutions through their relation to the limit-cases which manifest the boundaries that define normality. Such a critique of normality generates its own justification by proposing new critical subjectivities whose validity is *always-already-not-sufficiently* institutionally recognized. No matter how ubiquitous, the system can still be observed and described—an activity which constructs the identity of the observer and proposes new possibilities for action. In this way, it seems to me that social critique can be totalizing and yet maintain a difference between validity and power—which is perhaps opening enough to suggest that one can begin to think differently about enlightenment.

The intellectual tendencies that I have grouped as particularly embodying the danger that emerges with the postmodern discursive turn—social constructionism, hermeneutics and Wittgensteinian language game theory—are attempts to dissolve, rather than address, the constitutive paradox that Habermas calls a performative contradiction. They want to accept the main conclusion of the critique of philosophy—that all forms of thought are embedded in forms of life—without theorizing the standpoint from which such a conclusion can be arrived at and enacted. Thus, they may well argue that "in practice" there is no constitutive paradox, since any utterance will always be understood in a given context. This resort to common sense is valid enough, as far as it goes, but, if this is all that is said, it serves to cut off common sense from the epochal horizon that shapes the form of life itself, and thus to render invisible the shaping whereby common sense is given form. While the pragmatic effect of a speech act in a given language game is more or less determinable, it nevertheless exudes paradox in so far as it also participates in the shaping of an epoch. Every speech act both confirms the instituted horizon within which it makes sense and also re-enacts the shaping of the horizon. These particular and universal dimensions of a discursive intervention are always interwoven after the end of philosophy since their previously settled limits have become unhinged. Thus, the recognition of pragmatic meaning cannot serve genuinely to dissolve the paradox; it becomes a forced ignorance of the wider world-shaping activity of language—a cutting off of discourse from the horizon of the world that is a key danger after the linguistic turn. Thus, it must be recognized that the "critique of all values hitherto held to be highest" (Nietzsche) which roots them in forms of practice that cannot be taken to be universal, requires for its enunciation a standpoint which strains beyond any particular form of practice. The anti-metaphysical, anti-foundational stand is possible only because the philosophical tradition articulated a standpoint beyond practical involvements. Necessarily, the standpoint of totalizing critique comes at the end of a philosophical tradition upon which it depends for its concept of the universal in order, in its turn, to reveal this tradition as partial and, in that sense, ideological. In consequence, the genuine and unavoidable constitutive paradox that emerges with the totalizing of critique cannot be simply dissolved by embracing the multiplicity of forms of life. The dominant postmodern tendency, which I have called a danger, wants the consequences of totalizing critique without the labour that produces it. This flattening of the constitutive paradox, through its attempted dissolution, makes it impossible to address the present historical moment in which totalizing critique becomes both necessary and without foundation. To put it somewhat differently, one cannot simply discard universality for particularity at this point, but must radically deconstruct and reformulate the particularity–universality nexus itself.

This danger involved in recognizing that a culture enfolds the forms of evaluation is that it might attenuate the notion of critique sufficiently to amount to abandoning it altogether. The dominant tendency within the postmodern condition seems to encourage this route by saying that, since there are any number of discourses that claim both particular and universal dimensions of the present epoch, it is *impossible in principle* to legitimate one discourse over another. The only universal statement would thus be a denial of the legitimacy of universal statements covering an indefinite plurality of discourses. The pragmatic effect of this utterance is to withdraw concern for the world-horizon and it is in this sense ideological, but if one wants to accept the totalizing of critique, one must address the question of reflexive justification in a paradoxical context and show how ideology-critiques can be both moves within common sense and oriented toward the historical epoch as a whole. Paradox is not only a logical, and post-logical, appelation; it is constitutive of self-referring critique, in which utterances made possible by a form of life radically question that form of life itself. The standpoint of critique from within the epoch it criticizes does not discount its intervention in a form of life. Rather, it calls out for a critical practice which recognizes the passage of every utterance toward the world-horizon.

NOTES

1. Compare Edmund Husserl, *Die Krisis der Europaeischen Wissenschaft und die Transzendentale Phaenomenologie* (The Hague: Martinus Nijhoff, 1976) pp. 74–5, 386, with *The Crisis of the European Sciences and Transcendental Phenomenology*, trans. David Carr (Evanston: Northwestern University Press, 1970) pp. 73–4, 378. Maurice Merleau-Ponty, *Themes from the Lectures at the College de France 1952–1960*, trans. John O'Neill (Evanston: Northwestern University Press, 1970) Chapter 5 and "Indirect Language and the Voices of Silence" in *Signs*, trans. Richard C. McCleary (Evanston: Northwestern University Press, 1962) p. 59. Claude Lefort, *Democracy and Political Theory*, trans. David Macey (Minneapolis: University of Minnesota Press, 1988) pp. 10–12, 217, 219.

2. Lefort, *Democracy and Political Theory*, p. 222.

3. George P. Grant, "Ideology in Modern Empires" in *Perspectives of Empire, Essays Presented to Gerald S. Graham*, ed. John E. Flint and Glyndwr Williams (London: Longman's Group, 1973) p. 194.

4. Max Horkheimer and Theodor Adorno, *Dialectic of Enlightenment*, trans. John Cumming (New York: Herder and Herder, 1972) p. xi.

5. Ibid., p. xiii.

6. Max Horkheimer, *Dawn and Decline*, trans. Michael Shaw (New York: Seabury Press, 1978) p. 239.

7. Jürgen Habermas, *The Philosophical Discourse of Modernity*, trans. Frederick Lawrence (Cambridge: MIT Press, 1987) p. 119.

8. Jürgen Habermas, "Discourse Ethics: Notes on a Program of Philosophical Justification" in *Moral Consciousness and Communicative Action*, trans. Christian Lenhardt and Shierry Weber Nicholsen (Cambridge: MIT Press, 1990) p. 80.

9. Martin Jay, "The Debate over Performative Contradiction: Habermas versus the Poststructuralists" in Axel Honneth, Thomas McCarthy, Claus Offe and Albrecht Wellmer (eds) *Philosophical Interventions in the Unfinished Project of Enlightenment*, trans. William Regh (Cambridge: MIT Press, 1992) p. 266.

10. Jürgen Habermas, *The Philosophical Discourse of Modernity*, pp. 187, 197.

11. It is not my present purpose to analyse Habermas's discourse ethics itself in this context. My concern is strictly with its use to counter so-called

Nietzschean forms of cultural criticism. However, my analysis at this point does imply that one can accept the reciprocity and universalization conditions proposed by discourse ethics and not accept the limitation of criticism, nor its formalism. The three key assumptions made by Habermas at this point are that normative claims "can be treated *like* claims to truth" ("Discourse Ethics", p. 68), that the main problem of justification is defeating moral scepticism, and the reduction of the range of persuasive speech to the dualism of truth/lies ("Discourse Ethics", p. 90).

12. I have criticized Habermas's return to limited critique in more detail in "Habermas Confronts the Deconstructionist Challenge: On *The Philosophical Discourse of Modernity,*" *Canadian Journal of Political and Social Theory,* Vol. 14, Nos 1, 2, 3, 1990.

13. Jürgen Habermas, *The Philosophical Discourse of Modernity,* pp. 185, 193.

14. Ibid., pp. 119, 185, 188.

15. Mikhail Bakhtin, *Philosophy of the Act,* trans. Vadim Liapunov (Austin: University of Texas Press, 1993) and Ludwig Landgrebe, *The Phenomenology of Edmund Husserl* (Ithaca: Cornell University Press, 1981).

16. Niklas Luhmann, "The Autopoiesis of Social Systems" and "Tautology and Paradox in the Self-Descriptions of Modern Society" in *Essays on Self-reference* (New York: Columbia University Press, 1990).

3

THE REBOUND TO CONTINGENCY

The discursive turn in philosophy and the human sciences stems from taking language use as especially significant in illuminating the whole of social praxis. Philosophical and scientific activity itself, after the turn, takes language as the metaphorical basis for understanding its own theoretical formation. This reflexive application of the discursive turn to theory itself is one of the main sources of the power of the metaphor of language. It not only provokes interesting new descriptions of social praxis but also reconfigures the relationship of theory to social praxis. The metaphor of language gives itself to a concise formulation of the recursive doubling that is always present in the project of self-knowledge in philosophy and the human sciences since humanity is both known and knower. The project of self-knowledge in the human sciences produces a doubling of the subject which has been characteristic of modernity since the anchoring of knowledge in subjectivity by Descartes. It was called the empirical–transcendental doublet by Foucault and the transcendental and concrete egos by Husserl.[1]

Constitutive paradox is the contemporary form of this doubling which results from the collapsing together of the legitimating discourse formerly known as philosophy with the specific utterances of social critique. The loss of linkage between particular utterances and a legitimating discourse requires that the relationship between particular and universal, or immediacy and totality, be radically rethought. One important contemporary attempt to pose this question of linkage between is in the theory of articulation developed by Ernesto Laclau and Chantal Mouffe. I will argue that their conception remains within the metaphysical opposition that it attempts to displace in so far as its emphasis on the contingency of articulating linkages is still dominated by a rebound from necessity.

The concept of articulation emerged historically in the work of Ernesto Laclau through the development of the key idea of structuralism—that the only alternative form of explanation to "reduction to" a prior or underlying sufficient cause, or foundation, is structural determinism, or explanation with reference to the organizing scheme of a current totality. Thus, the idea of structural totality emerged in polemical opposition to reductionism, or explanation with reference to determinate empirical contents. Within Marxism, there is a continual resurgence of these two forms of explanation referring either toward totality or back to class origin. While these two types of explanation are different from each other, and one or the other is usually stressed by a given thinker or school, they are in a deeper sense mutually reinforcing. As Heidegger has shown and Derrida has elaborated, metaphysics consists in the mutual implication of origin and goal.[2] Thus, to argue for one trajectory of thought against the other misses the complementarity of the two. These local polemics do not alter the system of oppositions within which such reversals operate. Moreover, the ascription of origin and telos can shift their roles within these mutually reinforcing alternatives—class unity can be redefined as a goal and totality regarded as an origin. Since the complementarity of the two alternatives of structural totality and empirical location is now apparent, it is presently more to the point to rethink the theoretical basis of Marxism from the standpoint of the emergent concept of articulation. While the concept of articulation emerged from structuralism, or rather the unravelling of structuralism, it is not necessarily confined within the set of complementary metaphysical oppositions. I will argue that the break from structuralism allows for a new encounter with the phenomenological tradition, and that in this manner the investigation of cultural praxis can elude metaphysical closure in a new postmodern open field.

In these days when a quote from Althusser seems to begin every discussion of ideology, and in which everything prior seems to have faded from memory, it is necessary to recall that structuralism arose, not only in the local polemic against causal reductionism to empirical location and class content, but also in opposition to the global alternative of routing theory toward everyday experience and mundane existence that is characteristic of phenomenology. French philosophy in the 1950s was polarized between structuralism and existential phenomenology. It is in opposition to all theory oriented to finding its origin in experience (whether empiricist or phenomenological) that the idea of structural determinism was articulated. In this larger context, Althusser opposed all Hegelian and "humanist" interpretations of Marx which, he argued, were based on a concept of expressive totality.[3] The fundamental idea of expressive totality is that of a whole which develops throughout all its aspects through an internal unfolding of its essence. Against this, structuralism proposed the notion of "multiple planes of determination" whose "conjunction," or intersection, could not be conceptualized on any model of inner development. Whereas expressive totality, through its notion of internal development, relied on the mutual implication of origin and goal characteristic of metaphysical thought, structuralism remains caught in metaphysics in two ways: first, through the notion of structure as a closed system and second, externally, as it were, through its polemical denial of the relevance of origins and empirical contents.

Existential phenomenology—represented at that time in France primarily by Sartre, Merleau-Ponty and de Beauvoir—incorporated Marx by attempting a synthesis of Hegel and Husserl. Thus it is not surprising that the structuralist characterization of existential phenomenology followed their own prior self-conception in collapsing phenomenological (Husserlian) and Hegelian concepts of totality, though structuralism elaborated its own distinctiveness by rejecting them in one fell swoop as expressive. While this is not the place to offer a detailed critique of this attempted synthesis, it is worthwhile to point out two key points whereby French existentialism departed from phenomenology in a way that made this collapsing possible: First, they rejected Husserl's transcendental reduction in favour of a "mundane," or worldly, phenomenology. Second, they did not distinguish between Hegelian and phenomenological notions of immediacy. For a Hegelian, immediacy is always mediated; thus, the phenomenological retrieval of immediacy could be understood, in "expressive" fashion, to mediate itself toward totality. Immediacy in the Husserlian sense of self-evidence, or original evidence, is closer to the Hegelian concept of the "concrete," rather than Hegelian "immediacy." But immediacy, in phenomenological terms, is neither self-mediating toward a totality, nor a foundation that would be impervious to any further questioning. In the Preface to *Phenomenology of Spirit*, Hegel saw this as the only alternative: "Thoughts become fluid when pure thinking, this inner *immediacy*, recognizes itself as a moment, or when the pure certainty of itself abstracts from itself—not by leaving itself out, or setting itself aside, but by giving up the *fixity* of its self-positing."[4] Recognizing that knowledge does not consist in isolated assertions, Hegel claimed that it is the self-mediation of individual evidences toward a totality in which knowledge consists: "Through this movement the pure thoughts become *Notions*, and are only now what they are in truth, self-movements, circles, spiritual essences, which is what their substance is."[5] Thus, the Hegelian image of knowledge is a circle in which the beginning initiates the movement to the end—immediacy to total mediation or totality—and the end recaptures its own beginning—totality or Science becomes concrete in sensuous immediacy. Through its preformation in the direction of a presupposed totality, Hegel's immediacy is entirely carried up into the system without remainder. Husserl's concept of immediacy is more concerned with the second part of this movement than the first—the movement toward the concrete whereby structures of scientific knowledge are given evidence "originally" by the philosopher. Only through the rediscovery of original evidence by each investigator for him/herself do scientific edifices, in the sense of elaborated knowledge-systems, become lived and efficacious within the life of the one who *strives for knowledge.* It is the "reduction" of knowledge-systems to the striving that produced them and that can reanimate them that is the core of the phenomenological emphasis on immediacy. It involves neither an assertion that immediacy is fixed in the sense that it couldn't be modified by later evidences, nor an acceptance of the Hegelian view that such modification is a "mediation" that carries the experience of evidence entirely into the movement of knowledge. Husserl's concept of immediacy is existentialist in the Kierkegaardian sense that "the System is of course *ex post facto*, and so does not begin immediately with the immediacy with which existence began."[6] Immediacy in the Hegelian sense is a concept developed within, and only meaningful within, the System which presupposes its finishing in the totality. In contrast, phenomenological immediacy refers to the existence of any knowledge-structure in original evidence, as opposed to mere convention and taking over from others, and is thus the existential index of the striving for knowledge. It is not original in a historical or logical sense, but from the point of view of the striving for knowledge as an accounting for oneself—which is in the end an ethical task. The image of knowledge in phenomenology thus cannot be a circle, but is this combination of *immediate existence* with the *horizon* within which it occurs. There is always a remainder to any system. The task of phenomenological investigation is thus to investigate the space between these terminations. It is an infinite space, which has emerged from the loss of passage between origin and goal, near and far, that characterized the Hegelian mediation characteristic of modernity. As a consequence, a concern with the concrete can no longer take a Hegelian form either, as the *application* of a system that is finished, and must be rediscovered as immediacy or existence in a Husserlian manner. Despite the existentialist component to Husserl's phenomenology, it is not where French existentialism located it. This is a point with many implications. If a comparison between Hegel and Husserl were on the agenda, it would be between the "concrete" and "immediate evidence." The confusion of Hegelian and Husserlian concepts of immediacy was the main theoretical error of French existentialism. The upshot of this is that the structuralist characterization of existential phenomenology was not without justification in the French context, but does not apply to phenomenology as a whole. Thus, while I do not wish to rediscover unblemished the French phenomenological Marxism of the 1950s which was at that time the alternative to structuralism, I argue that the advances in Marxist theory that the concept of articulation achieves can, nevertheless, only be secured and developed within a theoretical perspective that retrieves a key experiential dimension based in phenomenology. This notion of experience is close to the question of the concrete in Hegel and, by virtue of a similar critique of Hegelian closure by Marx to the existentialist critique by Kierkegaard, to the notion of praxis in Marx.

The opposition between structural determinism and experiential immediacy, between which Marxism has lurched back and forth without resolution, must now be brought into the theory of articulation itself. Not only Marxism, but cultural theory in general, has been articulated in the tension between viewing humanity as from a distant star and capturing the presence of experience in its presencing. The concept of articulation emerged through the structuralist denial of immediacy-origin and, in the hands of Laclau and Mouffe, engages in a complementary denial of any closed, sutured, totality-goal. It attempts to deny both sides of the metaphysical opposition between totality and immediacy and, for this reason, proposes an exit from the metaphysical closure in which Marxism had become trapped. The new intellectual formation that has been coming into being in this space of metaphysical deconstruction denies the "foundationalist" and "essentialist" pretensions of modern thought and society. In particular, such a denial involves a rejection of the notion that the social totality is determinable as such because its formulation as a totality is always the product of a hegemonic political project—an effect of power. If totality is rethought in Gramscian terms as the horizon of a hegemonic project, the social totality is not claimed to be determinable as such, but only *through* the specific investigations (themes) undertaken. Thus, the concept of totality as horizon does not imply a political project of total transformation of the system but is rather connected to the less "totalizing" political projects of the new social movements. In Laclau's phrasing, a horizon is "an empty locus, a point in which society symbolizes its very groundlessness."[7] Simplifying somewhat in order to clarify: feminism wants to eliminate patriarchy; the ecology movement wants to eliminate industrial society; etc. Each movement has a definition of the system that pervades the system in its entirety. These are not reform movements in the sense that they point to systemic features. None the less, they are not exclusive definitions: the society is both patriarchal and industrial; and capitalist, and Eurocentric, etc. While new social movement theory has tended to characterize these as particular or restricted movements in distinction from the traditional Marxist project of transforming the system as a whole, there is actually a more subtle reformation of the nexus of particularity and universality at stake. One does not need to reject the notion of totality, but rather see that the totality in question is also capable of being put alongside other total definitions. The whole is thus a horizon always capable of further determination, but never finally determined, which thus issues in a political project of a plurality of social movements each oriented toward a given determination. The larger, "total" political project is thus oriented toward a Gramscian conception of the system as a hegemonic diversity of locations articulated through the leadership uniting a historic bloc and of a possible counter-hegemony understood in the same manner. Thus Laclau and Mouffe conclude their presentation with the claim that "It is only through negativity, division and antagonism that a formation can constitute itself as a totalizing horizon."[8]

The limit of the social attains a presence within the discursive formation by an operation that Laclau and Mouffe designate as "equivalence." They give the example of a colonized country in which differences of dress, language, skin colour and customs become equivalent, or substitutable, as evidence of the oppressiveness of the dominant power and remark that "[s]ince each of these contents is equivalent to the others in terms of their common differentiation from the colonized people, it loses the condition of differential *moment*, and acquires the floating character of an *element*."[9] This common differentiation should not be understood as various expressions of an underlying essentially antagonistic relation, which would be to revert to the positivity of the social that they criticize, but as the *construction* of equivalences that, through the antagonism, articulate the relation colonizer/colonized as domination, rather than as just a subordination. We may notice that the example in this case does not do the full duty that the theory requires. Actually, they speak of the dominant power being "made evident" in these different contents,[10] but this is a misleading phrase. If it cannot mean essential underlying relations of power which express themselves in various forms, as the phrase seems to imply (but which would be incompatible with their entire approach), then the issue is exactly how is this cultural unity of "the dominant power" constructed, and their terminology avoids this posing of the question. To clarify that this key issue of

antagonism has not been well-enough illuminated by Laclau and
Mouffe, let us instead refer to a dominated, but not colonized,
country like Canada in which, we may say, the dependent relations
between Canada and the US are "like" the relations of labour and
capital, which, in turn, are "like" the relations between Quebec
and the federal government, "like" relations between men and
women, and "like" relations between humanity and nature. This
collection of similitudes, or equivalences, is not pregiven but constructed in the practical politics in which one and/or more of
them is at issue. In each case, it is by no means self-evident that the
best way to push one of these causes is by alliance with the dominated part of another social difference. Why not ally oneself with
a dominant power in another discourse? And, of course, in the
practical politics of the last thirty years—both in Canada and else-
where—such alliances have indeed occurred. Feminism, to pick
just one example, has been most "successful" where it has allied
itself with the business mentality and possessive individualist
notions of equality. To assume from the outset that one subordinated social difference, when it is experienced through antagonism
as a domination, is in any "natural," or predictable, sense drawn to
alliance with other subordinate sectors, is a remnant of exactly the
Marxist essentialism that Laclau and Mouffe criticize. Let us finally
say it clearly: The standpoint of the subordinated is not an epistemologically privileged one, though it is crucial politically.

With the demise of foundationalism, this relation between
specificity and totality can be understood as an internal–external
relation, without any necessity to claim "fundamentalness," or priority, for either side. Social differences exist in all social formations.
Only in some cases do they become "antagonisms" pressing for
social change and invoking their centrality to the social form as a

whole. Such antagonisms have become visible in the new social movements of the last thirty years—ecology, anti-nuclear, anti-racist, ethnic, feminist, sexual liberation, regionalist, nationalist, and other, movements. In the new social movements there has been a "step back" with respect to more conventional political events: It is not only an issue of a power struggle within a deter-mined social formation, but primarily a question of under what conditions is a given social difference *experienced as insufferable* and imagination directed toward alternatives which, thereby, *unsettles the presupposed understanding* of the social formation and provides a *glimpse into the universal dimensions* of cultural life. At this junc-ture, the teleology of modern society toward the ideals of "autonomy and equality" is displaced by a concern with an "ethics of difference." These movements invoke boundary-phenomena pertaining to the relation between the internal social difference and its external context. The politics of articulation resides in this internal/external dynamism between common sense and the epochal horizon.

My criticism of Laclau and Mouffe centres on the concept of totality as horizon that they use without acknowledging its reso-nance with Husserl's use of the same term. I suggest that they utilize but do not develop adequately a notion of the "field of discursivity" because their conception of hegemony is too closely tied to the notion of "contingency" which cannot be purged of connotations stemming from its metaphysical polemical opposition to the notion of "necessity." My critique thus has two parts. The first suggests that Laclau and Mouffe's concept of the "field of discursivity" can be developed through a connection to the phenomenological concept of "world" based on the idea of "thematization." The second devel-ops the concept of "particularity" (in distinction from the more commonly used concept of "difference") in order to advance beyond the rhetoric of contingency, or unfixity, that is key to their text. Thus, I argue that against its intentions the concept of hegemonic totality which Laclau and Mouffe propose is itself still circumscribed by the complementary metaphysical oppositions it rejects. A genuine exit requires that the key terms of necessity and contingency be fundamentally rethought, criticized and reformulated, which this essay attempts to do by introducing the phenomenological term "world" and the philosophical concept of "particularity" into the space of the deconstruction of the metaphysical complementarity of origin and totality. The universalization of contingency, the expansion of hegemony to the limit of the social, requires a new conception of the relation of part and whole. The phenomenological concept of totality as horizon constituting a "world," derived from the theme–background relation, is distinct from the criticized alternatives of organic, logical or dissolved totality, and which is theorized beyond the negative statements of temporariness and unfixity. Such a phenomenological concept of totality does not fall into the errors pinpointed by Laclau and Mouffe and can be considered an extension of the concept of horizon which they propose themselves. This argument leads to the corollary that, while their post-structuralist conception of totality is not adequate to conceptualizing the origin of modernity, the phenomenological concept of the world as horizon proposed here can do so both specifically and conclusively.

Laclau and Mouffe locate the origin of the problematic of articulation in the rationalization and disenchantment of modern society. The elements on which articulations operate were specified in the eighteenth century as "fragments of a lost unity."[11] It is

significant they they turn from argument to narration at this point
in the text, as narration is a common strategy when one can not
give an adequate theoretical account. The analysis of modern society as a division and fragmentation was elaborated by German
philosophy in contrast to their conception of the natural, organic
unity of Greek culture. This unity could not be recaptured since its
very specification implies a conscious analysis that could not annul
its own conditions of emergence. With the displacement of totality from origin to telos the theoretical task became the *construction*
of a conscious and rational totality. Thus emerged the modern
concept of alienation. Laclau and Mouffe argue that this new form
of totality into which elements are to be unified may take two
forms: "either that organization is contingent and, therefore, external to the fragments themselves; or else, both the fragments and
the organization are necessary moments of a totality which transcends them."[12] While this is a clear alternative, one the theory of
articulation seeks to address, it is nevertheless the case that the history of modern philosophy has tended to fudge the alternative.
The history of Marxism has been no less clear in this respect.

A clarification of this alternative emerged in Louis Althusser's
structuralist critique of Hegel through the notion of "expressive
totality."[13] An expressive totality is a unity in which all of the elements and relations unfold from and therefore express an
underlying principle. This principle of unity encompasses all transitions such that they take on a necessary and logical character.
Hegel's rationalist totality claimed to be such a system of mediations through exclusively logical relations. Thus, his conception of
philosophy was based on the principle of the identity of logic and
content. Through dialectic, speculative philosophy established the
identity of Thought and Being.[14] Subsequent dialectical thought,

up to Adorno, has always been sceptical of any separation of logic, or "method," and content. However, this claim masked the fact that non-necessary, contingent relations were the basis for many so-called logical transitions, as any careful twentieth-century reader of the *Phenomenology of Spirit* will have noticed. In other words, the putative banishment of rhetoric from philosophy concealed its return, disguised as logic, to shore up the system. In contrast, Althusser, through the concept of "overdetermination," attempted to theorize the multiplicity of meanings inherent in any symbolic, or cultural, order. Laclau and Mouffe state the implication of this concept in the following manner:

> The symbolic—i.e., overdetermined—character of social rela-
> tions therefore implies that they lack an ultimate literality which
> would reduce them to necessary moments of an immanent law.
> There are not *two* planes, one of essences and the other of
> appearances, since there is no possibility of fixing an *ultimate* lit-
> eral sense for which the symbolic would be a second and
> derived plane of signification. Society and social agents lack
> any essence and their regularities merely consist of the relative
> and precarious forms of fixation which accompany the estab-
> lishment of a certain order.[15]

They point out that this implication of Althusser's concept of overdetermination co-existed in his work with an incompatible notion of "determination in the last instance by the economy" that held it within Marxism and, indeed, reduced it back to an essentialism very much like the Hegelian type it criticized.[16] The later deconstruction of Althusserianism allowed the possibility of merely shifting from an essentialism of expressive totality to an essentialism of elements—in other words, a lurch back from the whole to the parts, from rationalism to empiricism.[17] This alternative of expressive totality or disaggregated elements is thus a complementary metaphysical opposition within a similar essentialism (of part or whole). Laclau and Mouffe comment that this debate evaded the fundamental question: "by failing to *specify the terrain* in which the unity or separation among objects takes place, we once more fall back into the 'rationalism or empiricism' alternative."[18] Thus, it is only through the component of the "terrain," or "field," that the theory of articulation can avoid both a rationalist and an empiricist conception of totality.

The notion of politics as the construction and deconstruction of equivalences must incorporate some notion of the general discursive field as a whole, since it is across the plural discourses constituting this field that equivalences are constructed. In the course of their argument, the important concept of the *general "field," or "terrain," of discursivity* is often used but neither clarified nor addressed directly.[19] If we examine the manner of appearance of the field, the space of competing articulations, we can define specific conditions for its emergence. If there were an articulation so successful as to achieve an uncontested hegemonic organization of the entire field, it would be a Hegelian rationalist totality of mediations, rather than the space of articulations. But, also, the field cannot be simply a plurality of articulations, since it also constitutes the possibility of translation between them, through the construction of equivalences. Laclau and Mouffe thus say that "the *general field of the emergence of hegemony* is that of articulatory practices, that is, a field where the 'elements' have not crystallized into 'moments'."[20] The general discursive field thus cannot be subsumed under one (or any determinate number of) articulation(s), but neither is it outside the articulation(s) taken as a whole. Rather, it is to be sought in the very competition of articulations to hegemonize its space—a competition which, in principle, can have no decisive resolution without eliminating the entire problematic of hegemony and articulation. Thus hegemony cannot be conceived as radiating from a privileged point in the discursive field and power must be conceived as a product of opposed logics of equivalence and difference not as foundational. They define hegemony as "basically metonymical: its effects always emerge from a surplus of meaning which results from an operation of displacement."[21] It is for this reason that a rhetoric of the "lack of fixity of any meaning" is an often reiterated component of the text of *Hegemony and Socialist Strategy*. I want to suggest that these features of the field are captured in the phenomenological notion of horizon, which is based on the notion of a theme/background relation. The element is a theme focused upon which only appears against a surrounding background. The background shades off indefinitely in all directions. It is given as "there," but not with an explicit clarity. Of course, elements previously part of the undetermined background can become themes, but this occurs precisely through a shift of theme and, thereby, a shift of background. The background can only be determined by ceasing to be background. As an undetermined surrounding to the theme, the background is not *in* time and space, but is the place and duration implicit in the theme. The shading off of the background is indefinite, but not infinite, and terminates in a *horizon* that circumscribes the background as a whole. However, this limit of the background cannot be given as if it were a theme. There is a horizon because the background to any theme is specific to the theme due to the relevances (to use Schütz's term) to which it gives form. Related themes are related precisely by reference to an overlapping, but not identical, background and can be determined in their applicability with reference to the circumscribing horizon. The background and its horizon are therefore experienced in an entirely different manner than themes. As Husserl phrases it,

> these horizons, then, are "presuppositions," which, as intentional implicates included in the constituting intentionality, continually determine the objective sense of the immediate experiential surroundings, and which therefore have a character totally different from that of any of the idealizing presuppositions of predicative judging.[22]

The critical point here pertains to the extension of the theme–background relation through the notion of horizon into a new concept of totality which is known in phenomenological terminology as the "world." Though Laclau and Mouffe use the term horizon to refer to a hegemonic totality, they do not theorize the term itself and do not consider the phenomenological concept of totality as horizon as a possible complement to their intentions. On the basis of the theme–background relation, we can define the central problem of rationalist logical mediation succinctly: Rationalism is a totality of relations between thematized elements that presents the *relations between* elements as if they were themselves thematized *elements*. The impossibility of this total thematization of all elements and relations surfaces periodically as the empiricist disaggregation. This reciprocal opposition confirms the point that the opposition between necessary and contingent relations is an inadequate basis for the theory of articulation. Contingency is simply the absence of logical necessity. While the problematic of hegemony arises in this manner from within the rationalist dissolution, if it remains satisfied simply with the assertion of contingency, the elements are entrapped within the empiricist dissolution.

The figure–ground relationship means that any thematic unity is given within the context of a totality that, in principle, never appears thematically. The background of a theme shades off indefinitely, but not infinitely, and is circumscribed by a horizon. Since there is a plurality of themes, there is also a plurality of horizons. Husserl called the presupposed, non-thematic, *horizon of horizons* the "world" and emphasized the difference between the evidence of the world and that of objects within it. "There exists a fundamental difference between the way we are conscious of the world and the way we are conscious of things or objects . . . though together the two make up a fundamental unity. . . . We are conscious of this horizon only as a horizon for existing objects; without particular objects of consciousness it cannot be actual."[23] The totality of the world can never become an object. The indistinctness of the world, its characteristic of infinite continuation in time and space, provides the presupposed unity from which objects and their various backgrounds appear as belonging within the same horizon of the world. This is not to say that there is any object that cannot be thematized; on the contrary, thematization is inherently without barriers; any element can be picked up from the horizon and transformed into an explicit object. Rather, since thematization is itself the constitution of object-ness, or element-ness (in Laclau and Mouffe's vocabulary), the world is always "prior," presupposed by elements within it. As Husserl puts it, "All that is together in the world has a universal immediate or mediate way of belonging together; through this the world is not merely a totality but an all-encompassing unity, a whole (even though it is infinite)."[24] With this notion of world-unity as "belonging-together," the unity of the general discursive field can be understood without slipping into the difficulties with the modern notions of "totality" pointed out by Laclau and Mouffe. The theory of articulation needs some conception of unity which surpasses the temporary unity of articulations. Only if this unity can be satisfactorily distinguished from both logical totality and empirical contingency can the theory of articulation theoretically account for the conditions of its own operation. I am claiming that the conception of totality in the phenomenological concept of the world-horizon fulfils this function. The totality of the horizon of the world is not a "fixity" in any of its forms (organic, rationalist, empiricist), which imply the total thematization of objects and their relations. The horizon changes with respect to the theme, and the world has a different character, or style, in different socio-historical periods. None the less, the existence of the horizon as such does not change, as the presumption of a unitary world to which themes belong does not change. This relation between change and perdurance is characteristic of non-thematic totality. It is always there, yet its particular style changes; if one were to attempt to define this style, aspects of it would be transformed into themes and there would remain an unthematized background. Its style is contingent, but its existence necessary, though this horizonal necessity can never be transferred to any specific themes.

The "world" thus has two interrelated aspects:[25] On the one hand, the world is the culturally relative horizonal unity populated by social identities and with a characteristic spatial and temporal extension whose specific style is constituted by ongoing cultural practices. In this sense, the instituting expression enables a discourse whose centrality in defining the style of a world is due to its ability to translate the other culturally relevant discourses and thereby implicate the world-horizon. Thus, the "greater fundamentality," or "materiality," of some discourses depends on their ability to define the limits of the specific cultural world through its horizon. Similarly, the "unconscious" of a cultural unity can be addressed as "that which cannot be translated into a theme within this cultural unity," that is, as a limit-concept of the horizon rather than as a repressed within a discourse. It is the general possibility of translation that constructs the limits of a discursive formation. On the other hand, the world is a universality within which all these culturally relative worlds can encounter each other, and from whose relation global history and geography is constructed. This universality is not apprehensible apart from the culturally relative, but only *through* specific socio-historical worlds and is not revealed all at once, but only in glimpses.[26] It is especially important to pursue these glimpses in the turning point between two socio-historical worlds. It is this contemporary turning point that is now discussed, with widely varying degrees of adequacy, under the heading of postmodernity. One aspect of this turning point is that we should be able to account for the previous historical turning into the epoch out of which we are now proceeding. As a corollary of understanding the notion of totality as world-horizon, we can now address this question of the origin of modernity that is not theoretically accounted for by Laclau and Mouffe. They, as noted above, follow classical German philosophy in specifying the elements presupposed by articulatory practice as "fragments of a lost unity." But at this key point the theoretical status of this historically correct observation must be held up to scrutiny.

Now, either there is such a thing as an organic totality—that is, a non-constructed, immediately given totality which encompasses each of its moments, or there is not. If there is, or was, such an organic totality, how could it disintegrate into elements? Distintegration could not come from its parts, since they serve in every case to confirm the whole. The whole is, by definition, without contradiction and could not disintegrate itself. Thus disintegration would have to originate externally, to operate from outside on an organic whole. But then, of course, it would not be a whole, but a merely apparent whole whose real partiality was later discovered. "Greek unity" was, it would seem, either a false unity sustained only by ethnic arrogance and destined to be revealed as merely partial and dissolved from outside, or it was a real organic unity and has not dissolved—we have merely forgotten it, but it is there for us to recapture. The progressive and conservative alternative here stems from the idea of an organic whole with which the analysis began. It is insoluble on this basis. Laclau and Mouffe's failure to investigate the notion of the "field of discourse" which they use makes it impossible for them to say anything about this crucial issue of the origin of modernity. Consequently, their starting point on this issue is narrative, rather than theoretical. When one cannot formulate a theory, one tells a story. They simply use the characterization of fragmentation that was classical for German philosophy from Schiller to Hegel and Marx. But this characterization takes its content from a field defined through two totalities: The memory of a prior (Greek) organic totality and the anticipation of modern rationalist totality. But one cannot theoretically reject the Hegelian rationalist concept of totality, as well as organic totality, and simultaneously utilize the classical diagnosis of the modern world as "fragmentation," when it is precisely these conceptions of totality that make the diagnosis possible.[27]

However, on the basis of the phenomenological critique sketched above, this issue can be sorted out. Organic totality may be defined as ascribing to thematic elements a real independence, ignoring their common relation to the world as horizon, in combination with the metaphoric elevation of one of these independent elements to the rank of a principle capable of subsuming all the rest. This is what Max Scheler called a "relative natural world-view."[28] One example of this is the paradigmatic character of craft production throughout Plato's, and indeed Greek, philosophy.[29] Unity is thus achieved by a subsumption which remains concrete since it derives from an element within the unity. Organic unity is thus a "tyranny of the part," elevated to an organization of the whole. The paradigmatic part thus metaphorically defines the horizon of the world. Such traditional world-views, though they are relatively stable in their own terms, do indeed have problems when they encounter an outside. This outside reveals the partial character of the organizing principle by confronting it with other organizing principles. The experience of "fragmentation" is thus a perennial possibility for such traditional organic unities, but it needs another condition for its emergence. The plurality of organic wholes can also lead to a simple eclecticism, which was indeed widespread in late antiquity.

Only with the rise of a new idea of universality, one that encompasses not merely elements but entire world-views, can there be an analysis of modernity as a decay into fragments. This is a universality based, not on a substantive organizing principle (which I have called here a "metaphorically elevated element"), but on what Husserl called the "bare possibility of an organizing principle at all"[30]—that is, a merely formal and therefore cosmopolitan claim to unity. This brief theoretical account does not provide a crucial historical linkage between the decline of organic unities and the emergence of modern universality. The universal religions played a key role in this respect since "the pure possibility of organization as such" could not, in the first place, be conceived as the object of positive knowledge, but had to be placed beyond the knowable world. This principle defines the modern epoch. Its paradigmatic expression is, of course, Descartes' arraying of the world before himself as representation and securing its knowability in the self-evidence of immediate subjectivity, which is accomplished through the synthesis of formalism and subjectivism.[31] The new idea of universality reaches its apogee in the rationalist notion of a purely logical totality which is emblematic of modernity. Only on the basis of this twofold development—the combination of memory of substantive unity with the initial idea of formal cosmopolitan totality—could the emergent modern era be described as a fragmentation. The centrality of the notion of formal rational totality to modernity ensures that the diagnosis of fragmentation and the project of a recovery/discovery of wholeness continually re-emerges, especially in times of crisis. This leads to the subsequent, and most characteristic, modern attempt at logical totality in Hegel, where the formal array of knowledge is acknowledged as insufficient but there is also an attempt to retrieve the fundamental project of modern subjective representation. This was attempted through accounting for the rationalist project as a historical culmination and thereby claiming to include all experience within its purview. Thus, the key role played in both modern philosophy and social criticism by the notion of alienation, which charts a temporal path of the loss and recovery of totality—organic social totality, fragmented individualism, new rational social totality incorporating individualism. This should serve to indicate that we can no longer simply appropriate the diagnosis of modernity as described through the alienation story by German idealism, but must regard this story itself as characteristic of modernity. Indeed, a large part of what is going on in the debates surrounding post-modernism is that it is impossible to imagine putting the fragments together again. But, in this case, they really shouldn't be called "fragments" any more and the starting point of social critique must be reformulated.

The modern rationalist option begins from the elements but (unlike organic totality) cannot raise one of them into a substantive principle. Thus, it begins from the pure principle of organization itself ("the bare possibility of an organizing principle at all"), not any particular organizing principle and attempts to turn this formal-logical system into a substantive one by sleight of hand—though we should recognize that this "sleight of hand" is a fundamental and defining component of modernity. It consists in maintaining the concept of logical totality alongside the critique of formalism. But the critique of formalism, though valid, cannot of itself generate concreteness. Thus, we may say that the modern rationalist totality understood as the "unconditioned condition of conditions," or "undetermined totality of determinations," in Kant and Hegel mis-interprets the horizon of the world as if it were the totality of conditions. It does not view the whole as itself conditioned, as in organic unity, but views the whole as the sum of conditions. The unthematic horizon is thus treated as if it were the sum of thematized elements. Thus, in both ancient organic unities and modern rationalist totalities there is an obscuring of the horizon of the world as an unthematized background. The project of hegemony can only emerge, as Laclau and Mouffe rightly assert, with the decay of these two inclusive wholes, but the absence of a developed account of the field of discursivity makes it impossible to theorize the transition to modernity and the subsequent decay of rationalism that enables hegemony to emerge and, as a consequence, for the whole of the practice of articulation itself. By way of contrast, the present phenomenological reformulation of the concept of articulation begins from the undeveloped, but key, concept in Laclau and Mouffe's work of the "field of discursivity" to develop a conception of the world as the unthematized horizon of horizons that can address the shifts between types of world-horizons that can be called historical epochs.

The other aspect of my critique of the work of Laclau and Mouffe in *Hegemony and Socialist Strategy* centres on the persistent reference to contingency as the defining characteristic of a hegemonic totality. In discussing the Althusserian notion of overdetermination as the origin of the concept of articulation, they suggest that the "logic of articulation" emerges through "the critique of every type of fixity, through an affirmation of the incomplete, open and politically negotiable character of every identity." In an articulated identity "the presence of some in the others hinders the suturing of the identity of any of them."[32] In fact, the main characteristic of an identity that Laclau and Mouffe formulate in *Hegemony and Socialist Strategy* is the negative one of its lack of fixity, its temporary character, its contingency. The negative character of this assertion indicates that it makes sense only as a polemical assertion of postmodern anti-totality in relation to the conceptions of totality to which it is opposed—Greek organic unity, modern rationalist logical totality and the empiricist decomposition of totality into elements. I want to argue in this connection that the theorizing of the logic of articulation would benefit from the replacement of the emphasis on contingency and unfixity with the positive concept of particularity. This will be done by developing the concept of "particularity" to allow a distinction of particularity from contingency—which is the main term through which the non-necessity of contents or linkages is expressed in contemporary philosophy.

Contingency is the metaphysical complement of necessity and an exit from their mutual implication can only be achieved by means of the further term "particularity." The rhetoric of "it is no accident that . . ." was characteristic of Weber and, through the influence of Lukács, much of Western Marxism.[33] Such a manner of speaking supposes that, even if the necessity of a given fact or element is not immediately apparent, it is "really" rationally comprehensible only within a totality of determinations. In other words, the apparent contingency of a given event is overcome theoretically through a commitment to logical totality. However, because it is always problematic for logical totality to define the manner in which a given concrete event is determined through the totality, this determination is expressed in principle, as it were, through the negation of non-necessity. "It is no accident that" does not exactly say that "it is thoroughly determined that"— which is very hard to prove and probably always unconvincing in a specific case. The rhetoric of no-accident is thus the insinuation of a necessity that is nevertheless not named, or nameable, due to the continually postponed character of the final explanation that covers every concrete case. It is a perpetually delayed promise to explain. In recent years this rhetoric of "it is no accident that" has passed into history along with the expectation of the final coming of logical totality. But it has been replaced by a complementary rhetoric that works within the same opposition of terms. The assertion of contingency is an assertion of non-necessity whose polemical object is a necessity defined through rational–logical totality. The rhetoric of contingency is thus as empty as the rhetoric of no-accident. It is a rhetoric of no-necessity whose proclamation that there is no "ultimate"—that is to say foundational, essential, logical—explanation serves to avoid any form of explanation at all, when precisely the issue for a hegemonic conception of totality is to explain how a particular hegemony comes to be formed, and remains effective, despite its non-necessity. Contingency only asserts the abstract possibility of difference, that things in principle may change, but says nothing concrete about why such change does or does not happen. The concretion of a hegemonic concept of totality requires the development of a concept of particularity that is situated at precisely the point of an *identification* with a certain definition of the social whole which is universalizing but which nevertheless encounters other competing definitions.

George Grant introduced the term "one's own," or "particularity" (which he derived by rendering Heidegger's term "*Eigentlich*" into English), in order to defend the existence of Canada against its incorporation into the United States. In his famous short book *Lament for a Nation* he phrased the philosophical issue in this way: "The belief in Canada's continued existence has always appealed against universalism. It appealed to particularity against the wider loyalty of the continent. If universalism is the most 'valid modern trend,' then is it not right for Canadians to welcome our integration into the empire?"[34] This embracing of a poetic expression of what is one's own has significance beyond the polemical context in which Grant discovered the concept of particularity. We know the universal *through* the particularities which make it concrete for us. But, even more, we are cut off from such a passage toward the universal if we must sacrifice our own along the way. When a culture is sacrificed, when I must forget my own in order to pass on toward the universal, the universal remains without incarnation in my world. It becomes necessarily abstract, in the sense of lacking relation to the here and now, and my own becomes *merely* my own, parochial. This opposition between a local parochiality and a distant universality is the experience of all those who live in the shadow of empires.[35] Within the United States, or France, or Britain, every place has its own uniqueness and yet partakes in the national identity. It is this *passage between* the particular and the universal that is blocked for those who live in a particular condition which is not taken up into the larger identity. Thus, the particular seems to be completely arbitrary and the universal a merely dry abstractness. A philosophy concerned to address this situation must address both the *justification of the particular* identity and a version of the universal that allows its *inclusion in universality* in order to restore a relation between the local here and now and the connection with humanity as such. This is the situation as described from within the sense of loss, of being cut off, experienced by identities which are not recognized by the prevailing hegemonic formation. This description seems to me apposite to the further development of the concept of articulation which requires a rethinking of the complementary concepts of necessity and contingency. The concept of particularity is used, I believe without exception by Grant, in order to defend a particular allegiance in a moment in which it is perceived as threatened.

The concept of particularity is importantly distinguished from the concept of contingency which is widespread in contemporary philosophical discourse. The discourse of contingency and its defence as a proper concern for philosophy was most forcefully argued by existentialism. The first appearance of the term "contingency" in Jean-Paul Sartre's *Being and Nothingness* is in the context of explaining human being as always existing in a "condition which it has not chosen." Humans are thrown into a "situation" in so far as one's being is bound up with factuality and does not provide its own foundation. Here, contingency refers to the fact that "the explanation and the foundation of my being—in so far as I am a *particular being*—can not be sought in necessary being."[36] The immediate structure of human being is in its presence to a world which cannot be derived from structures of universality. The introduction of the term "contingency" is thus a way of introducing into philosophy a concern with non-necessary, non-universal elements of a particular being's situation—in fact, of bringing philosophy down from the clouds of what is everywhere and always the case to issues which arise for a temporally and spatially particularized concrete being. It is not too much to say that the term "contingency" is part and parcel of a critique of traditional philosophy and a turning toward particularity. The term itself, however, is especially derived from "non-necessary," in the sense of that which cannot be accounted for or explained. There are actually two different inflections compacted here: One, the contingent cannot be *derived from* the universal; it is more than a mere example. Two, it cannot be accounted for or explained. These two inflections appear to be identical if the accounting for or explaining is understood on the model of derivation from the universal—i.e. a mode of explanation characteristic of the traditional philosophy that is here being criticized. Therefore, we may say that, to the extent that a new mode of philosophical discourse is achieved, and "accounting for" no longer takes this traditional form, the difference between the two inflections becomes more marked. Sartre's use of the term compresses two meanings which it is now necessary to distinguish. In the terminology which I would like to suggest, particularity is more than an example of universality; it refers to the fact that a temporally and spatially bound being is thrown into a situation that it does not create. Contingency, by way of contrast, refers to the non-derivability of particularity from traditional modes of philosophical discourse. The notion that particularity cannot be accounted for or explained is based upon Sartre's maintenance of a traditional version of what philosophical explanation would consist in. Thus, his use of contingency inflects the concept in the direction of non-accountability, inability of explanation, and arbitrariness that characterized the existentialist notion of choice. To the extent that philosophical explanation can turn, or has been turned, towards human situations—as Sartre himself recommended—and the model of explanation itself reformulated as a result, then the term "contingency" is no longer appropriate. The particularity that requires philosophical articulation is cut off from philosophical articulation if it is interpreted as *purely contingent* in the manner of Sartre. The distinction between particularity and contingency, in sharp contrast, opens up the particularities of human situations to philosophical articulation and, in the same moment, implies a reformulation of the concept of philosophy. From this standpoint, Sartre's role was to have opened up a new conception of philosophy that his own formulation prevented from emerging properly. Particularity need no longer be defined as against universality but as the very *condition for* whatever universality the human being may be able to apprehend.

The more recent use of contingency by Richard Rorty in *Contingency, Irony and Solidarity* contains a similar slide between the terms "particularity" and "contingency"[37]—even connecting them with idiosyncrasy—suggesting that it is a characteristic of contemporary philosophy to identify the two, not merely an individual proclivity. Rorty introduces contingency in order to oppose the notion that there is a "core self" to all human beings regardless of their spatial and temporal location. He claims that "what counts as being a decent human being is relative to historical circumstance, a matter of transient consensus about what attitudes are normal and what practices are just or unjust."[38] All human characteristics are plunged into a social and historical relativism such that the question of why not to be cruel to other human beings is denied the possibility of any non-circular answer.[39] Sartre would certainly not have gone so far; none the less, it does seem to be a consequence of making contingency basic to philosophical discourse. The interpretation of morality as a language and languages as historical contingencies has, Rorty claims, the consequence that moral action is a matter of "identifying oneself with such a contingency."[40] The action of identifying with a contingency, however, does not have any theoretically relevant force. The contingency simply remains a contingency. This occludes at a deeper level one of the key components of the distinction for which I am arguing. While the components of socio-historical location are contingent, in the sense of non-necessary and non-derivable from universals, such components are essential, even necessary, for the identification which constitutes the individual or group in question. Identity comes about through precisely such processes of identification with practices and components of a world. They no longer merely surround the actor, but become part of the self-definition of the actor. Rorty's conclusions only appear to follow because contingency, in his view, is necessarily opposed to universality.

Thus, he denies any meaningful possibility of identification with the universal category of human beings as such, claiming that any "we" is necessarily contrasted to a they.[41] The origin of this error can now be defined clearly: First, in the slide between the meanings of particularity and contingency, and, second, in the failure to account for the *effective power of identification*.

If I can generalize from these two examples, it seems that twentieth-century philosophical discourse is paralysed by a contradiction. One the one hand, it wishes to open up the realm of the specificity of spatial and temporal location to investigation as opposed to the straightforward universals of traditional philosophy. But on the other hand, it opens up this territory solely, or at least mainly, in contrast to traditional philosophical categories and thereby misrepresents the phenomenon. As a consequence, contemporary philosophy tends to take a sceptical and relativist turn that may be anathema even to many of its practitioners. As long as it remains at this point, the assertion of contingency is merely a rebound from universality and has not yet been pushed toward an adequate philosophical expression.

Laclau and Mouffe address the relation of contingency and necessity in the context of explaining their concept of articulation. Their intention is to subvert the opposition. The concept of hegemony emerged from Marxist theory in order to theorize situations, or conjunctures, that could not be adequately subsumed under the logic of modes of production that is its main explanatory scheme. The history of modes of production proposed a historical necessity within which contingent hegemonic conjunctures functioned as "exceptions" or delays in the arrival of an adequate explanation. Laclau and Mouffe reverse this function of contingency and expand its logic to encompass the necessity in contrast with which it was originally defined. Necessity is defined from contingency, not the reverse. This is why the rhetoric of contingency and non-necessity is so pervasive in *Hegemony and Socialist Strategy*. They argue that "for the social, necessity exists only as a partial effort to limit contingency," that the two "cannot be conceived as relations between two areas that are delimited and external to each other," and thus that necessity cannot be a principle or a ground but rather an "effort of literalization which fixes the differences of a relational system."[42] Necessity is thus defined as the effort to fix an unfixity, to literalize a discourse which is constructed through metaphors, in short, as an effect of contingency. They attempt to undo the opposition of the two terms in a deconstruction which shows the first and defining term to be an effect of the second and partial term. This is a more radical shift than that performed by Sartre and Rorty in so far as these two remain caught in describing contingency as, in Laclau and Mouffe's terms, two delimited and external areas. Sartre's contingent human choice was based on the opposition between Nothingness and Being, in which the necessity of Being was the basis for scraping out a space of lack within the fullness of Being. Rorty's hermeneutic conception of contingency is even less radical in so far as it is contrasted with, not the fullness of Being, but merely the supposed necessity of a concept of a core self independent of its worldly involvements—an idea that seems virtually a caricature. Both remain caught within an opposition of contingency and necessity in which, in the final analysis, necessity has the last word. Laclau and Mouffe attempt a radical shift in which necessity would become only a limited and unsustainable strategy within a field of contingency. It is for this reason that their conception of hegemony utilizes a deconstruction of metaphysical oppositions. However, this deconstruction cannot lead toward an alternative theorization of the particularities of mid-range identities. It tends to remain caught at the point of its deconstruction of the opposition and thus issues in a reiteration of the rhetoric of non-necessity and contingency. The distinction between contingency and particularity would avoid this consequence by paving the way for a renewal of the particularity–universalizing nexus instead of remaining within the contingency–necessity dead-end. Grant's polemic against universality had a certain similarity to that of Sartre and Rorty in its critique of deficient universals but with the crucial difference that it was concerned to justify the legitimacy and transformative power of mid-range identifications. This is the point at which Grant's concept converges with that of Laclau and Mouffe. For this reason the concept of particularity contains the possibility of a further development beyond its original polemical context that can address, rather than succumb to, the contradiction opened up by contemporary philosophy.

The definition of this concept of particularity requires that one take a "step back" with regard to one's everyday involvements in a collective identity in order to recognize that it *is* endangered, that it *should* be preserved and extended, and that this project requires that such a right be extended to *others* as well.[43] It thus concerns the common origin of ontology and axiology. The reflexive step back turns the purely inherited, or socially formed, character of collective identity into a process of identification amenable to rational justification. Such reflexion is concrete in the sense that it does not pulverize the belonging upon which it reflects but rather articulates it and preserves it in a new form. In this sense the reflexive turn constitutes a new mediation between particularity and universality by originating the possibility of a rational discourse concerning belonging. It is a reflexive turn from within social action, not epistemology, and therefore occurs within the realm of love and hate, suffering and joy, and concerns their opening out to philosophical articulation. Particularity thus involves an *embracing* of a cultural identity, not just inheriting it. The step back begins from the experience of affective belonging that is one's own, which requires that other belongings be seen from the outside and justified in an ethics of difference. The step back thus discloses that the condition for the appearance of any universality is the particularity that can connect one to the universal only through others. Access to the universal requires respect for other particularities.

Ernesto Laclau has used the term "particularity" to define the hegemonic conception of totality as "the presentation of the particularity of a group as the incarnation of that empty signifier which refers to the communitarian order as an absence, an unfulfilled reality."[44] While this definition invokes a particularity–universality relation, it treats particularity as equivalent to particularism, which my discussion attempts to separate. This is a consequence of the definition of universality as an empty signifier, or an always unfulfilled absence. Since universality is a mere absence, it is filled by a particularity that presents itself as universal. A particularity which claims to be a universality is always a particularism, that is, a limited whole that denies the legitimacy of other particularities. If a supposed universality is always a stand-in particularism and particularism always seeks to fill an empty univeralism, then the field of discourse is never anything other than a generalized war between discourses that I will criticize in a later chapter as a "general rhetoric." What this contingent switching offers may be at times diagnostically powerful, but it undercuts the possibility of a hegemonic politics with anything more than a purely arbitrary claim to universality. As Slavoj Žižek has argued, and I have also pointed out above, the chain of equivalences that such a hegemonic politics could construct will necessarily include elements that do not fit into an egalitarian, Left politics. Žižek has extended this self-reinforcing conception of empty universalism versus ambitious particularism to suggest that Left politics should identify with the symptom, that is, "an element which—although the non-realization of the universal principle in it appears to hinge on contingent circumstances—*has* to remain an exception, that is, the point of suspension of the universal principle."[45] However, such a political practice is self-defeating in the sense that, while it can show the necessary limit in the prevailing universalism, any further hegemonic universalism that may be proposed would be open to exactly the same form of criticism made in the same way. In short, the particularism–universalism short-circuit elaborated by Laclau separates social critique from any genuinely universal claims.[46] It remains stuck at the stage of showing the failed universality of the predominant system, disallowing the notion that social transformation needs to propose a new universality—however tentative and open to revision.[47] The rebound to contingency cuts the ground out from under any affirmative conception of universalization.

The preliminary reformulation of the particularity–universalizing relation that I have suggested through introducing the term "particularity" seeks to open up this issue in another direction. Particularity is not the opposite of universality, but its condition, as universality is not the transcendence of particularity, but its articulation. Philosophy must thus be understood not as a universal, but a *universalizing* discourse—that is, a discourse that proposes a universal to the affective reception of others. The distinction between universal and universalizing goes back to Kant's *Critique of Judgment* and has been used and developed by many twentieth-century thinkers in order to theorize the intermediate realm, "aesthetic" according to Kant, "political" according to Hannah Arendt, in which judgments have a claim upon others but cannot be shown to be necessarily universal.[48] Reflective judgment, as Kant termed it, moves from an exemplary particular to the universal, rather than by subsuming a particular under a universal, proposes a sensuously, material universality to the desired approbation of others rather than making a claim that would overreach any further discussion. The present argument has not pursued this reworking of the conception of universality as such, but it is implied in the concept of particularity that I have proposed.

I introduced the phenomenological notion of the world as horizon and the philosophical concept of particularity into a critique of the work of Ernesto Laclau and Chantal Mouffe in order to clarify what is needed for a theorization of the linkage between particular interventions and the social formation as a whole, between common sense and the epochal horizon. With the loss of mediation between near and far represented most clearly by Hegel's concept of *Aufhebung*, contemporary philosophy has opened and begun to investigate this space. My arguments have not revoked the advances made by Laclau and Mouffe in theorizing this space, but have attempted to push beyond to further "positive" determinations of articulation that are not dominated by its polemical objections to classical modern conceptions of universality and necessity. The interplay of particularity with the horizon of the world is the context in which a revised concept of ideology-critique as epochal criticism can operate in the postmodern condition.

NOTES

1. Michel Foucault, *The Order of Things* (New York: Vintage, 1973) pp. 318–22 and Edmund Husserl, *The Crisis of the European Sciences and Transcendental Phenomenology*, trans. David Carr (Evanston: Northwestern University Press, 1970) pp. 178–86. Foucault's later work tries to avoid this doubling through a return to "practice," though this is an unlikely solution since it tends to find the same duality concealed in practice. See on this point Hubert L. Dreyfus and Paul Rabinow, *Michel Foucault: Beyond Structuralism and Hermeneutics* (Chicago: The University of Chicago Press, 1983) especially Chapter 9.

2. Martin Heidegger, *Identity and Difference*, trans. Joan Stambaugh (New York: Harper and Row, 1969) and Jacques Derrida, "Signature Event Context" in *Margins of Philosophy*, trans. Alan Bass (Chicago: University of Chicago Press, 1982) p. 329.

3. Louis Althusser, *For Marx,* trans. Ben Brewster (New York: Vintage, 1970) pp. 202–4.

4. G. W. F. Hegel, *Phenomenology of Spirit*, trans. A. V. Miller (Oxford: Oxford University Press, 1979) p. 20.

5. Ibid., p. 20.

6. Søren Kierkegaard, *Concluding Unscientific Postscript*, trans. David F. Swenson and Walter Lowrie (Princeton: Princeton University Press, 1968) p. 102.

7. Ernesto Laclau, "Politics and the Limits of Modernity" in *Universal Abandon: The Politics of Postmodernism*, ed. Andrew Ross (Minneapolis: University of Minnesota Press, 1988) p. 81.

8. Ernesto Laclau and Chantal Mouffe, *Hegemony and Socialist Strategy* (London: Verso, 1985) p. 144. I believe that this is the only place in this book where the term "horizon" is used to characterize hegemonic totality. Laclau has subsequently used the term more extensively though he has not referred to the use of the term by Husserl and phenomenology in this context. My interpretation of phenomenology and of Husserl specifically is significantly different from Laclau's in a manner which is indicated in the text through the discussion of French phenomenology but cannot be thoroughly discussed here. See Ernesto Laclau, *New Reflections on the Revolution of Our Time* (London and New York: Verso, 1990) pp. 200, 212, 220 and also *Hegemony and Socialist Strategy*, p. 105.

9. Ibid., p. 127.

10. Ibid.

11. Ibid., pp. 93–6.

12. Ibid., p. 94.

13. Louis Althusser, *For Marx*, pp. 101–4.

14. See especially G. W. F. Hegel, *Phenomenology of Spirit*, pp. 33–5.

15. Laclau and Mouffe, *Hegemony and Socialist Strategy*, p. 98.

16. Ibid., p. 98. See Louis Althusser, *For Marx*, p. 111.

17. Ibid., p. 103.

18. Ibid., p. 104, emphasis added.

19. Ibid., pp. 104, 111, 134, 135, 138, 182.

20. Ibid., p. 134, emphasis added.

21. Ibid., p. 141.

22. Edmund Husserl, *Formal and Transcendental Logic*, trans. Dorion Cairns (The Hague: Martinus Nijhoff, 1969) pp. 199–200.

23. Edmund Husserl, *The Crisis of European Sciences and Transcendental Phenomenology*, p. 143.

24. Ibid., p. 31, emphasis removed.

25. Edmund Husserl, *The Crisis of European Sciences and Transcendental Phenomenology*, pp. 139, 147.

26. This is the point at which the possibility of the transcendental reduction emerges. The suggestion that the universality of the world is only apprehended in glimpses (*Abschattungen*) entails a revision of Husserl's notion of the transcendental reduction. But, I believe, it is a consistent extension of his late view that the reduction needs to be continually carried out anew. Part of this revision is the suggestion that the term "transcendental subjectivity" is, in a certain sense, misleading. On these grounds, I am bound to disagree with the second part of Husserl's claim that we may attend to the general structure of the lifeworld "in its generality and, with sufficient care, fix it once and for all in a way equally accessible to all" (1973, p. 139).

27. Laclau and Mouffe themselves make this point about the rhetorical framing of the notion of fragmentation as a category of analysis in a footnote to a previous chapter. However, they do not incorporate this insight when they utilize the story of fragmentation in Chapter 3, which I am currently criticizing. See *Hegemony and Socialist Strategy*, p. 43 footnote 15 and pp. 93–7.

28. Max Scheler, *Die Wissenformen und die Gesellschaft* (Munich: Francke Verlag, 1960) pp. 60–3. See my discussion in *Technique and Enlightenment: Limits of Instrumental Reason* (Washington: Center for Advanced Research in Phenomenology and University Press of America, 1984) pp. 49–50.

29. Reiner Schürmann, *Heidegger on Being and Acting: From Principles to Anarchy* (Bloomington: Indiana University Press, 1987) pp. 95–105.

30. Edmund Husserl, *Formal and Transcendental Logic, passim.*

31. Ian Angus, *Technique and Enlightenment*, pp. 59–98.

32. Ibid., p. 104.

33. Max Weber, *From Max Weber: Essays in Sociology*, trans. H. H. Gerth and C. Wright Mills (New York: Oxford University Press, 1976) p. 155.

34. George Grant, *Lament for a Nation: The Defeat of Canadian Nationalism* (Toronto: McClelland and Stewart, 1970) p. 85.

35. A deconstruction of this opposition is presented in my *A Border Within: National Identity, Cultural Plurality, and Wilderness* (Montreal and Kingston: McGill-Queen's Press, 1997).

36. Jean-Paul Sartre, *Being and Nothingness*, trans. Hazel E. Barnes (New York: Philosophical Library, 1956) pp. 79, 81.

37. Richard Rorty, *Contingency, Irony and Solidarity* (Cambridge: Cambridge University Press, 1989) p. 33; see also pp. 41, 61 and *passim.*

38. Ibid., p. 189; see also p. 45.

39. Ibid., p. xv.

40. Ibid., p. 60. The possibility that a language may be a mode of action in the world with characteristics that carry it beyond contingency is therefore ruled out by Rorty. His claims do not follow directly from the linguistic turn in philosophy and the human sciences, but from a specific theory of language.

41. Ibid., p. 190. As, interestingly, so does Sartre; see *Being and Nothingness*, pp. 413–15.

42. Ernesto Laclau and Chantal Mouffe, *Hegemony and Socialist Strategy*, p. 114.

43. The notion of a "step back" is taken from Heidegger's reformulation of the transcendental reduction. See Martin Heidegger, *On Time and Being*, trans. Joan Stambaugh (New York: Harper and Row, 1972) pp. 9, 28, 45–7.

44. Ernesto Laclau, "Why Do Empty Signifiers Matter to Politics?" in *The Lesser Evil and the Greater Good*, ed. Jeffrey Weeks (London: Rivers Oram Press, 1994) p. 176. See also, Ernesto Laclau, "Beyond Emancipation" in *Emancipation(s)* (London and New York: Verso, 1996) p. 15.

45. Slavoj Žižek, "Multiculturalism, Or the Cultural Logic of Multinational Capitalism," *New Left Review*, No. 225, September–October 1997.

46. The origin of this conception of particular–universal is Lacan's notion of suture. See *Hegemony and Socialist Strategy*, p. 88, footnote 1.

47. Laclau criticizes deconstruction at this point, though he is uncertain about whether it applies to Derrida, for suggesting that the democratic option is in any sense a more justifiable ethico-political claim than a totalitarian one. "The Time is Out of Joint" in *Emancipation(s)*, pp. 77–8.

48. Interestingly, Max Horkheimer and Hans-Georg Gadamer also began from this part of Kant's work to explicate the type of judgments pertaining to Critical Theory and hermeneutics. I think that this indicates something fundamental about twentieth-century philosophy's imperative to approach what Husserl called "material universals." See Hannah Arendt, *The Life of the Mind, Vol. 1, Willing* (New York: Harcourt, Brace, Jovanovich, 1978) Appendix "Judging"; Max Horkheimer, *Kants kritik der urteilskraft als bindeglied zwischen theoretischer und praktischer philosophie* (Stuttgart: Verlag von W. Kohlhammer, 1925); Hans-Georg Gadamer, *Truth and Method* (New York: Crossroad, 1975); see also Ian H. Angus, *Technique and Enlightenment*, Chapters 4 and 5. This issue of the relation of the universal to the exemplary individual case has been taken up also in the work of Jacques Derrida through the questions of undecidability and the ethical relation to a singularity, or justice. See, for example, Jacques Derrida, *Specters of Marx*, trans. Peggy Kamuf (New York and London: Routledge, 1994) p. 75 and *The Gift of Death*, trans. David Wills (Chicago and London: University of Chicago Press, 1995) pp. 84–5.

4

EPOCHAL CRITICISM

In restricted critique the dominant values of freedom, autonomy and fulfilment of human needs which motivate specific ideology-critiques are either not held up to scrutiny or are considered to be independently legitimated in a different discourse (usually philosophy or science, but sometimes avant-garde art) whose validity is not impugned by the specific critiques themselves. Once it is accepted that these values that sustain the critical enterprise are the product of the very tradition that is being revealed as ideological, the activity of critique and the overarching justification of the values which guide critiques can not be held external to each other. A constitutive paradox is enacted in the performance of social critiques in which the justification of critiques itself becomes radically problematic in the enactment of critiques. While it is tempting to rebound from the predominant philosophical doctrines of the necessity and universality of such a justification toward the sheer contingency and particularism of articulations that would submerge issues of totality and the epochal horizon within common sense, the complementary concepts of particularity and horizon suggest another route. I will argue that a concept of epochal criticism can be sustained within the discursive turn in philosophy and

the human sciences through attention to the medium of communication in which an utterance takes place. The constitutive
paradox of the interplay of particularity and world horizon
becomes visible through the primal scene of the medium of communication in which every utterance is inscribed.

This reformulation of the concept of totality can be clarified
through a comparison of the concept of "horizon" in Nietzsche
and Husserl. The end of metaphysics is formulated in Nietzsche's
description of the death of God as the loss of a totality in which
every part derives its significance from its place in the whole:

> The madman jumped into their midst and pierced them with
> his eyes. "Whither is God?" he cried; "I will tell you. *We have
> killed him*—you and I. All of us are his murderers. But how did
> we do this? How could we drink up the sea? Who gave us the
> sponge to wipe away the entire horizon? What were we doing
> when we unchained this earth from its sun?"[1]

The key to this passage is a human act of unchaining which establishes a difference between a past and a present condition and
thus originates the questions of how the act could have been performed. What happens to human experience, or the "earth," in
relation to the totality of which it is a part, the "sea" and the "horizon"? The sea is a metaphor for the totality of the surrounding
world and the horizon refers to the limits which human perception
of the surrounding world encounters. Both of these metaphors for
totality are used to express a new relation to totality that has been
made perceivable by a human action. The earth was, until now,
chained to the sun and it is "we" who have unchained it. The
chain holding the earth to the sun refers to the metaphysical

interpretation of the relation between earth and sun, between the nearest and the furthest-highest. As for many religions, the sun stands for the highest divinity and the earth for our mortality. We may also hear an echo of Plato's use of the metaphor of the sun to indicate the necessary medium that makes possible the perception of things. This necessary medium is not a specific perceived thing, nor the perceiving subject, but the surrounding medium of light in which the subject and the object can coincide such that perception can occur. The "chain" suggests that the human world has in the past taken its structure and meaning from its dependence on the highest value—God, the sun, the eternal, truth. This highest value was also taken as the foundation, or origin, of the human. Nietzsche's metaphor thus establishes a connection between the surrounding world of the sea, or horizon, and a relation of "chaining" whereby they were connected in the past. It also, by means of the decisive human action of unchaining, reveals that this relation was a *specifically metaphysical interpretation* of the relation between the surrounding world and its foundation. In this metaphysical interpretation the sun was the origin of the meaning of the earth such that the earth reflected the sun. In other words, there used to be a mutual implication between earth and sun expressing the unity of origin and goal, the dependence of the temporal on the eternal, and that the meaning of human events derives from their relation to a foundation and higher purpose. This enfolding metaphysical totality was lost with the death of God, but totality itself is not lost after the decisive act. The sea and the horizon remain, but the earth is not chained to them in the same way as it was chained to the sun. We may even say that the sea and the horizon really only appear as such after the decisive act of unlinking to the sun. They are the contemporary experience of totality after its specifically metaphysical interpretation that took them to be the sun. The death of God is therefore the revealing of the sun to be the sea, the unveiling of the highest to be really the surrounding horizon.

It has been supposed that the end of metaphysics is a loss of totality *per se*, but it is really a loss of the metaphysical interpretation of totality, of what we might call an *absolute totality* that enfolds each part and determines its meaning through the whole. The postmodern break does not annihilate either the nearest (common sense) or the furthest (world-horizon) but rather their mutual implication such that the assumed passage between them is lost such that the question of their relation becomes raised in a radical manner. From this loss of mutual implication emerges a postmetaphysical perception of totality as simply "horizon," as standing behind and emerging through particulars, but as incapable of systematic organization or directing force. Edmund Husserl arrived at just such a conception through his radical critique of logic and truth:

> To judge in a naive evidence is to judge on the basis of a giving of something itself, while continually asking what can be actually "seen" and given faithful expression—accordingly it is to judge by the same method that a cautiously shrewd person follows in practical life whenever it is seriously important for him to "find out how matters really are." That is the beginning of all wisdom, though not its end . . . further reflective inquiry always follows . . . We have the *truth* then, not as falsely absolutized, but rather, in each case, as within its *horizons*—which do not remain overlooked or veiled from sight, but are systematically explicated.[2]

Every perception involves a claim to truth, but is presented within a horizon. The horizon is always presented through a given perception and thus cannot be directly perceived as such. Explication of the truth of a given perception leads further onward to its horizonal context, but the horizonal contexts of a plurality of perceptions cannot be totalized in an absolute metaphysical closure—it is unchained from the sun. The end of metaphysics thus opens up the surrounding world, the sea, to more detailed explication than when its meaning was circumscribed by its relation to God, or the highest. Human experience on the earth involves an interplay between the unthematic surrounding world and its horizonal limits. The specifically metaphysical interpretation identified horizon in this sense with the highest or the sun. The surrounding world within which the senses of specific perceptions converge can be therefore distinguished from the metaphysical closure of this earth by its linkage to the idea of the sun, or God. The parts all remain. What is key is the unchaining, the loss of "passage between," or a settled connection of the two which requires a redefinition of the two extremes outside of the metaphysical assumption of mutual dependence and implication: the sun falls from its height to become the sea; earth loses its ground to become common sense.

The interplay of common sense and the world-horizon constitutes the paradox of epochal critique, which is instituted by the becoming incredible of the interpretation of the totality as the unity of origin and goal, of the chaining of the earth to the sun. When the mutually implicatory unity of metaphysical oppositions falls apart, a space emerges which is stretched between immediate perception, or common sense, and the horizon of the world. Epochal critique emerges with the opening of this space through the loss of foundation.

Any utterance, or expression, occurs through a fusing between a meaning, message-content, or sense, with a medium of communication in which it is expressed. In any expression a meaning is always embodied in a medium. For the moment, we may use the term "inscription," even though it is derived from the specific medium of writing, to refer to the "materiality" of any medium of communication. This "external" materiality is fused in a given expression with a specific sense that refers to the senses expressed in previous utterances in a manner that forges the coherence of a discourse. Let us begin by noting how the thematic concern with meaning, or content, necessarily tends to underplay the medium of communication in a manner that ultimately severs discourse from the world-horizon, in order subsequently to turn attention to the activity of world-inscription. If we regard expression from the viewpoint of its sense, or content, it always refers back to previous contents and forward to future ones (both actual and anticipated). This thematic continuity of mutual reference and relevance thus constitutes a discursive unity. There is a discourse concerning free trade, for example, or for the 1991 war in the Persian Gulf. Such a discourse is situated within an institutional framework that constitutes its external horizon, which often includes several centres of power. While this external horizon may itself be altered by the continuing discourse, it entails a greater perdurance, or "solidity," than specific contributions to the discourse, and often of the whole discourse itself—we expect the Pentagon to survive the Gulf War, for example, though there is no guarantee that it will do so. In this sense, the external institutional horizon is outside the thematic discourse although it continues to affect it. Contributions to the discourse are expressed in various media of communication. With respect to free trade, and the war in the Gulf, relevant expressions are situated in newspapers, television, memos and documents, telephone lines, word of mouth, and so forth. Moreover, weapons of war would have to be included in this list in so far as they express a meaning-content which contributes to the ongoing discourse. Without intending this list to be exhaustive, the point is that expressions are possible because of a medium of communication that is fused with a message-content in a given expression. Moreover, there are a plurality of such media. In so far as we usually focus attention on the "sense" of an expression, the medium itself is relatively overlooked. Indeed, this is not accidental. Attention directed toward the thematic unity of a discourse will underplay the role of media of communication precisely because relevant expressions originate from a plurality of media and converge on an identical theme. It is true that the difference between media might affect the discourse in so far as it is relevant to the impact, or "weight," of the sense in affecting the theme, but this consideration can only become a secondary variable in so far as the legitimation for its introduction derives from the theme that constitutes the unity of the discourse. Thus, a thematic, or sense-oriented, focus on discourse necessarily overlooks the full significance of the medium of communication which is essential to any expression. Consequently, the institutional framework which is operative in a discourse, giving greater weight to some message-contents, cannot be accounted for within the discourse itself. It remains an external variable: "who speaks" is an external factor in comparison to "what is said." This thematic focus allows for a relevance of discourse studies to a hegemonic politics of common sense. They gain relevance to immediate politics by leaving aside any characterization of the historical epoch as a whole. But, as the above discussion attempted to show, this discursive focus runs the unavoidable danger of being *severed from* a theory of the social totality. Thus, an unsatisfactory alternative emerges: Either a theory of the social totality is regarded as unnecessary and perhaps even impossible, or such a theory is assumed externally to be the wider context for the discourse study—in which case the turn toward discourse in the human sciences is not really accepted, but is seen as merely providing a newer and perhaps brighter tool to aid social analysis.

The discursive turn in philosophy and the human sciences does not necessarily reach such an impasse if it focuses on the medium of communication that is co-present with sense, or message-content, in an expression. Through the medium of communication an expression is connected to the given arrangement of media that characterizes a historical epoch. This approach reverses the predominant focus on the meaning of utterances with a focus on their manner of inscription. Therefore, it must be admitted, it tends, at least in the first place, to downplay content. The advantage is that it opens the possibility of connecting discourse, and the discursive turn in philosophy and the human sciences, to epochal criticism. The medium of communication in which an utterance is inscribed is a forming, shaping, instituting influence on the world. It may be called a "materiality" in the sense that it is distinguished from the ideal meaning which inheres in content, but should not be thought of as merely an external physical and dispensable vehicle for supporting content. The influential transportation model of communication reduced and misunderstood the medium as a "channel" in precisely this manner. A channel allows a passage between two pre-existent points, but neither brings the origin and destination into existence nor forges the spatial relation between them. The term "medium" is intended to refer to the shaping of spatial relations that is the origin of locations and also to the instituting of temporal relations that are the origin of historical events. Used in this way the term "medium" makes a connection between the phenomenological concept of institution and the shaping of social relations by forms of inscription. This difference between channel and medium is the same as that drawn by Husserl between the physical body (*Korper*) and the living body (*Leib*).[3] The physical body is objectified by science and understood as a necessary support to a supposedly internal mind or spirit. While a physical body is a necessary carrier of the mind, it is not understood as a forming influence on the ability to think and perceive. This mind–body relation is of course dependent upon the prior distinction between mental and physical substances stemming from Descartes. The living body, however, is the body as experienced in which the separation between "I" and "my body" is not there, in which, as Husserl says, my body "holds sway" in the world. *I am my body* and the developed abilities of my body not only belong to me but form the very manner of my experiencing the world. If I learn to play a musical instrument or to use a machine such as an automobile, for example, my perception of the world is changed along with an enhanced ability to act in it. The most primary communicative act is, from this perspective, not the word but the gesture and the fundamental issue of communication is the cultivation of the body through which the entirety of human culture is developed. A medium of communication is the embodiment of meaning in this sense. In Husserl's words, "these systems of 'exhibiting of' are related back to correlative multiplicities of kinesthetic processes having the peculiar character of the 'I do,' 'I move,' (to which even the 'I hold still' must be added)."[4] Media of communication are thus extended bodily kinaestheses whose materiality consists of animated modes of expression. It shapes the very ability to express as well as the world in which expressions take place. All expression requires a medium of communication. The plurality of these media, and their interrelation, should be seen as the embodiment of human culture, not merely as a container for transporting contents. To return to a previous example, while weapons and indeed all human artefacts can certainly be interpreted as signs—and this is the basis for both semiotic and systems approaches to communication—they also destroy and disrupt the embodied social form and that of individuals. While a weapon is *also* a sign, it is also a sign that is a *weapon*. To the extent that communication is understood in opposition to such embodied, material disruptions it becomes partial and ideological by concealing its role in the larger social formation.

The distinction between meaning, or message-content, and medium has its origin in the metaphysical conditions under which rhetoric and hermeneutics emerge. Alongside a transformation *of* orality pertinent to the origin of rhetoric, I will consider the transformation *from* orality to writing as discussed by hermeneutic philosophy. With their metaphysical formation, both of these transformations are held within bounds such that they can be interpreted as "transformations" of an identical substratum. This substratum is the meaning-content of an expression which is assumed to be the fundamental datum of communication. By dropping this assumption the radical nature of the formation of cultural experience by a plurality of media of communication comes to the fore.

The problem of a message's effect on an audience, which is the defining focus of rhetoric, arises as soon as there is a suspension introduced between speaking and replying. In conversation there is a continuously re-established reciprocity because each is, in turn, both speaker and audience. This allows a checking of audience reception through the speech that it motivates and, thus, through the further audience reaction to this motivated speech. The process of mutual checking of speech act and audience effect occurs through the production of further speech acts which refer continuously backward and forward to the exchange which enables the conversation to continue. Interruption of this conversational reciprocity separates production from consumption, speech act from audience effect, and therefore raises the problem of their relationship. By suspending an immediate relation of reciprocity, the scope of communication is expanded in space and time, thus instituting the possibility of a culture dispersed throughout various forms with different relations between production and consumption. This expansion raises the general question of the various types of mediated relationships that are possible, and predominant, between communication acts and their effects. Specifically, the problem of audience effect arises when the meaning of a communication act is stretched between its production and its effect—in conditions in which the direct reciprocity of mutual checking is suspended. Such a separation can be introduced from "outside," as it were—from factors external to the act of producing and consuming the communication act itself. For example, although conversation allows reciprocal turn-taking, a speech in a public arena does not. Reciprocity is transformed into the understanding of the speech, internal evaluation of it, and, possibly, heckling. If one is socially recognized as being allowed to do so, there may be the possibility of making another speech in rebuttal. But this is *another* speech, with the same features of relationship between speaker and audience, not an immediate reciprocity in the same communication act. In fact, it is often precisely because of such immediate non-reciprocity that political bodies devise rules which institutionalize the right to reply. Audience response is suspended, though not altogether nullified, because a given communication act does not occur alone, but in the context of a socially organized plurality of communication acts. Nevertheless, once reciprocity is pushed outside a given communication act, institutional rules and procedures are required to re-establish a certain kind of reciprocity through the "right to produce similar and related acts." At this point, reciprocal exchange can only be established by producing more similar communication acts, not by continuing in the same act.

Basic features of political regimes can be delineated by the different ways they deal with this issue. Democracy, for example, is the attempt to push the right of reply prior to decision-making to its furthest extent. The turn-taking of conversation can be called a single communication act because the structure of each intervention is formed by the prior and subsequent reciprocity from which the specific intervention gains its meaning. One public speech and a subsequent rebuttal, in contrast, must be regarded as two separate communication acts because the structure of a speech is independent of the existence or non-existence of a rebuttal. Thus, the very constitution of the audience of the first speech means that "reciprocity" is possible only through subsequent speeches. Whereas the reciprocal turn-taking of conversation includes a before-and-after reference to other parts of the same communication act, the mutual referencing of separate acts (such as speeches) is established at a higher, more inclusive level that can be called a discourse. The suspension of reciprocity thus simultaneously constitutes an audience and divides the communication act into a plurality of acts. This splitting of a continuous communication act into several chronologically related acts originates the problem of assuring the effect of a message that cannot be checked through the continuous process of the same communication act. It motivates the institutionalization of rules concerning the "right to reply," i.e. the right to add another communication act. The very constitution of an audience poses an issue for democratic theory of another forum in which the broken reciprocity can be repaired.

The external transformation of conversation into speechmaking is an institutional transformation within the oral medium of communication. This is by no means a negligible transformation. Such external social and institutional forces contribute to the meaning of any specific communication act. Some political regimes do not, after all, institutionalize the right to reply, or, perhaps more important, the right to initiate speech. Often, only some people in positions of influence are allowed to produce relevant speech and have the right to make pertinent replies. It is the considerable merit of democracy to base its political theory on the principle of an institutional right of everyone to initiate and reply. In practice, this principle is probably always curtailed to some degree. To this extent, democracy may be a regulative ideal capable of greater degrees of approximation, but not of final actualization. Such a transformation of conversation into speechmaking with an audience is a result of "external" institutional forces. The suspension introduced between speaking and replying is not inherent in the medium of communication that we can call "orality," but depends on social, economic, and political forces acting upon orality and giving it a particular socio-historical form. This distinction between speech-making and conversation determines the point at which Aristotle's investigation of rhetoric emerges and finds its place in the ethical–political determination of political regimes. He states that "rhetoric falls into three divisions, determined by the three classes of listeners to speeches. Of the three elements in speech-making—speaker, subject, and person addressed—it is the last one, the hearer, that determines the speech's end and object."[5] Rhetoric in the classical sense emerges precisely because of the suspension of turn-taking and allows the classification of speeches by their different relations to an audience. Rhetoric could thus be defined by Aristotle as "the power of observing the means of persuasion on almost any subject."[6] Rhetoric emerges through the constitution of the audience at the point where the reciprocal checking of conversation is suspended from outside and, consequently, the problem of the persuasive force of a speech can be posed independently of its content.

The emergence of an independent concern with persuasion involves a simultaneous reformation of the concept of truth, whose internal content can now be conceptualized apart from its persuasive force. In Aristotle, and in ancient Greek philosophy generally, this was conceptualized as the distinction between dialectic and rhetoric. Dialectic was concerned with the discovery of truth, rhetoric with its persuasive dissemination. This distinction is applicable not only to questions of truth, but to all use of language. Frege and Searle, for example, distinguish in similar fashion between the "sense," or propositional content, of an utterance and its (illocutionary) force.[7] We may say, in a general way, that language has both a semantic, descriptive dimension and a pragmatic, active dimension. This distinction between the "inherent content" of an utterance and its "effect, or force" has persisted in various forms precisely because it is constituted by the emergence of the audience. It is not the specific forms in which this distinction can be made that concern us here, but rather the suspension of reciprocity from which emerges a space in which this distinction can and must be made. This space can be called "metaphysics" in so far as it opens up the possibility of a "foundational" discourse centred on an "internal" truth distinct from its persuasive effects. While this account of the emergence of the metaphysical space is obviously rather truncated, the main concern here is to show how the traditional notions of rhetoric, persuasion and audience-effect are circumscribed within this space despite the fact that its key instituting moment is the discourse of truth, or "philosophy." While the notion of truth is key to this metaphysical space, nevertheless it simultaneously involves a related (though devalued in relation to truth) conception of persuasion. The suspension of reciprocity institutes rhetoric as a concern with the persuasive means of accomplishing an audience-effect in the same moment that it formulates a distinction between the internal content of an utterance and its external effect—dialectic and rhetoric.

Let us now make a preliminary conclusion based on this analysis of the suspension of reciprocity. The problem of audience-effect as it emerges within metaphysics is parasitic on the central organizing notion of the internal content of an utterance. Thus, any investigation of audience-effect that takes place within this distinction, and therefore inquires into persuasion *as defined in distinction from* inherent content, presupposes that effect is a function of factors external to the communicative act itself. In so far as the separation between truth and persuasion determines the space of investigation, the process of formation of the subject-positions of speaker and audience are thrust outside the communicative act. Rhetoric, of course, has investigated the strategies of speech that have commanded a persuasive energy on an audience. Nevertheless, the actual effect of these persuasive strategies depends on the audience "itself." Rhetoric presumes the audience "of" the communicative act as already-there prior to the utterance. The constitution of the audience through the suspension of reciprocity expels the formation of the audience outside the communication event. The effect that emerges from the impact that the persuasive strategies have on an audience is thus defined outside the communicative act itself. Investigation of the audience in this manner will necessarily become essentially a positive, empirical description of an audience whose main features are presupposed prior to the communicative act. Thus, the process of communication under investigation will be denied a constitutive function in forming its audience. The same point can be put in a slightly different way. The metaphysical distinction between internal content and persuasive effect locates persuasion ambiguously: Is persuasion located in the style (formal, metaphorical, etc.) of the speech or in the actual persons persuaded? Both? Neither? Perhaps persuasion should be located in the *connection between* the speech act and its "actual" audience, but this connection cannot be properly investigated within the metaphysical space because the separation of all persuasion from internal content necessarily undercuts the possibility of thinking these two components together. We may say that the primary distinction relegates the secondary one to irrelevance. Because the rhetorical study of persuasion is instituted by the internal content–effect distinction, it cannot investigate the actual locus at which persuasion occurs—"between" internal and external, or at the point of their "connection." The Aristotelian formula "speaker—subject—person addressed" leaves the formation of the "person addressed" outside the communicative–rhetorical–persuasive act, at the same moment that it is concerned with the

107

effect on this already formed person. Similarly, this formula leaves out the formation of the "speaker" as well because the "subject" is already understood on the basis of the prior model of internal content. But it is precisely this formation of the *relation between* speaker and audience that is the main effect of a speech act. This "consubstantiality" and "identification" of speaker and audience through the speech, in Kenneth Burke's terminology, is the key concern of persuasion after metaphysics.[8]

To sum up, the suspension of reciprocity institutes a distinction between internal content and external effect that, in turn, requires that the effect of this content be investigated in relation to an audience that is formed outside the given communication. The key question is thus the relation between a specific communication act and the social context in which it occurs. The prior formation of the audience is either left uninvestigated (within traditional rhetoric) or shunted off to be covered by an entirely separate social theory (social scientific studies of the audience). A dilemma must arise: Either the audience is presumed to be preformed, in which case the communicative act is investigated simply as representational and denied any constitutive power; or, the communicative act is regarded as constituting its audience-effect, in which case it seems to be all-powerful. Avoiding this dilemma requires that the instituting metaphysical distinction between inherent content (philosophy, science) and rhetorical force be held up to scrutiny.

Rhetoric thus arises with the suspension of reciprocity in orality and the definition of meaning as an internal content to the speech. This opens a space in which the question of the effect of a speech on an audience can be posed. There is another, more radical, irruption of reciprocity when we consider a transformation that is not *of* orality but *from* orality to writing. A phenomenology of the radical distinction between speech and writing is opened up by the work of Paul Ricoeur and Hans-Georg Gadamer, though I will argue later that this phenomenology is later revoked by hermeneutic philosophy by returning it to a presupposed unity of meaning that confines it within metaphysics. A subsequent analysis which retains the radical difference between speech and writing and, by implication, between all distinct media of communication therefore must be proposed.

Ricoeur defines a text as "any discourse fixed by writing." This fixture is an "intentional exteriorization" which transforms both the event of speech and its meaning. We need to distinguish here between the written transcription of an oral speech event and a writing "occurring where speech could have emerged."[9] In the case of transcription, such as the written transcription of speech in a courtroom, the writing in question clearly refers back to an anterior speech act which it preserves but does not replace, and therefore can be regarded as a representation and extension of that original act. In contrast, the specificity of writing as a medium of communication only emerges when there is no prior speech act, when the meaning is written, as Ricoeur says, "instead" of being spoken. If we regard this as a mere replacement, as simply a different location for an identical meaning, we altogether miss the productive and forming characteristics of the medium of communication. But by focusing on the characteristics of direct inscription in writing we open up the possibility that the materiality of a communication medium is not merely an external coat that can be sloughed off at will, but constitutive of both the event and the meaning of the communication itself. In an oral speech event, speaker and audience are present to one another in a common situation in the here and now. The positions of speaker and hearer can be exchanged repeatedly and, consequently, difficulties in understanding can be removed by clarification of the speaker's intention through further discussion. Reference in such an encounter is primarily ostensive and speech is above all an engaged presentation, rather than an imaginative representation of the world. Speaking is immediately rhetorical and agonistic since there is little space for a separation of knower and known.[10] The inscription of a written text shatters this reciprocity of speaker and hearer in a common situation and disperses the analogous relations in both space and time. Writer and reader probably never meet except through the text. Their roles are not reversible. Rather than addressing those present at the moment of speech, writing addresses, in principle, all who can read. It is not an immediate act presenting an intervention in a situation, but a delayed representation. Thus, it manifests a distinction between an event and the meaning of that event. It is only the meaning that is fixed in inscription, not the event of communicating, or the act of inscribing itself. Consequently, the reference of a text is not directly to the world of the author but to a world opened up within the text, which must then be mediated by the reader's interpretation to his or her world. Historical consciousness derives from the experience of the tension between the horizon of the text in the past and the horizon of the present reader. By this "fusing of horizons," in Gadamer's phrase, the text mediates across space and time:

> The projecting of the historical horizon, then, is only a phase in the process of understanding, and does not become solidified into the self-alienation of a past consciousness, but is overtaken by our own present horizon of understanding. In the process of understanding there takes place a real fusing of horizons, which

means that as the historical horizon is projected, it is simultaneously removed.[11]

Thus, the possibility of distance between the reader and the meaning in the text calls for an active interpretation that produces the unity of a tradition in history. The distinction between the saying and the said in writing is a distantiation that calls forth the subsequent activity of interpretation that aims to close the distance and create continuity. Consequently, Ricoeur claims that writing requires the act of "application" which can "fulfil the text in present speech."[12] In short, inscription creates distance, therefore the possibility of misunderstanding, and consequently the eventual possibility of a hermeneutic re-establishment of a "conversation" that produces a much more extensive continuity over the dispersal.

The hermeneutic distinction between speech and writing thus concludes by postulating a twofold mutual relation that encloses them within the same hermeneutic circle of tradition. It is this presupposed *relation between* speech and writing that encloses the hermeneutic comparison of media of communication within classic modern cultural theory. First, the separation of event and meaning by writing is said to clarify what is only a "virtual," or occluded, distinction that is nevertheless operative in speech.[13] Even in speech, event and meaning, or rhetoric and truth, are not identical—though we might never have seen this without writing. Thus, hermeneutic philosophy suggests that writing brings forth the concealed possibilities of speech. In Gadamer's words, "that language is capable of being written down is by no means incidental to its nature. Rather, the capacity of being written down is based on the fact that speech itself shares in the pure ideality of meaning that communicates itself in it. In writing this meaning of what is spoken exists purely for itself, completely detached from all emotional elements of expression and communication."[14] This hermeneutic centring on the ideal meaning-content of expression is a key assumption of metaphysics essential to its conception of totality: It is by centring on a meaning-content (supposedly) independent of the materiality of inscription that the plurality of media of communication can be totalized. It is for this reason that, for Ricoeur and Gadamer, as for all hermeneutic philosophy, the model of the text is in principle applicable to the entirety of human action, and therefore is the most complete method for the human sciences.[15] Even in the case of history, where event and meaning seem to be identical (as in the case of orality) this separation is taken to be an emergent one, rather than an external imposition. Second, hermeneutics argues that the distance instituted by writing must be hermeneutically "fulfilled" in the present speech of the interpreter. "All writing is . . . a kind of alienated speech, and its signs need to be transformed back into speech and meaning" since "language has its true being only in conversation, in the exercise of understanding between people."[16] Thus, the ideality of the meaning-content is replaced within social relations such that expression can matter in the conduct of human life. This completes the hermeneutic circle, which could not span the plural materialities of media of communication without assuming an underlying identical site of expression. In this way, the assumptions of the ideality of meaning-content and the singularity of the site of expression reinforce each other. Hermeneutics, though it opens up the discourse on a plurality of sites of inscription, nevertheless simultaneously closes down the implications of the different materialities of media of communication through these two assumptions.

With the assertion of this double hermeneutical relation of "virtuality" and "fulfilment," the initial distinction between different characteristics of speech and writing due to the materiality of their inscription in different media of communication is tamed and shelved. Tradition can be a hermeneutic unity because the plurality of media is transcended by an account of meaning that suspends the plurality. To put it succinctly, if writing occurs at the *site* where speech "could have emerged," the hermeneutic taming occurs through the assumption that this site is, in principle, identical for both speech and writing. Speech and writing are enfolded within a unity of "language" as the virtuality and fulfilment of the expression of meaning, and meaning is assumed to be the one and only site of human being. In hermeneutic philosophy, the distinction between media of communication becomes, in the final instance, a secondary variable dependent on meaning-content. We are now in a position to follow up the focus on media of communication with a full sense of the radical attention to the materiality of discourse that it requires in order to come to grips with postmodern culture and not be reinscribed within a metaphysical totality. In short, we are confronted not simply with a plurality of discourses, but a plurality of sites of discourse and a critique of meaning.

The focus on the forming significance of sites of discourse instituted in media of communication is an established, though minority, tradition in communication studies. Consider, for example, the contribution of Jack Goody and Ian Watt to social anthropology, based on the key observation that oral and written modes of transmission affect differently the cultural heritage passed on. They argued that the "relative continuity of the categories of understanding from one generation to another is primarily ensured by language, which is the most direct and comprehensive expression of the social experience of the group" and, in particular, that "the intrinsic nature of oral communication has a considerable effect upon both the content and the transmission of the cultural repertoire."[17] Also, Claude Lévi-Strauss has suggested that the existence of writing is what makes the difference between Western and so-called "primitive" societies that is constitutive of anthropology.[18] Similarly, Harold Innis has pointed out that a "concern with communication by the ear assumes reliance on time. Persistence of the oral tradition in Greece implied an emphasis on poetry intimately associated with music and a time art. Verbal poetry goes back to the fundamental reality of time. . . . The oral tradition in the Homeric epics reflected the character of early Greek society."[19] This interrelation between the "character of a society" and its shaping by a dominant medium of communication can be generalized beyond the specific medium of orality. The poetic instituting is not simply an emergent "national narrative," but also a specific formation of perception that shapes the "national character" far beyond the storyline of the narrative. Innis called this a "bias" inherent in a medium of communication whereby its characteristics were extended to the experiential formation of an entire civilization. "The bias of modern civilization incidental to the newspaper and the radio will presume a perspective in consideration of civilizations dominated by other media. . . . We can perhaps assume that the use of a medium of communication over a long period will to some extent determine the character of knowledge to be communicated and suggest that its pervasive influence will eventually create a civilization in which life and flexibility will become exeedingly difficult to maintain and that the advantages of a new medium will become such as to lead to the emergence of a new civilization."[20] The medium of communication, understood in this way as embodied inscriptions, shapes national character and history in constituting the epochal horizon.

Thus, a medium of communication is not to be opposed to social institutions, as meaning-content necessarily is, but should be understood as the shaping origin of institutions—an origin which may become "foundational," though it can always be unsettled by other media. For example, in Canada the railway was constructed to facilitate the extraction and export of raw materials and staple goods (such as grain) from the interior of the country. In so doing, the railways linked the interior to the St Lawrence River in an East–West axis that connected back to the European imperial centre. This means of transportation was built upon the earlier maritime East–West axis established through the extraction of previous staple goods, such as fish, wood and beaver, but also extended this axis in a manner that became a cultural transformation. The very notion of "railway" thus encompasses technology, the traversal of space, a plurality of relevant social actors, and relations of dependence between colony and empire in a tension between history and transformation. It was articulated against a background of earlier maritime imperial relations. This East–West axis was the condition for the existence of Canada as a separate, though dependent, country in North America. The progressive weakening of this axis in favour of a North–South one in the twentieth century has led to the gradual weakening of Canada's already tenuous independent sphere of action. The recent free trade agreements with the United States, and later Mexico, have probably definitively undermined the communicative axis that brought forth the possibility of Canada. It is concretely entangled with the new shaping of the world through electronic media in the sense of both transborder data flows and commercial messages. In a very real sense, a historical epoch is coming to a close—an epoch whose horizon is indicated by the medium which instituted it. In focusing on the embodied side of a communicative act, the influence of embodied materiality on the formation of human meaning is crystallized. But this is not a circumscription of culture, or discourse, from outside. It is inherent in the world-inscribing of the medium of communication itself. A medium is the solidity of discourse, that whereby the world becomes more than what we say it is. This is a way of theorizing constraint, but *constraint within human culture*, not constraint *of* culture by an external materiality, like the base–superstructure formulation of Marxism, for example, which is precisely what is denied by the linguistic turn. After the railway, the canoe becomes a kind of return. No longer an institution, it becomes an instrument of leisure, as McLuhan pointed out, an art form. It is precisely this founding of a before–after that shapes institutions.

At such turning points, the *archai* that institute and shape discourses become visible in their own right. Discursive thought emanates from a primal, originating figure, or primal scene, back toward which the deconstructive strategy is oriented.[21] The postmodern condition is an opening, made possible by a fissure between origin and goal, universal and particular, such that metaphysical oppositions lose their mutually implicatory character. They do not disappear, but begin to float apart. Such is the loss of foundations. In such a moment, thought and practice experience a radical groundlessness. It is this void that has given rise to the turn toward discourse in the human sciences. This void gives rise to a radical questioning of the *archai* that settle the metaphysical oppositions in a given historical epoch. It opens to the tension in practice from which *archai* emerge and which apparently propels

them beyond practice to become a foundation for it. Any historical epoch is instituted through such a "propelling-forward" of an
originating figure, or primal scene. In the moment when this
becomes visible, one is no longer within a historical epoch, but at
the turning between them where their institution originates.

Whether it be in the context of a diagnosis of contemporary
society or a re-evaluation of modern views of non-Western, previously so-called primitive, societies, the focus on media of
communication marshals a critical tendency through a focus on
the materiality of forms of expression. This focus finds its place in
phenomenology in connection to the notion of *institution*, or the
instituting of a primal scene whereby a new formation is brought
into being such that it becomes a pervasive influence throughout
later developments to constitute a tradition. The instituting of a
historical epoch occurs through a given complex of media of communication. It is crucial that the development of this thought of
instituting sites is tied to the contemporary situation in which it
has emerged. Eric Havelock has claimed that the literature that
argues for a focus of media of communication sprang on to the
stage in 1963 and has grown by leaps and bounds ever since.[22] The
rediscovery of orality that characterized this literature emerged in
the contemporary historical shift away from a predominantly literate civilization under the influence of new electronic media such
as radio and television, and which has accelerated more recently
with the introduction of computers, satellites and so forth. His
appreciation of the prior oral culture of Homeric Greece led
Havelock to suggest that philosophy itself was formed by the shift
from orality to writing. The separation of the knower from the
known, the condition for the emergence of philosophy, lies in the
new conception of language as descriptive, material and visual

rather than rhetorical, agonistic and acoustic. From this shift emerged both the Socratic practice of "essential definition," whereby an answer to the "What is x?" question was sought, and the Socratic conception of the self which, through the process of dialectic, formed itself in the image of justice.[23] It was thus suggested that the very form of knowledge in the culture of the West was initiated by a civilizational shift which was not itself fully comprehended by those who underwent it. In this sense, the literature in communication studies that argues for the shaping influence of sites of inscription has an affinity with the nineteenth-century critique of philosophy by Marx, Nietzsche and Freud, who suggested that the project of knowing could only be formulated under conditions that prevented its adequate self-knowledge.

The separation of knower and known emerges with the decline of mythic narrative and provokes the philosophical attempt to close the gap. Plato likened knowledge to vision and pointed out that the seer and the seen could only coincide in the presence of light. Similarly, the co-presence of knower and known can only occur in the presence of a medium of connection that Plato called the Good.[24] When the philosopher emerges from the cave and gazes on the sun, the soul is formed to resemble the order of the cosmos.[25] But the sight of the sun is not "another" knowledge, however exalted. It is the point of coincidence between the ability to see and the source of light that makes any and all connections between knower and known possible. Philosophy thus grounds the very possibility of rational civilization through the encounter with the origin of connection between human perception and extra-human order. The notion of sites of inscription links historical changes in media of communication to human perception of Being. In so far as a given medium becomes metaphorically illuminative of the ground of this connection between humanity and Being it circumscribes an epoch of awareness. The history of Being, in Heidegger's phrase, is thus the history of these media of connection that open the possibility of, and assign a characteristic form to, the web of meaning that characterizes the world in a given epoch—which includes the constitution of a relation between knower and known. Communication, in this sense, is not a question of the transmission of a priorly articulated thought. It is the form of awareness that shapes the articulation of thought. Thought itself is understood less as an "internal" activity than as the multiplicity of connections that is spread out throughout the material forms of social communication. From this perspective, the media of communication that have been developed through-out human culture are expressions of the socio-historical Being of human life. They are the embodied rhetorical form that institutes, or establishes, a world.[26]

The basic philosophical formulation of the role of media of communication in the human sciences that I am proposing here is of the body as the root-phenomenon of expressive forms, media of communication as embodied material expressions, a particular complex of expressive forms as the construction of a world, and the historical succession of worlds as manifestations of Being. This conception is the extension of the phenomenological concept of institution, or *Urstiftung*. This constitution of a world of meaning can also be formulated as a rhetoric of forms of expression centring on media of communication. "World," in the phenomenological sense that I am using it here, does not refer in an objectivist sense to a reality presupposed as existing prior to human meaning nor in a subjectivist sense as a projection of mental acts, but rather to the totality of meaning that is immanent in practical involvements.[27]

It is a contemporary formulation of the relation between humanity and nature sketched by the early Marx, in which the externality of nature and humanity produced by modern alienation is replaced by a conception in which "nature is man's body."[28] In recent years, this world of meaning has been investigated through the metaphor of language, since language-use is the most characteristic activity enacting human meaning. In arguing for the site of inscription as a fundamental notion in the theory of discourse, I am suggesting the possibility of understanding a complex of media of communication as constituting a human world. Even more, one may become attuned to the historical disclosure of a succession of these worlds—what we might call the embodied history of human Being. It is important that the institution of a world be understood as an articulation of a complex of media of communication. Since a world does not derive from a single primal scene but from a complex of such scenes, the possible misunderstanding that it has a singular and overriding origin or destiny is dispelled—a notion that seems to be operative in the singular and virtually determining character of "destiny" in Heidegger's philosophy. Only through the plurality of its scenes in a historical instituting can the embodied history of human Being escape being enclosed between a fixed origin and destiny.

A constitutive paradox emerges when one attempts to describe the embodied history of forms of inscription within the sites that are formed by this very same embodiment. A contemporary thinking of media of communication must address the inevitability of expressing the forms of awareness in terms drawn from the historical forms of expression. This constitutive paradox of communication stems from the fact that every "communication" as expression, or sense-content, is a metaphorical formation of the very possibility of "communication" as shaping a form of connection, or institution. To state it somewhat differently, the representative and constitutive aspects of communication are interwoven in the same communicative act. In phenomenological terminology, every communication act is simultaneously a "mundane" act within the given world-horizon and a "transcendental" act of constitution of that horizon. This suggests that the medium of communication is actually the transcendental aspect of a communication act, always presented through a specific content, but never in it. A contemporary rhetoric thus has less to do with persuasion in the sense of yielding assent to a given content, than with a deeper persuasion, inherent in every expression, to assent to the form of awareness that is manifested through the content. It is a rhetoric of sites of inscription. It is also within this loop that the postmodern connection between the human sciences and philosophy is to be found, which requires a thorough rethinking of the relation between rhetoric and philosophy—a relation whose terms have been largely settled since the Greek division of territory.

It is in this postmodern context of a newly unsettled relation between rhetoric and philosophy that the sphere of rhetoric can be expanded to deal with media forms, rather than just their contents, even though the rhetoric of media forms is only itself expressable as, or through, a content. The metaphorical, and even allusive, level at which discourse about the institution of historical forms of discourse is articulated remains tied to the contents of human expression— though in a reflexive manner. The thesis proper to communication in this expanded sense is that media of communication constitute human experience in its perceptual, institutional and cognitive aspects, which are elaborated in the dimensions of space and time, such that a specific cultural form is given to the lifeworld of a social group. Culture, in this usage, is not understood as distinct from society, economics, politics and so forth, but in a more anthropological sense as the "specific pervasive style" (Husserl) that pervades these areas and unifies them into a "form of life" (Wittgenstein). Any communication, besides taking place within the horizon of this cultural form, contributes to the definition of the cultural form through its medium. If the thesis proper to rhetoric in its historical form concerns the persuasive power of language, the theory of sites of inscription is a "media rhetorics" in so far as it pertains to the institution of a cultural form—not the persuasion to see the world in a certain way, but the image-ing of the world as such.

The notion of the institution of a cultural form through a medium of communication suggests that the making-common that is communication occurs more at the level of the type of social interaction that predominates rather than the contents of specific communications. In this manner the study of the interaction of a plurality of media of communication, or a dominant media complex, defines a historical epoch. Arguing that consciousness is a product of the need to communicate, Nietzsche suggested that consciousness is, by its very nature, oriented to what is communicable and therefore superficial and average. Grammar is the metaphysics of the people, from which epistemologists do not extricate themselves.[29] Each communicative form, each consciousness, is thus traversed by a non-communicable, an unconsciousness, whose uncommon-ness may be taken to define the limit of the form. If this were taken to refer to a communicative content, the argument would not refer to more than an empirical limit. It would express the difficulty, but not the impossibility, of expanding the limit. If Nietzsche's "pressure of the need for communication"[30] is interpreted as such, it must refer back to a presupposed, and dubious, anthropological psychology. But if the "pressure of the need" is interpreted in a constitutive manner, it refers only internally to the reciprocal need constitutive of a human group as such. It is not the content of expressions that forges socio-cultural relations, but their form. In short, it is the dominant medium of communication, patterning the media ecology, that circumscribes the perceptual, institutional and cognitive style of a culture. This limit is not empirical and is not definable from within a culture. Every cultural form is haunted by its unconsciousness, every communication by that which escapes expression. This unheard, unfelt, unthought limit can be approached through the medium of communication and, in this way, communication studies can address the interdisciplinary project of self-knowledge that defines the human sciences. The thesis proper to communication studies does not stop short of the incommunicable, not being limited to the culture in which it comes to expression. Ordinarily we read the marks on paper, being oriented through their materiality to the meaning they signify. Occasionally, this inscription, the wonder of meaning's embodiment, comes to consciousness. Rarely, we focus behind the marks to the paper which has been inscribed. Here the transcendental limit to the cultural inscriptions may be encountered. The event of communication occurs at the moment when pen touches paper. To write of a blank sheet of paper is to turn communication toward that which makes it possible, the point at which it emerges from the incommunicable, the unsaid, the unconsciousness which haunts human events. The theory of media of communication investigates human meaning not only as content but primarily as the circumscription of common sense within a horizon. The dominant medium, or

media, of communication—including their prevailing relationships, or "translations"—connects the given formation of common
sense to its horizon in the historical epoch. It thus accounts for the
greater immovability, or solidity, of some discourses over others.
From this perspective, power is not understood as the "repression"
of existing alternatives, but as the predominant thematizations
that prevent, or impede, the very formulation of alternatives.
Moreover, alternatives are more likely to emerge from media that
are not tied into the dominant power formation, and to unsettle
common sense much more by invoking different social relationships and perceptual formations than by providing new
content—though it is often the case that such alternative media do
provide different content.

At this point we can return to explicate the key theme in my argument concerning understanding epochal critique through the notion
of constitutive paradox. This paradox is expanded and explored,
though not dissolved, through the focus on media of communication.
Every expression is a fusing of message-content with a medium of
communication. Thus, every expression acts both to contribute to the
content of an ongoing discourse and also to shape an experiential formation with perceptual and institutional–technological consequences
which constructs social relationships and thereby forms human
experience within a world-horizon. These aspects of any communicative act mean that every expression is simultaneously a
specific statement within a discourse, an invoking of a social relationship, and an experience of the horizon of the world. It is thus
self-referential in a threefold manner. At this moment in the manifestation of human practical involvement with the world, it is not
our task to dismantle the paradoxes that emerge from this self-
referentiality, but to use them to productively investigate the

manifold co-enactments in every expression. It is the very fact that these three aspects are now manifested as the "complex self-references" of a single communication act that both sustains the constitutive paradox and situates it in our current postmodern condition where the *archai* of civilizational character become visible. If the epochal horizon is taken as settled, poetic expressions become foundational *archai* and these three aspects are separated into different axes of civilizational character—such as literature, social relationships (studied by the social sciences), and religion and philosophy. Within the postmodern constitutive paradox, these are not archaic axes but a cross-referencing perceptual–social–historical formation. It is apparent, from this perspective, why the settling of the boundaries of knowledge and action is a key concern for the philosophy of the human sciences today.

Any act of communication consists of these three aspects—which we may call a said, the saying and the site. By a "said," I mean the meaning or content of an utterance, but also its enunciation in the here and now with a rhetorical force in an argumentative field that is constructed through its reference to other statements in a discourse such that it is an intervention within a constituted discourse, or a move within a given language game. The danger is that the human sciences tend to become ideological by confining themselves to this dimension of language. The "saying" is the face that articulates the said; it is a concrete encounter with an otherness that constitutes a social relation. Concerning the said, criticism is a rather attenuated matter of representations, their completeness and adequacy, and constraints to what is represented. With the "saying" one is directed to the social relation, or set of identities, instituted by the communication itself. The event of inscription shapes forms of social interaction. Every saying, in constituting a social relation, occurs within a site. Perhaps it is more accurate to say "is a siting." A communication clears a space, or opens a horizon of the world, within which a social relation appears. Characteristic sites shape socio-historical formations; such clearings tend to persist over and throughout a social form. In siting, a medium of communication institutes the poetics of social history, but, despite this "foundational" persistence, siting is a permanent characteristic of communication. Every communication either reinstitutes a characteristic site or founds another one even though this possibility only becomes apparent and relevant at historical turning points. The notion of a postmodern turning suggests that the present moment consists of a shift between sites, and, to the extent that one embraces the plurality opened by this shift, one takes part in characterizing, and is shaped by, a shift that is beyond control. It is at this juncture that communication takes us beyond the content of human expression, and beyond the saying in which the faces of others emerge, to the siting of the world-horizon which gives our civilization its character. Here we encounter the threshold beyond which there is only Being itself. These are not separate destinations; they are present in every word. Their manifestation is a becoming-conscious of practical action. In this sense, a conception of epochal critique that centres on the medium of communication radicalizes ideology-critique, and saves it by going beyond, toward the epochal horizon.

NOTES

1. Friedrich Nietzsche, *The Gay Science*, trans. Walter Kaufmann (New York: Random House, 1974) p. 181; Book 3, aphorism 125.

2. Edmund Husserl, *Formal and Transcendental Logic*, trans. Dorion Cairns (The Hague: Martinus Nijhoff, 1969) pp. 278–9.

3. Edmund Husserl, *The Crisis of the European Sciences and Transcendental Phenomenology*, trans. David Carr (Evanston: Northwestern University Press, 1970) p. 107.

4. Ibid., p. 161.

5. Aristotle, *Rhetoric*, trans. W. R. Roberts (New York: The Modern Library, 1984) pp. 31–2, 1358a–b.

6. Ibid., p. 24, 1355b.

7. John Searle, *Speech Acts: An Essay in the Philosophy of Language* (Cambridge: Cambridge University Press, 1971) pp. 30–3.

8. The significance of Kenneth Burke's introduction of the concepts of con-substantiality and identification is therefore to undo and rethink the separation between speaker and audience through analysing speech as constitutive of their relation—which accounts for his importance for a contemporary theory of rhetoric and communication. See *A Rhetoric of Motives* (Berkeley: University of California Press, 1950) especially pp. 55–8, 19–23.

9. Paul Ricoeur, "What is a Text? Explanation and Understanding" in *Hermeneutics and the Human Sciences*, ed. and trans. John Thompson (Cambridge: Cambridge University Press, 1981) p. 146.

10. Ibid., pp. 148–9.

11. Hans-Georg Gadamer, *Truth and Method* (New York: Crossroad, 1975) p. 273.

12. Paul Ricoeur, "What is a Text?", p. 158. See also Gadamer, *Truth and Method*, pp. 274–8.

13. Paul Ricoeur, *Interpretation Theory: Discourse and the Surplus of Meaning* (Fort Worth: The Texas Christian University Press, 1976) pp. 25, 91.

14. Gadamer, *Truth and Method*, p. 354.

15. Paul Ricoeur, "The Model of the Text: Meaningful Action Considered as a Text" in *Hermeneutics and the Human Sciences*; Hans-Georg Gadamer, "On the Scope and Function of Hermeneutical Reflection" in *Philosophical Hermeneutics*, trans. D. Linge (Berkeley: University of California Press, 1977) and *Truth and Method*, pp. 153–344; Clifford Geertz, *The Interpretation of Cultures* (New York: Basic Books, 1973).

16. Hans-Georg Gadamer, *Truth and Method*, pp. 354, 404.

17. Jack Goody and Ian Watt, "The Consequences of Literacy" in *Literacy in Traditional Societies*, ed. Jack Goody (Cambridge: Cambridge University Press, 1968) pp. 28–9.

18. Claude Lévi-Strauss, *Myth and Meaning* (Toronto and Buffalo: University of Toronto Press, 1978) p. 15.

19. Harold Innis, "The Problem of Space" in *The Bias of Communication* (Toronto: University of Toronto Press, 1973) p. 106.

20. Harold Innis, "The Bias of Communication" in ibid., p. 34.

21. See Ernesto Grassi, *Rhetoric as Philosophy: The Humanistic Tradition* (University Park and London: The University of Pennsylvania State Press, 1984) and Jacques Derrida, "White Mythology" in *Margins of Philosophy* (Chicago: University of Chicago Press, 1982).

22. Eric Havelock, *The Muse Learns to Write* (New Haven and London: Yale University Press, 1986) pp. 24–9. This must refer mainly to popularization, however, since it ignores the prior work of Harold Innis and others.

23. Ibid., pp. 105–16; Eric Havelock, *Preface to Plato* (Cambridge: Harvard University Press, 1963) pp. 208–10.

24. Plato, *Republic*, trans. Paul Shorey in *The Collected Dialogues of Plato*, ed. Edith Hamilton and Huntington Cairns (New York: Pantheon, 1966) pp. 742–4, 507b–9b.

25. See, for the philosophical intuition of cosmological order, *Republic*, 518c, 540a, 585a–6a, 611a–12d; *Phaedo*, 90a–d, trans. Hugh Tredennick; *Seventh Letter*, trans. L. A. Post, 433b.

26. Heidegger described poetry as the "projective saying of world and earth" in "The Origin of the Work of Art" in *Poetry, Language, Truth*, trans. Albert Hofstadter (New York: Harper and Row, 1975) p. 74. This Heideggerian conception of poetry has been developed into a conception of rhetoric as the institution and confirmation of human dwelling in the world by Ernesto Grassi in *Rhetoric as Philosophy* and Michael J. Hyde in "Rhetorically, Man Dwells: On the Making-Known Function of Discourse", *Communication*, Vol. 7, 1983. This conception of poetry, even as developed into rhetoric, contains a mystifying temptation for misunderstanding language due to the loss of its material component. The notion of sites of inscription attempts to remedy this mystification of Heideggerian origin.

27. See, for a more complete account of the phenomenological concept of the world, Edmund Husserl, *The Crisis of European Sciences and Transcendental Phenomenology*, pp. 103–89 and Martin Heidegger, *Being and Time*, trans. John Macquarrie and Edward Robinson (New York and Evanston: Harper and Row, 1962) pp. 91–148.

28. Karl Marx, "Economic and Philosophical Manuscripts of 1844" in *The Marx-Engels Reader*, ed. Robert C. Tucker (New York: Norton, 1978) p. 75.

29. Friedrich Nietzsche, *The Gay Science*, pp. 298–300; Book 5, aphorism 354.

30. Ibid., p. 298; Book 5, aphorism 354.

5

RECONSTRUCTING DEMOCRACY IN THE
MEDIA ENVIRONMENT

In their contemporary postmodern moment, social and cultural studies run the danger of rejecting the component of ethico-political evaluation that is essential to critical social theory in favour of a cultural relativism that supposedly better recognizes the legitimacy of the plurality of cultures. To the extent that the evaluative component is regarded as entirely internal to cultural forms, and therefore as incapable of radically criticizing them, social and cultural theory is pushed toward a pluralism that is practically indistinct from a relativism that undermines social critique. Here I want to redesign the ethico-political evaluative component that is essential for a critical theory of society and which can serve as the basis for a concept of radical democracy that is pluralist in the sense of fostering many speaking-positions but which halts the slide toward relativism. That is, it begins to renegotiate the particularity–universality nexus instead of either rejecting contemporary critiques of universality and totality out of hand or asserting contingency against necessity and plurality against unity in a manner that will suggest a future rebound back. In the context of the spatialized moment of global culture, I argue that the concept of critique can be reinvented through a focus on the materiality of media of communication which can root the interpretation of symbolic representations in the more fundamental issue of the constitution of social relations. An adequate theory of discourse for radical democracy must focus on the transversal relations between sites of inscription and the cultural horizon in the postmodern cultural field.

Genuine democracy requires widespread public participation in the process of deliberation and decision-making. For this reason, the ideal case of Greek face-to-face participatory democracy retains an appeal even while it seems unrealizable in a large-scale industrial capitalist society. Relations of immediate reciprocity such that each can speak and listen in turn, combined with access to relevant social knowledge, ideally guarantees that deliberation and decision-making cannot be monopolized by powerful interests. Democratic theory and practice therefore rely on a normative conception of communication. Even in a complex society where representative procedures must supplement citizen participation, the ideal of reciprocity seems essential to rule by the people. Freedom of speech in its classic form was fundamental to democratic societies because it intended to guarantee both widespread access to relevant social knowledge by banning government censorship and widespread ability to articulate opinion and engage in decision-making. The main issue for a radical democratic theory of the media is the political principle of reciprocity in contemporary conditions such that the "right to speak" can have real efficacy as a "right to be heard."

In contemporary capitalist societies, democratic theory must address two main sources whereby reciprocity is attenuated: The monopolization of access to relevant social knowledge and the inability of listeners to transform themselves into speakers. Both of these may be posed as questions of the extent to which an audience also produces and circulates social knowledge and engages actively in the process of deliberation and decision-making. The tendency of the most significant contemporary communication systems is to produce audiences without this capacity. Audiences tend to remain simply audiences; that is to say, communication systems tend to sever audiences from reciprocal production of social knowledge and engagement in decision-making. Even if projected advances in communication technologies were to allow for inputs and plebiscites on various public issues, as several authors including C. B. Macpherson have argued, we must recognize "an inescapable requirement of any decision-making process: somebody must formulate the questions."[1] It is this fundamental non-reciprocal component of contemporary media of communication that is problematic for radical democracy. For this reason, a critical theory of society dedicated to the recovery and extension of democracy must analyse the role of audiences in contemporary communication systems. This issue for a democratic theory of audiences is not limited to coverage of news and politics in the usual sense. A genuinely democratic theory requires that the very definition of what is newsworthy and what is political emerge from the process of reciprocal communication. It therefore implies a focus on the constitution of audiences as non-speakers in the whole of cultural production. In a real sense, the audience is the key mediating link between cultural production in general and the possibilities of radical democracy. The articulation of the classic principle of reciprocity in contemporary conditions of cultural production suggests that democracy is not merely a matter of political institutions, but is a whole way of life that is uniquely and newly endangered by the constitution of audiences, and can only be recovered and extended by being diffused throughout the entirety of cultural production. This theoretical investigation of the role of the audience for a contemporary democratic theory begins with a historical situating of the problem of the audience in the contemporary postmodern cultural condition which shows why the notion of plural interpretations now takes on such a key legitimating role.

Any cultural object can be viewed from the perspectives of its production, its audience and its critical evaluation. Cultural production today is increasingly monopolized by the cultural industries, whose replication and transmission of the productions selected for promotion crowds out locally produced and nonprofit cultural forms. Yet, in this situation, the plurality of audience interpretations of any given mass media text is often presented as evidence that the audience is always "struggling to establish its own meanings" and is not a simple dupe of media moguls. While the latter may well be so, the polysemy of mass media texts is a *condition* for their commercial success, especially in a culturally diverse world characterized by transnational media flows, and doesn't go any distance at all toward proving that the audience isn't hindered from wider social critique or action by the mass media. The assumption that texts must transmit a univocal meaning in order to play an ideological role is a caricature that serves to let virtually everything off the hook. The contemporary postmodern cultural field exhibits a remarkable duality with respect to the role of the audience: On the one hand, contemporary cultural theory has been concerned to argue for an expanded capacity of the audience to engage in active interpretations of mass media texts. On the other hand, the notion that there is a plurality of audience interpretations of any text has come to play a key legitimating role in so far as it appears to render moot the issue of the centralizing of media ownership, the non-reciprocality of many contemporary media and the consequent constricting of access to cultural production—the inability of those confined to being audiences to be heard amid the noise produced by the mass media. In order to develop a critical cultural theory of the mass media, it is essential to theorize the plurality of interpretations along with the constraint visited on the audience by the medium of communication. It is much easier for the new pluralist apologists to celebrate the ingenuity of "people" to use the products of mass culture in diverse ways despite their control by increasingly fewer hands, than for critical theorists to define precisely the constraints that foreclose political alternatives. Such celebrations leave the larger context of cultural production and reception undisturbed: the globe is being carved into competing free trade zones reinforced by political and military power legitimated, in large part, by a transnational cultural system in which consumption is promoted as the model of social life. In short, the plurality of audience interpretations of a given cultural production is often interpreted in an ideological way as a pluralism that tends to legitimate monopoly by the cultural industries. In so far as no one can claim today that there is widespread democratic access to production of cultural products through the mass media, the plurality of audience responses is the key term through which this ideological legitimation operates. But it is important to notice that the audience responds in a plurality of ways to the content represented on the media; it does not have the option of being in a plurality of relations to the medium itself and for this reason it cannot make itself heard.

The present analysis focuses on the preconditions for "being heard" in order to argue that a new political principle must be advanced in order to extend democracy in consumer capitalist societies. This principle suggests that every lack of reciprocity in a medium of communication must be compensated by the "right to speak" in another forum of equal social significance—i.e. where one is likely to be heard. This amounts to a reassertion of the principle of reciprocity in a context in which it is impossible to rely primarily on face-to-face communication to guarantee democratic participation. Such a reassertion requires that the different characteristics of media of communication—such as speech, writing, radio, television, and so forth—be identified and clarified in a comparative fashion. It argues that democracy must now be addressed through the social relations that various media institute and emphasize. For "the people"—as an effective or passive political force—are constituted through the media of communication that predominate in a society.[2] The radio broadcast was discussed in this manner by Jean-Paul Sartre as an indication of the predominance of what he called "serial" social relations that inhibit the possibility of collective action:

> But the important point is not whether a particular radio listener possesses his own transmitter and can make contact, as an individual, *later*, with some other listener, in another city or country: the mere fact of *listening to the radio*, that is to say, of listening to a particular broadcast at a particular time, establishes a serial relation of *absence* between the different listeners.[3]

Listeners are grouped together through the medium of the radio broadcast and have relations only through it. Consequently, it is impossible for them to act collectively; their action can only be the sum of individual actions, so that the meaning of this sum is not an intended outcome of any member. As Sartre continues,

> my impotence does not lie only in the impossibility of silencing this voice: it also lies in the impossibility of convincing, *one by one*, the listeners all of whom it exhorts in the common isolation which it creates for all of them as their inert bond.[4]

The speaker–listener relation of one-way transmission and the listener–listener relation of seriality are constituted simultaneously by the broadcast such that the audience's seriality inhibits the collective political action that democratic participation requires. There is no need to deny that each listener may interpret the content of the broadcast in a relatively unique manner. The emphasis here is on the constitution of social relations, not on the circulation of opinions and interpretations.

Within the closure of metaphysics, every expression is subdivided into internal meaning-content, or sense, and external persuasive force. Any investigation of audience effect within this framework remains caught within this duality that creates an insoluble dilemma at each level of the inquiry. In this context we can appreciate the radicalness of Marshall McLuhan's claim that the content of a medium is its users, or that internal sense is entirely present in persuasive force.[5] A media theory for radical democracy must provoke a questioning of the metaphysical distinction that has set up our separation between content and effect, or dialectic and rhetoric. The present strategy for so doing centres on the "external" materiality of the medium of communication. This is not the relative, secondary externality of persuasive effect—which is constituted in opposition to internal content. The "material

Externality" of the medium of communication, whose distinctiveness we may designate with a capital E, undercuts the sense-force, or content-effect, of the expression as a whole and pertains to the structure and consequences of the communicative act itself. This radical Externality opens up the possibility of undercutting the metaphysical distinction between internal content and persuasive force, between truth (philosophy) and rhetoric, by subjecting it to a more fundamental axis of investigation as the constitution of social relations within which issues of truth or persuasion arise. The metaphysical tradition and the dependent conception of rhetoric have been formed by the focus on speech—from which the very term "audience," or "hearers," is formed—as has been argued by Jacques Derrida for example.[6] The discussion of the rhetorical tradition here indicates a support for this claim independent of Derrida's account. Nevertheless, I do not regard Derrida's claim as fully justified in so far as it involves a confusion between the two e(E)xternalities that I distinguish.

The present inquiry, by way of contrast, centres on the comparison between different media of communication. It was noted previously that rhetoric came into being as an external transformation of the medium of orality such that the reciprocal turn-taking of conversation was suspended. This suspension is the condition for the emergence of the question concerning persuasion, or audience-effect. If we wish to formulate generally the limits within which all interpretations are constrained, it will necessarily depend upon the entire social and institutional complex of the social formation of the audience. We may formulate the conclusion of this inquiry in general terms: The suspension of reciprocity within a medium of communication pushes the constraints on interpretation outside the given communication

136

act and, thereby, to the social formation as a whole. In the most general terms, this is where the interplay of constraint and plurality that fixes meaning must be located. There is a different form of suspension introduced when we compare the reciprocal turn-taking of conversation with writing. This is not an external institutional transformation of orality but a transformation to a different medium of communication altogether. The relation between writer and reader is analogous to, but not the same as, the relation between speaker and audience. Because the materiality of the medium of communication is different, writing is not a transformation of the social and institutional setting of orality but a transformation of orality itself, of the medium in which the communication act occurs. In the case of writing, there is instituted a separation between producer and consumer within the medium itself—which is analogous to the separation introduced into orality by its institutional transformation into speech. This "internal" separation in writing may be called the *context of the medium*. It inaugurates a different type of suspension of reciprocity that puts into play an internal set of social relationships within the writing-reading, or literate, complex. One may go even further, to observe that writing is not necessarily a "transformation" of speech at all. One may write, as Ricoeur says, *instead of* speaking.[7] One may write where there is no need, desire, or possibility, of speaking. In this sense, and despite the hermeneutic attempt at recuperation, writing must be understood as simply "another" medium of communication that allows communication acts of a different type. There is a plurality of communication acts here too, but it is not the simple plurality of acts of speech-making in the same oral medium of communication. Every speech act occurs in relation to a plurality of speech acts (interorality). Also, for example, every act of writing occurs in relation to other acts of writing (intertextuality). It would not be meaningful otherwise. But there is also a plurality of media of communication in relation to the materiality of expression. It can only be addressed by putting the various media in relation to each other by discussing the context of the medium in a comparative manner.

These two forms of suspension of reciprocity are based in the plurality of media of communication. The first refers to external institutional transformations within a medium. The second refers to the External plurality of media of communication themselves. It was stated above that the fixture of meaning in the audience in the first case is dependent on the social formation as a whole. When we add the notion that the social formation as a whole consists, not merely of one medium of communication, but of a plurality of media that interact with, or "translate," each other, this fixture can be seen to be dependent on the general interaction of media. For example, the fixture of meaning in the audience for a book is established, in the first place, in relation to other forms of writing and the different institutional relations that this implies. But, in a second and larger sense, the fixture is dependent on the relation of writing to the whole social formation (defined as the interaction of all existing media of communication). When we consider the medium of writing thematically, the social formation stands as a background constituted by the interaction of all media of communication except writing—which is exempt from the background because it is the current focus of analysis. We have here a dual externality: An externality "internal" to the medium— other forms of writing, other forms of orality, for example—that is based on institutional influences on the medium. Also, there is a more general Externality designated with a capital "E." This

Externality refers to the media environment in the social formation—the plurality of media of communication, their interactions,
and also the translations "in" and "out" of the medium in question.

The question concerning the audience emerges at the site of the
suspension of reciprocity, a suspension that takes two forms: One
oriented to the external institutional transformation of a medium
of communication and another pertaining to the External formation of the institutional complex itself. Thus there are two kinds of
fixture of meaning in the audience: One which pertains to the
mirroring of all external social differences in different interpretations of a given meaning-content. Here one expects to see the
influence of other social variables affecting the plurality of audience interpretations. And a second which pertains to the very
formation of these social differences themselves through the media
environment. After metaphysics we cannot simply presuppose a
formed audience and must therefore venture into the Externality
of the totality of the media environment. It is in the interplay
between these two e(E)xternalities that the connection between
expressed content and audience effect can be formulated—a connection that evaded metaphysics. The medium of communication
is a medium precisely in so far as it establishes connection and, in
that sense, there is a presumption toward (some kind of) reciprocity in the very idea of a medium. A medium of
communication is neither internal sense nor persuasive force, but
the establishment of the ground of their connection, a primal
scene that institutes relational social identities. For orality, it is
the space that allows speaking and hearing; for writing, it is the
paper behind the marks of a pen; for video, it is the tape and
recording/playing apparatus. Even more precisely, the medium of
writing is the connection of pen with paper enabled through the

alphabet. Metaphysics consists in asserting a definite complex of a dominant medium of communication in order to stabilize an internal meaning-content whose external effect can then be posed. The question concerning the audience is circumscribed within the metaphysical space as long as it accepts this stabilization. The shift toward the comparative theory of media of communication is a postmetaphysical inquiry that formulates the fixing of meaning by situating the audience within the social formation in a double sense. From this perspective both the conceptions of pure interpretive plurality and single injections of meaning-content are ideological deformations. Human expression is the instituting of connection. Connection itself can only be theorized through the medium of communication by which it is instituted and which establishes the interplay of plurality and constraint within a social formation.

Let me illustrate with respect to the current social role of the commercial use of video technology—the medium of television. The first fixture of meaning refers to the institutional complex of television in relation to the other (discarded or marginalized) possibilities of video. Constraint at this point is focused through the political economy of television that consists in delivering audiences to advertisers.[8] The plurality of audience interpretations can be expected to mirror the social differences of the entire social formation, but this mirroring is "focused," or thematized, through the necessity that the audience as a whole must fill the social role allotted within the political economy of television. Anything else will spell the quick demise of this audience, and its plural interpretations of the previously selectively produced fare, in the face of the commercial imperative. The second fixture of meaning refers to the internal social relations of the medium of television in relation to the Externality of other media. In this connection it is the one-to-many relation of a centralized source broadcasting to a plurality of isolated receivers that is most important. Constraint, with respect to this plurality of interpretations of television content, consists in the fact that *any content whatever* on this medium connects the audience into this social relationship with the centralized information source. While this relationship is currently exploited in the commercial form, it is open also to other appropriations such as use by a central government in "informing" subjects, etc. The issue for radical democracy is whether this medium of communication can be used without invoking the one–many social relationship that obviously has political implications. My argument is that it cannot. At this point, the relevant comparison is with other media of communication that allow for more participatory social relations and less centralized sources of information. The institutional complex of the medium provides the constraint through which audience interpretations mirror wider social differences. It is with respect to the External context of the medium that the role of the social relations within the medium are placed in relation to the social formation as a whole and the necessary constraint upon the audience by this subject-positioning can be formulated. The hegemonic role of television in contemporary society operates in both these dimensions, but, while issues of content are remediable in the short term through political action, the question of the politics of the site of inscription is less readily so.

This analysis of the ideological functions of contemporary communication systems aims to reinvigorate democratic theory. In so far as reciprocity in communication is built into the very idea of democracy, radical democratic theory must analyse failures and suspensions of reciprocity. An audience is constituted by just such a suspension of reciprocity. It is not that an audience is entirely passive with regard to the content of the medium. It is merely that its active response is expelled to another communication act. Reciprocity can thus be salvaged to the extent that there is a political right to produce other communication acts. One may be compensated, as it were, for being an audience by the right to initiate and reply in another forum, but this "right to speak" in another forum requires a forum of equal social significance if it is to be able to counterbalance the non-democratic suspension of reciprocity. Since an entirely face-to-face democracy is no longer viable, a principle of equal compensation for the constitution of an audience would amount to a reassertion of the democratic participation in a context dominated by cultural industries. Every medium occurs in the context of two e(E)xternalities: The institutional context of the medium and the media environment. To the extent that the suspension derives from the first externality, equal compensation takes the form of the traditional "right to reply"—to reply to a news editorial, for example; to produce another speech in a political forum; or to gain access to television for minority opinion. This right is recognized in democratic theory, and it would make a great deal of difference to contemporary society if it were fully put into practice. As John Keane has argued, freedom of expression in the contemporary context requires "the power to *seek* points of view."[9] None the less, the present analysis suggests that there is a further issue with regard to the right to reply which has not been addressed at all by content-oriented analyses and which stems from the second Externality. How would this right of compensation work? To the extent that one becomes an audience for television, one has a right to compensation in another medium of equal social significance. The right to reply on television deriving from the first externality is not sufficient to address the fact that—whoever is speaking on television—all television reinforces the one-to-many structure that constitutes the audience in their mutual seriality and absence. While Keane mentions that "dispersed networks of communication can more easily penetrate the pores of civil society and build networks of meaning among various groups of citizens," the content-orientation of his analysis of communication doesn't allow this possibility to be genuinely followed up; in the end, he relies on the competition between elites over the definition of social reality to secure "an abundance of information flows."[10] In contrast, the present analysis suggests that "information flows" are not enough and that the materiality of sites of communication must be the core of a theory of democracy in a media environment. It is the genius of social movements to have invented and relied upon forms of communication such as consciousness-raising, leafleting, folk songs, and so forth, which bring people into different social relations than the predominant media. Throughout its history the Left has been permeated by such alternative forms even though it has not often enough taken them seriously and has been hampered by an envy of the power of the mass media. The political issue is how such incipient sites of inscription can infuse the whole of social life with democratic social relations that contest the dictatorial social relations of television. The Externality of a single site with respect to the media environment can only be addressed by compensation in another medium which, rather than reinforcing the television audience, would institute a different set of speaker–audience relations.

The problem, of course, is that there is probably not another medium of equal social effect as television. This compensation would thus have the effect of requiring institutional support (of the type of the first externality) for other media, such as public meetings, art shows, guerrilla video, etc. The upshot of this principle is thus to require that audiences be compensated for the monopolization of cultural production by pervasive media such as television. The effect of this compensation would be to reduce this monopoly—not only to produce more access to television as it exists, or to produce better television, but to reduce the monopoly that the medium of television holds over cultural production. In the long run such a principle would undermine the ability of any medium to effectively control cultural space. It would be a democracy not only of citizens but of media themselves. This is the only long-run means whereby we can transform the contemporary media environment in a democratic direction.

New political principles are hard to come by, but something such as this is needed to reform the democratic tradition so that it can deal with the contemporary proliferation of media. Here I have attempted to address this issue through the problem of audiences who are spoken to on the condition that their replies cannot be heard. Let me end by stating the principle of the second Externality in a general form: The creation of any audience in any medium, in so far as it suspends the reciprocity on which democracy depends, requires the compensation of that audience by the institution of other media in which that audience can attain active expression in such a manner that the social decision-making process can be influenced to the extent of the suspending medium. It would take this much to establish as a social principle the reciprocity upon which participatory democracy depends. If it seems too much, then let that serve to measure the distance we have to go.

I want to conclude this argument with a reference to cultural interventions that connect to this reformulated postmodern conception of ideology-critique. This approach centres on the specific characteristics of each medium of communication and argues that the horizon of the historical epoch can be named through the transversal intersection of a plurality of media. It is the contribution of each specific cultural production to the naming of this horizon that constitutes its capacity for ideology-critique. While the plurality of sites of discourse cannot be totalized through a temporal recovery, neither are the sites simply external to each other. The sites of discourse interact transversally with each other in a spatial dispersion, or, as we may also say, media *translate* other media. While there is, in principle, no closure to possible translations, neither are they all actually accomplished in any given social formation. Thus it is the specific character of the existing translations that defines a prevailing socio-cultural form. Or, to reverse the proposition, a given socio-cultural form is defined by those translations that are, viewed from within it, "impossible." Consequently, a specific media comparison, such as that between speech and writing, occurs against a background environment that is itself constituted by translation between all other media of communication. Media theory is, then, not a secondary analysis based upon a more primary, foundational reality—such as the mode of production—though neither is the "totality" within which a specific comparison occurs simply ignored—as it is in both mainstream media analysis and much "postmodern" social theory. Rather, the mode of production itself is understood as an environment constituted through the totality of media translations, against which specific media forms, and comparisons, stand out. It is the impossibility of totalizing all translations that constitutes the "postmodern" aspect of media theory, not a supposed absence of totality as such. In short, totality is understood as a horizon rather than a self-referring system.

Understood in this way, media institute forms of social interaction and related modes of representation. Media are not secondary to an externally defined social form; rather, a specific medium occurs against the background constituted by the present state of media translations. Thus, the phenomenology of media of communication, which was sketched through the contrast of speech and writing, is not simply concerned with comparisons of internal characteristics of media, but also with the institutional weight and perceptual engagement that they embody. Media of communication are thus most fundamentally *constitutive* of social relations but, based on the plurality of media constitutions, also produce *representations* of the world. Let us state more generally the hypothesis that the materiality of media of communication inform both the event and "ideal" meaning-content of discourse: The performance of a communication act in a medium of communication constitutes both a distinct set of social relations and also a characteristic type of reference to, or representation of, the world—though the "world" in this formulation cannot be understood as prior to that constituted by media, but as a *horizon* formed through the interactions between media constitutions. In shifting the focus from the "inside," or meaning-content, of discourse to its "outside," or materiality of inscription, the world—as the totality of what can be experienced in whatever manner—is not merely represented within media but is formed through them. The world is thus understood as the horizon of the constitutive function of a given medium, and thus capable of being represented within that medium, and, also, as itself given its prevailing form by the mutual translations between media of communication. There is a plurality of sites of discursive acts which constitute distinct sets of social relations; the representational aspect of a given medium is possible because these sites are not simply external, but interact with each other. The world, as the horizon of these interactions, is the largest context of a given discursive act. Therefore, the specific form that a given cultural world takes is constituted by the actual extent of media "translations" between sites—and the limit of a cultural form is defined by the impossible translations.

The ethico-political component that can ground a theory of radical democracy is located in the relation between the site of a given inscription and the horizon of the world, a relation which was previously understood as an *Aufhebung*. The most basic philosophical issue here can be generalized from the transformation introduced by writing into the consciousness formed within an oral culture: By making marks, the limitations of unaided memory are overcome. By persisting in an external materiality, which can therefore be reactivated at will, human culture gains the ability to extend itself in time and space. As Jacques Derrida has put it, "the durable institution of a sign" is "the only irreducible kernel of the concept of writing."[11] Once the connection between the hermeneutic focus on internal meaning-content and the occlusion of the forming influence of the materiality of media in hermeneutics is apparent, attention must shift to the Externality of meaning in the marks that institute the durability, or "delay," of human culture in space and time. Delay in communication is produced by a mark that produces a "trace" of the act of inscription. This trace indicates a meaning that can be reactivated. Inscription is thus most fundamentally the inscribing of a trace that allows a later repetition. The plurality of sites of discourse suggests a plurality of modes of traces. If each medium is a fixing of discourse in a specific mode of inscription, then one must investigate a plurality of modes of tracing. Culture is constituted by the mutual translation of these modes of tracing and delay.

Then we may say: It is the relation to its horizon that determines the effect of the site of inscription. Every specific inscription is constituted by its horizon through its medium. The horizon determines what can be expressed within the medium and that which remains outside. In the case of writing, the horizon of existing translations determines the unwritten. The cultural horizon similarly determines the unsaid, the unradioed, the unvideoed, and so forth. And since each medium is a formation of the senses, the horizon determines the unseen, the unheard, the unfelt, the unthought—in every case, the limit of contemporary expression. This limit of the cultural formation is no longer a single limit, but a plurality of limits. Every medium of communication has its own limit. In translating from one medium to another, there will always be something that does not translate. A residue, or silence, is produced by the act of translation. Hegel dismissed this left-out residue as "lazy existence" due to the metaphysical assumption that in the passage to totality nothing of significance was left out. But translation does not produce an identical meaning-content in another medium. Otherwise, it would not be translation into a *different* medium that constitutes social relations differently. In translation, something drops out. A medium is constituted not only by its own characteristics, but also by its horizon, which determines that which drops out in translation. Thus, we may say retrospectively that in modern cultural theory the edge of culture could be thought of as nature, as that which is outside all cultural forms, because of the exclusive concern with meaning-content. But once we focus on the forming of expression by media of communication, which implies a plurality of media of communication, there will be a plurality of limits, of edges. Culture is like a polygon which we are inside, and which refracts a plurality of internal silences. These limits are what is excluded by the present cultural formation. Each medium has its own inner horizon, in the sense that the horizon of the world determines that which cannot be translated into the medium in question. Each medium thus has an outside in relationship to the cultural environment. The function of translating from one medium of communication to another is precisely to take that outside and bring it inside, but this will, in the same moment, constitute something else that is pushed outside. The outside is not eternally outside. Limits, edges, appear through the activity of translating between media of communication. In translation, the edge of another medium of communication can appear.

There is a piece of music by Laurie Anderson called "Talking About Music is Like Dancing About Architecture," which raises some important questions in this regard. In the first place, consider the unspoken assumption of music criticism that we can get to the truth of music by translating it into words. Such criticism is really translation into another medium, but one tends to think that there is more truth there. Why? The answer will have to do with the horizon of music for self-understanding in relation to our commitment to a verbal or written model of self-understanding. The eye dominates the ear. We tend to suppose that dancing about architecture doesn't make much sense, whereas talking about music does. In the second place, maybe dancing about architecture makes just as much sense as talking about music. What is the function of a prohibition against translation at this point? To the contrary, more translations are possible than we normally think; and it is only through such "impossible" translations that the limits of our present cultural formation can appear. From this point of view, the impossible and ridiculous translations are the most valuable ones for socio-cultural criticism.

The limit of a cultural form will appear natural and immovable unless one does all translations. But, of course, one can never do all translations, so from within a socio-cultural formation some culturally formed aspect always appears as if it were precultural, or immovable. Any state of human culture can thus be circumscribed. All our perception has limits, but these limits can be expressed. The limits come into human experience not by remaining forever outside it but by being brought in by some other medium whose limit is different. Whereas modernist avant-garde cultural practice consisted in designing productions that reflected on their own constitution in a medium, in the postmodern field the critical point has shifted toward translation. Artists and critics who engage in translations that point cultural productions to their horizonal context can uncover limits within the cultural field. In a similar fashion, we can define reactionary cultural practice as the attempt to seal borders and prohibit translations—which is the practice of all fundamentalisms. The practice of producing "impossible translations" is thus the most radical democratic practice for politicizing the Externality of media of communication. In bringing silences, and limits, to expression it opens up the speaking–hearing relation upon which democracy depends to the widest ambit, not limited to forms of government but throughout the socio-cultural field. But this practice can never be complete since it is characteristic of any socio-cultural form, even the most radically democratic, to have limits which define it as a specific form. In this sense, radical democratic critical practice is a project that could never fulfil its teleology, which could never usher in a final institutionalization, which is also to say that there is no society or culture without silences.

Silences, especially in the context of opposing translations to fundamentalisms, tend to appear as entirely constraints, or limits in the "negative" sense. The political practice of breaking limits in this sense corresponds to traditional socialist-universalist practice and retains a validity in the reconstructed context for which I have argued. However, I also want to argue that there can be a "positive" rendering of limit. In the contemporary global context, a defence of breaking limits runs the danger of complicity with the globalizing push of capital. One should remember, of course, that global capital itself imposes limits and that impossible translations will confront it in this sense. None the less, it may be suspected that an acceptance of some limit that is not a fundamentalism needs to be a complementary part of the project of radical democracy. One might phrase this issue in terms of how the open socio-cultural horizon can become defined by drawing a border. Having shown, I hope, that the notion of horizon is essential to the project of epochal criticism, I will argue below that the totality of cultural productions must be reconceived through the notion of a border, understood as the institution of a limiting separation that demands an ethical response to the other, which becomes a root metaphor behind the project of radical democracy. To do this, one must recover a conception of the transformational power of silence, a silence which will distinguish itself from the silences that define the limits of a culture, and which might justify a border that does not defend a fundamentalism. A horizon refers to the unthematized limits of common sense which lie behind every concrete perception or thought. The whole field of cultural production and consumption nowadays stands simply as a "horizon" behind each specific work—neither as an enfolding totality, nor merely as a dis-aggregated empirical sum. Husserl used the term "horizon" to describe a "constant halo around the field of actual perception" in which what is determinately perceived is "penetrated and sur-rounded by an obscurely intended horizon of indeterminate actuality."[12] It is unmarked and never within perception as such since it is the ground of any actual perception. A border, by way of contrast, is a line within the field of perception or thought. It is concerned with dividing something up within common sense, and in that sense tends toward a definition or concept. As Heidegger says, a boundary is "that from which something *begins* its presenc-ing."[13] It is only possible to perceive the question of how to draw a border as a radical question if the existing borders have been unsettled and the obscure horizon of perception or thought hovers in the background. Such is the postmodern condition in which an obscure awareness of the unperceived and the unthought hovers over every actual thought or perception. In this way, the discovery of the horizon is the condition for posing radically the question of drawing a border—Husserl's horizon is the condition for Heidegger's border. Within the postmodern condition, a border is that which lets one's own home appear. Difference from the other is essential to one's own identity. A border is where the othering of the self begins.

NOTES

1. C. B. Macpherson, *The Life and Times of Liberal Democracy* (Oxford: Oxford University Press, 1977) p. 95.

2. I discussed the media of communication present at the founding of modern republics and the political principles that allowed them to constitute a democracy

in "Circumscribing Postmodern Culture" in *Cultural Politics in Contemporary America*, ed. Ian Angus and Sut Jhally (New York: Routledge, 1989).

3. Jean-Paul Sartre, *Critique of Dialectical Reason*, trans. Alan Sheridan-Smith (London: Verso, 1982) p. 271.

4. Ibid., pp. 272–3.

5. Marshall McLuhan, *Letters of Marshall McLuhan*, ed. M. Molinaro, C. McLuhan and W. Toye (Oxford: Oxford University Press, 1987) pp. 427, 443, 448 and Paul Marchand, *Marshall McLuhan: The Medium and the Messenger* (New York: Ticknor and Fields, 1989) pp. 34, 114, 167, 255.

6. Jacques Derrida, *Of Grammatology*, trans. Gayatri Chakravorty Spivak (Baltimore: Johns Hopkins University Press, 1976) and *Writing and Differance*, trans. Alan Bass (Chicago: Chicago University Press, 1978).

7. Paul Ricoeur, "What is a Text? Explanation and Understanding" in *Hermeneutics and the Human Sciences*, ed. and trans. John Thompson (Cambridge: Cambridge University Press, 1981) p. 146 and *Interpretation Theory: Discourse and the Surplus of Meaning* (Fort Worth: The Texas Christian University Press, 1976) p. 25.

8. Sut Jhally, *The Codes of Advertising* (New York: St. Martin's Press, 1987) Chapter 3.

9. John Keane, *The Media and Democracy* (Cambridge: Polity Press, 1991) p. 131.

10. Ibid., pp. 145, 190. In only one place in his text (p. 153) Keane does mention "sites of signification," but only in the context of contrasting market-influenced media with monopolies run by churches and states. The absence of a theory of site, or medium, of communication is connected also to Keane's defence of a governmentalist conception of democracy (p. 149) rather than the democratization of civil society.

11. Jacques Derrida, *Of Grammatology*, p. 44.

12. Edmund Husserl, *Ideas Pertaining to a Pure Phenomenology and to a Phenomenological Philosophy, First Book: General Introduction to a Pure Phenomenology*, trans. F. Kersten (The Hague: Martinus Nijhoff, 1982) p. 52, emphasis removed.

13. Martin Heidegger, "Building Dwelling Thinking" in *Poetry, Language, Thought*, trans. Albert Hofstadter (New York: Harper and Row, 1975) p. 154.

6

ETHICS AT THE END OF PHILOSOPHY

Once upon a time, there seems to have been a continuity of belonging: place, sacred locations; rites of passage, time out of mind; world extended, thick with meaning in a community before reflection. Displacement from this encircled world is the condition of our modernity—schism in time which gives rise to history; cut in space that amputates an individual from the social body; pain of separation, an individualized fear, in response to which our modern projects are elaborated. Yet through this pain there remain memories of the enfolding world; often idealized, as if this world was only a comfort, in utopias of beginnings, of returns, or re-creations of the end in a world without the pain of displacement. Yet there still remain unclarified memories of when place and time were indices of belonging rather than arbitrary nodes on an infinite continuum. These memories are "other" to the modern project of autonomy, recalling social connections that were unchosen, but enfolding and demanding—that which claims us, which we may only create by re-creating, and refuse only with an inner tremor. Involuntary belonging, a claim from without, must seem a scandal in our devotion to autonomy. Ethnicity, race, sex, class—all raise the figures of that which cannot be made uniform, that which is not equally available to all. So, in devotion to autonomy, to equality, one hides such differences by figuring them as "choices" of a subject that is presumed to stand behind them. Not to say they all are identical. Race and sex are ineradicable. Class, perhaps not so, unless it becomes just a name for the division of labour. Ethnicity, in our time, is caught between multiculturalism and fundamentalism. In each case, the encounter with otherness is constituted by a border, a boundary, that divides a "self" from an "other," a "here" from a "there" and connects them in a relationship. Most simply, one human encounters another, but a similar relationship occurs between social and cultural groups of many kinds—all of which have their distinctive characteristics. But there is a core of meaning which bears investigation in the postmodern context of describing the ethical encounter with an other. Without a universalizing inquiry into the self–other relation, its various modes cannot be understood together—we are left with the inconclusiveness of social scientific methods or casual observation. Thus, we must risk inquiry into otherness in general, in the hope of gathering these concerns in the context of contemporary culture. If we are to found a new possibility of belonging, it will be through a reckoning with the claim of the involuntary—at bottom, the body in its essential tension between empathy and display. For it is clear enough that the end of modern ethics has made homelessness universal in the name of autonomy.

Throughout the history of modern ethics the recognition of all as free and equal subjects is the *telos* of ethical and political action. This ethical project encompasses two related aspects: Ethical action requires the self-identity of the subject and the reconciliation of all subjects in the ethical universe. The metaphysical *telos* of modern ethics is the synthesis of identity and reconciliation. In this respect a crucial aspect of modern philosophical articulation was discovered by Kant, who clearly recognized the essential ethical form that is compatible with and gives meaning to the domination of nature initiated by Bacon and Descartes. The utilitarian strain in modern ethics, which posits the happiness of individuals as the paramount ethical goal, is in tension with the claim to autonomous subjectivity that arose from the new science. Either it merely reproduces heteronomy, in which case the individual ultimately becomes the mere object of a social-scientific calculus of desires, accomplished in practice by the marketplace, or happiness must be founded on autonomy—a task taken up by Hegel. The relation between happiness and autonomy devolves upon an evaluation of the morality inherent in modern political economy. Kant recognized that nature, the "merely given," could no longer be regarded as comprising a moral order to be assented to by human subjects; the basis of moral subjectivity had to be found in this capacity to "give order" itself: Autonomy, the "giving of one's law to oneself" superseded any claims to "fitting into" a pre-existent natural order. Ethical subjectivity rested on universality and autonomy, on the claim to be an "end in itself" and not only a means to other ends.

> Everything in creation which he [man] wishes and over which he has power can be used merely as a means; only man, and, with him, every rational creature, is an end in itself. He is the subject of the moral law which is holy, because of the autonomy of his freedom.[1]

This disposition of humanity over nature leaves aside the "natural" basis of humanity—most clearly in the family, but also the formation of community in prereflective tradition and locale—as a virtually pre-ethical state. Such involuntary community is a pre-modern relic which, after the Renaissance assertion of the domination of nature, must appear as a constraint, albeit a necessary one, to be transcended by the ethical subject. As Hegel put it,

> The family, as the immediate substantiality of mind, is specifically characterized by love, which is mind's feeling of its own unity. Hence in a family, one's frame of mind is to have self-consciousness of one's individuality within this unity as the absolute essence of oneself, with the result that one is not in it as an independent person but as a member.[2]

It is Hegel's attempt to synthesize substantial unity, particular happiness and universal recognition that situates him at the culmination of modern ethics.

It is from the fundamental insight of Kant into ethical autonomy that Hegel draws a distinction between civil society and the state—between the sphere of particular needs and goals and the sphere of universal human ends. In civil society we are each means for all others in so far as we work and exchange. There is only a formal universality here, in so far as we are each members, but there is no relation between subjects as ends—others are merely means to my separate and particular ends.[3] By contrast in the state, or ethico-political life, it is the relationship between subjects as ends in themselves that is at issue. This is no mere formal universality, but is concretely universal in so far as it is the formation of the rational and ethical community as such that is the content of the mutual relationship of subjects.[4] Whereas Kant was content to discover the principle of modern ethical life in the recognition of human subjects as ends in themselves and stress its difference from the satisfaction of needs and desires, Hegel claimed that the formal universality of multiple particular wills "pass over" into the universal will of the state. Thus, the concept of *Aufhebung* is the central discovery of Hegel since it unites the domination of nature and ethical autonomy through historical synthesis.[5] For Kant, virtue does not provide happiness and can only be regarded as "at least [a] possible" consequence of morality whose connection with it cannot be known.[6] By contrast, Hegel claims that, though the state transcends individual happiness, it should nevertheless provide it.[7] While the state transcends political economy, nevertheless political economy is its prerequisite. Modern ethics struggles to differentiate and synthesize these two concepts of the self: One in which the mutual use of subjects as means to the satisfaction of particular, separately defined, ends is legitimate; and, as the condition of this legitimacy, that subjects are also recognized as ends in themselves. The condition for the appearance of this modern ethical problem is the sundering of "natural community" by the Renaissance domination of nature which enters ethical theory through Kant's concept of autonomy. The participation of modern subjects in the involuntary immediacy of "natural" life is seen as an unavoidable constraint to be transcended by the modern mind. The sundering of immediate connection to the "here and now," of continuity in place and time, is the condition for the metaphysical *telos* of reconciliation in which modern ethics seeks to justify and transcend the historical project of dominating nature by reconciling the self with itself and with the other. Once the ethical subject is defined by its autonomy, it projects its identity with itself and its reconciliation with others. This project can be called metaphysical in so far as it attempts to *re-establish* (though of course in a new form) the identity and community which modern displacement sunders, but the possibility of this *telos* is never accounted for. It turns out to be a refigured memory of a continuity of belonging transformed from origin to goal. The account of displacement in modern ethics is underwritten by the *telos* of its cancelling. A radical investigation of displacement shows that the conditions under which the goal of identity and reconciliation is formulated blocks its realization.

Displacement in both space and time is the condition for modern ethics. The pain of schism and of cut which defines this displacement survives the attempted metaphysical cure. In order to probe this pain at the root of modern identity, this instituting displacement must be clarified. The modern conception of subjectivity becomes questionable in the works of Marx and Nietzsche. With their aid we can define the fundamental issue which a contemporary investigation must raise: The conditions under which the distinction between "essential" and "accidental" attributes in the self and its relations to others arises. In continuity with German Idealism and with modern philosophy as a whole, Marx regarded the tendency of capitalism to break down immediate, natural social groups as a salient failure of modernization.[8] The other major feature, the production of "wealth," is also a consequence of the domination of nature through political economy. Capitalism replaces "organic" social groups embedded in nature with exchange relationships based on the sale of labour power. Only by the separation of individuals from an encompassing, and to the modern mind domineering, community, could the capacity of individuals to labour be regarded as their property, which they can therefore exchange as a commodity on the market. As with Hegel, the separation of individual and labouring capacity, personality and ability, essence and accident, was co-extensive with exchange relations between individuals in civil society. Marx observed that the market exchange of labour power divided individuals into two major modern classes, a structural antagonism which had to be resolved before universal autonomy could be attained. In tracing the origin of exchange, where each is a means for the privately chosen ends of the generalized other, he accounted for the historical relationship between "natural" community and isolated individuals. Exchange began on the edges of communities, in their relations with other communities. Through a long historical process it migrated from the outside to the inside, eventually becoming the central organizing structure of society and of the activities of individuals. The distinction between labour and labour power, between the concrete activity of an individual and the "capacity" for such activity, arises with the universal exchange society of capitalism in which the creative activity of individuals becomes a commodity.[9] The alienation of the capacity to labour requires that the individual be distinguished from his or her activities. At this point the distinction between the person abstractly considered as a possessor of capacities and the actual excercise of capacities in concrete activities becomes the central structuring principle of society. In short, the subject is seen as *essentially* a possessor of human powers which are *accidentally*, under contingent historical conditions, put to determinate uses. Such a perspective is possible only "in abstraction," that is to say, when it is a question of objectifying the projected possibility of acting prior to its execution, as occurs in the wage contract. Concretely, "in use," there is no distinction between the individual and the exercise of capacities. A society based on labour power as a commodity enforces an abstract relation of the self to its activities and of the individual to the combined activity of a group. In each case, the total relation is only

established externally as a subordination of activities and individuals to the mechanism of coordination of the whole. In short, the
relation of part and whole is only possible as an absolute sovereignty
of the whole over subordinated parts—the abstract totality as
essence and the particulars as accidents without effect on the whole.
The path to a reconciliation of self and other is blocked by the separation of essence and accident. While Marx shares much of the
analysis of civil society with Hegel, he shows that its origin in displacement subverts its transcendence in the concrete universal of
the state. The Marxist procedure is to dismantle the social rein-
forcements of displacement.

In questioning the nature of modern morality, Nietzsche performs a similar regressive, or "genealogical," move. Both thinkers
turn from the metaphysical *telos* to a "beginning" understood as a
displacement—a separation at the source that precludes the reconciliation of essence and accident in self-identity. For Nietzsche,
the separation of self from its expressions gives rise to the myth of
freedom:

> For just as the popular mind separates the lightning from its
> flash and takes the latter for an *action*, for the operation of a
> subject called lightning, so popular morality also separates
> strength from expressions of strength, as if there were a neutral
> substratum behind the strong man, which was *free* to express
> strength or not to do so. But there is no such substratum; there
> is no "being" behind doing, effecting, becoming; "the doer" is
> merely a fiction added to the deed—the deed is everything.
> The popular mind in fact doubles the deed; when it sees the
> lightning flash, it is the deed of a deed: it posits the same event
> first as cause and then a second time as its effect.[10]

161

In the nineteenth century, the works of Marx and Nietzsche brought the metaphysical *telos* of modernity into question by a geneaology which refused to write back the *telos* of authentic identity and reconciliation into an origin. It is not possible to simply step beyond metaphysical closure, since the description of the closure occurs initially in terms still wedded to the metaphysic and risks terms for new experiences at the price of misunderstanding, but with these two thinkers the presuppositions of the modern framework began to be clarified and overcome, a task which, as it proceeds, can achieve formulations which do not simply repeat the metaphysic. By taking the standpoint that they both called "history," Marx and Nietzsche thus showed that in "use," in the concrete experience of self in social relations, the essence–attribute distinction does not arise. There is only production, will-to-power—the originating praxis which constitutes history. This is prior to the separation of self from capacities, or the ability to act from action, or the other from self, prior to object and subject. It is the fecundity of world-origination. Such a standpoint shows first that the essence–attribute distinction in modern ethics is a "representation" which is not present in the ongoing praxis of productive power. Second, that certain social institutions reinforce this representation as a method of understanding and concrete organization. Third, that the distinction only arises in particular historical conditions—that only the displaced define essence and attribute in self and other in order to elaborate a *telos* in which the distinction is cancelled and preserved. The goal of modern ethics as identity and reconciliation is undercut by the recognition that schism in time and cut in space cannot be reassembled from its incomplete representations, rather, displacement must be probed in its productive praxis, in the loss of *telos* and origin, in the ongoing stream of experience. The dismembered body of the world cannot be reassembled, but we may probe wreckage of the enfolding world for the involuntary body of otherness.

The self–other relation is a further doubling of the essence–attribute relation established in the self by the positing of a substratum behind its expressions. The metaphysical *telos* of reconciliation that oversees modern ethics can no longer be redeemed once the displacement of modernity has been unravelled. In order to think the "other" outside the metaphysical frame of identity and reconciliation, we must probe displacement—the sundering in history and geography that defines the pain of schism and cut on which the programme of modernity is elaborated. With the infinite delay of this *telos*, we must now return to the fundamental experience from which the part–whole doubling of the self and its redoubling in the other proceeds. The postmodern situation requires a return to the most fundamental condition of ethics—the constitution of the other in immediate experience by the self. Without a metaphysical principle of reconciliation modern ethics could not be taken up into a philosophical articulation that completed and justified the domination of nature. This specific predetermined interpretation of the self–other relation defines a central affirmation of modernity. In the present postmodern situation radical investigation of the constitution of the other within the immanent sphere of ownness is required to renew questioning of the ground and *telos* of ethics. In the fifth of his *Cartesian Meditations*, Edmund Husserl described the evidential basis for the belief in the existence of the other. It is from this primary constitution of the alter ego that higher-level cultural unities are built up. Our present situation is without a metaphysical guarantee of reconciliation of subjectivities. Thus, it cannot begin from a "dialectic" which presupposes the other as *given* in order to assure the *telos* of mutual recognition. Rather, we must risk the asymmetrical constitution of the other as ground of an ethics which responds to the postmodern situation. In order to inquire radically into the origin of one's experience of an other ego it is necessary to begin by setting aside two assumptions that function throughout common daily experience: The belief in an objective world apart from my experience of it; and, the belief that other subjects like myself populate this common objective world. These assumptions are not regarded as false; rather, it is only if they are dropped that the "constitution of the other" can be recognized as a genuine and fundamental question: How, in the indubitability of the ongoing stream of my experience, does the experience of others arise? How, when I can only experience my own consciousness firsthand, do I come to experience and believe in other consciousnesses "like" my own? Only by setting aside these two assumptions that are necessary to everyday experience and action can the proper wonder at the most basic facet of the social world be aroused. Such wonder may be unsettling, certainly of a metaphysic of reconciliation, but it is the only starting-point for a contemporary philosophy of cultural identity and civilization.

This does not imply that socio-historical life is regarded as ontologically built-up out of the activities of individual consciousness. Rather, it means that, while ongoing life rests on the ontological assumptions of the socio-historical lifeworld, for these assumptions to be made known, they must be suspended in order for their structuring accomplishment to be clarified. In short, the epistemological priority of the suspension of assumptions—which is at its apogee in the transcendental reduction—does not imperil the fact that such assumptions do, and continue to, function in life and action. Indeed, it is just this fact that makes them significant for phenomenological analysis. The movements of ontology and epistemology are inverse: No more can scientific knowledge of the lifeworld be considered a prerequisite for its accomplishment than the presuppositions of ontology can be regarded as a prior delimitation of epistemological warrants. Restricted to the stream of immanent experience as it bears the index "belonging to me"— what Husserl calls the "sphere of ownness"—it immediately appears that one aspect of this experience bears a specific and distinctive characteristic: My own body as a field of perception and source of action that necessarily accompanies the experience of other bodies and, also, reflexively experiences itself.

> Accordingly this peculiar abstractive sense-exclusion of what is alien leaves us a *kind of "world"* still, a Nature reduced to what is included in our ownness and, as having its place in this Nature thanks to the bodily organism, the psychophysical Ego, with "body and soul" and personal Ego—utterly *unique* members of this reduced "world."[11]

This fusion of sensuous nature and psyche is the sense of my embodiment as an animate organism. It is in this evidence that the experience of the other is founded. When the body of the other is perceived by me, there is an "analogizing transfer" from my psychophysical unity to the psychophysical unity of the alter ego. While only the body of the other is presented in immediate evidence, the psyche of the other is appresented *through* the body. Appresentation is a "pairing" such that along with an immediately presented datum a mediately appresented datum is given. In an external perception, for example, the front of a physical thing appresents a back side. This is not a deduction, or an inference of any kind, but a characteristic of perception. In the case of a physical object, it can be viewed subsequently from another aspect such that the "back" side is directly presented and appresents another unseen side. This phenomenon of "turning around" is a peculiarity of the case of physical objects. The appresented psyche of the other cannot *in principle* be presented directly; moreover, the body of the other is *continuously* present as itself and also as the vehicle for the other's psyche.[12] Thus, the other is given within my sphere of ownness through an appresentation based on the similarity of the other's body to mine. However, the precise character of this givenness is such that it can never be immediately present to me—the "otherness" of the other's psyche remains separate from the "ownness" of my psyche. Thus, "similarity" or "likeness" is not an "identity" or "sameness."

The constitution of the other, of a "there" which complements my "here," accomplishes an expansion beyond my sphere of ownness: I am no longer simply at the centre of the world but can be looked at from over there. Similarly, objects can be looked at from various sides simultaneously. Thus, we inhabit an objective world upon which higher levels of cultural meaning are founded. Most important in this context, the other is not given in empty fashion merely as an other. Rather, the other's body *continuously appresents* the "contents" of the other's ego. In other words, most fundamentally the other is given as "other" but, continuously founded on this, it displays itself as "this" other—now angry, now sad, now responding to my initiative.[13] Other social and cultural relations to an other thus encompass "specific contents" which are appresented to me through a pairing with my own cultural "body." There are three significant "self–other" relations for cultural identity which can be mentioned here. First, a cultural group requires "communication" whereby internal relations are established between the members of the group.[14] Thus, "accessibility is not unconditional,"[15] as with objective nature, but depends on the performance of certain communicative acts which define the content of the cultural group. Second, there is the level of intercultural communication and the empathic procedures requisite to understanding another culture. In Husserl's words,

> Here I and my culture are primordial, over and against every alien culture. To me and those who share in my culture, an alien culture is accessible only by a kind of "experience of someone else," a kind of "empathy," by which we project ourselves into the alien cultural community and its culture.[16]

Third, there is the level of civilization which, although it must arise from humans in specific cultural unities, actualizes the possibilities of humanity as such.

Husserl's description of the constitution of the other begins from the entry of an other into my perceptual sphere and remains geared to perception. However, I encounter the other, also and simultaneously, in the sphere of action, which Husserl considers merely as one possible modification of the ego's content.[17] In the primordially reduced sphere of ownness, I am an "animate organism" and the most basic element in this animation is the body's motility. Thus, the "I can" must be added to the "here" as a praxical modification of the perception of the other.[18] The practical dimension of the self rests on the ability to define projects, goals, and design courses of action to bring them about. A project is an organization of the world, both planned and materially inscribed, such that the meaning of things or people within the world derives from their furtherance or hindrance of the goal. Within this context the encounter with the other presupposes his or her existence and is directed to what Husserl called the "content" of consciousness—specifically the relation of this content to my goal. As described by Jean-Paul Sartre,

> I group the other's look at the very center of my *act* as the solidification and alienation of my own possibilities. In fear or in anxious or prudent anticipation, I perceive that these possibilities which I *am* and which are the condition of my transcendence are given also to another, given as about to be transcended in turn by his own possibilities. The other as a look is only that—my transcendence transcended.[19]

The look of the other encloses me as a factor within the organization of the world around a goal that is alien, and possibly unknown, to me. With this the centre of my world slips from my grasp and is lodged with the other. I am reified by my original conflict with the other; unless, of course, I am able to reify first—for this description is two-sided and can in principle, even if often not in historical fact, be reversed. However, it is not reciprocal in the sense of occurring simultaneously from both sides *in the same manner*, nor does it move toward dialectical resolution by a successive oscillation *tending toward synthesis*.[20] Thus, the "I can" in the motility of the other may be called a "decentring" of my orientation. In his early work Sartre did not analyse any further this original conflict, though later he came to regard it as deriving from the fact that human action, in all societies known thus far, operates within a condition of scarcity. Consequently, the other is

a threat to my life and that of my cultural group. Social organization in scarcity defines some as expendables, and we all scramble to
reserve this designation for the other—and, in so doing, become
the other ourselves.

> *His own activity* turns back against him, and reaches him *as
> other* through the social milieu. Through socialized matter and
> through material negation as an inert unity, man is constituted
> as Other than man. Man exists for everyone as *inhuman man*, as
> an alien species.[21]

This concept of scarcity is appropriated by Sartre from a Marxist
philosophy of history that is embedded in the modern conception of
the domination of nature for a free and equal society described
earlier. However, Sartre's formulation escapes this origin and approx-
imates a more general phenomenological description. While the
concept of "scarcity" may seem to be a materialist "cause" of social
conflict due to an objectivistically defined, perhaps biological,
notion of need and satisfaction, in fact, in its perceptual–praxical
description there is no basis for an external grounding of this sort.
Rather, "scarcity" has come to mean, in this context, the most general sense of "incompleteness"—an unfulfilled project of inhabiting
the social domain. It refers to the entire complex of contested terrain
in social relations, which carries as a moment that the other may see
me in ways I do not recognize, incorporate me in projects I neither
invent nor share, and construct a world in which I am a stranger.

The four "self–other" relationships mentioned here—self–other,
cultural unity, intercultural communication, civilization—are thus
constituted both perceptually and praxically. In perception a
here–there relation is set up in which there is an appresentation of

meaning in a one-way direction from a primordial sphere of own-ness to an empathy with the other. In action the motility of the embodied psyche is overlaid on the here–there relation: the there can be transformed into a here (and vice versa) and the objective, common world which this constitutes is organized around the projects of the actors. As long as the common world exhibits the characteristic of scarcity with respect to these projects, there is resulting conflict over who is to become expendable. In this sense action reverses the primordiality of the sphere of ownness in per-ception. The centring of the "I" in the body becomes decentred in the field of action of the hostile other. The body becomes "like" an object, reified, rather than "like" the appresented psyche. The look of the other freezes the body of the self "in" space, whereas centred motility is the source of spatial orientation. Thus, we may speak of a "double non-reciprocity" essentially constituted in all self–other relations.[22] It is important to note here that there is no metaphys-ical guarantee of reconciliation in this description. Indeed, the metaphysical character of modern ethics consists in interpreting the doubleness of these two non-reciprocal relations as inherently reversible, as if the two subjects could be assumed as essentially equivalent in their autonomy from concrete determination, so that their relation could be described as a "dialectic" and synthe-sized.

It must be noted that the centring–decentring relation between self and other is not equivalent to the perceptual–praxical dimen-sions of experience. Perception and action are simultaneously present in any consciousness. It would be misleading to regard per-ception as more primordial than action. (This may well be a version of the modern metaphysic of authentic origin.) Action involves perception; perception is essentially constituted by its praxical possibility. The body does not perceive *and then* actualize a modality of movement. Rather, constitution of the perceived world is through a motile openness to the world. This motility is entwined with intersubjective praxis. Praxical decentring and perceptual centring are equi-primordial. While perceptual and praxical emphases serve to introduce and illustrate the self–other relation, the root phenomenon of centring–decentring is present throughout all its dimensions. Husserl recognizes the significance of the continuous appresentation of the specific contents of the other's consciousness, which I will term "display," but because he regards action as merely a modification of perception, he downplays that aspect most apparent in action—decentring. While we have access to the consciousness of the other, the other does not "look" back in Sartre's sense. Thus, Husserl's assertion of the priority of the self as against its empathic transfers to the other must be modified and clarified. Decentring by the other is an equi-primordial experience of the self as objectified *within* a spatio–temporal field; thus, in such a respect, the self cannot simply be the *source* of empathic transfers. Only the centred self can be a source, not only in perception but also in action. Rather, there are two senses of "source" which need clarification here: Husserl's "priority of the self" must be understood as a "priority of *access*" through empathic transfer, but the condition of this access is that the other *display* itself—externalize its contents of consciousness. Display refers to the other's perceptual and praxical effect on the self, that corresponds to the "I can" as "there" corresponds to "here." This concept of display is the most primordial form which underlies the decentring described in Sartre's "gaze." In order for the gaze to decentre me within the perceptual–praxical field, the contents of the other's consciousness must be displayed to me as an organization of this field, apparent throughout its many parts but centred through the other. In the case described by Sartre, the gaze disguises its projects and objectifies me as an alien within its field. This is only one of several possible modifications, however, not all of which are reifying. The reifying modifications are dependent on the appearance of the essence–attribute distinction. In this wider sense, the gaze is also apparent in the case of one's sexual "surrender," for example, which is a decentring display of otherness, but is not necessarily reifying. Sartre's analysis of the sexual act in *Being and Nothingness* could be rewritten from this point of view. The description of the reifying gaze forgets the empathic non-reciprocity, indeed as social forces may repress it, and therefore describes display incorrectly as if it were necessarily reifying. Once we have fixed on this fundamental phenomenon of *display of otherness*, the modes of its appearance can be clarified. The self–other relation is at bottom a double non-reciprocality in which the self is a source of empathic transfer conditional upon displays of otherness. The former is a means of access to cultural unities, while the latter is the condition for the actualization of cultural unities as such.

The encounter of self and other is a non-reciprocal centring–decentring without a *telos* of reconciliation whose modalities occur both from the side of the self and from the side of the other. For simplicity's sake the following descriptions consider the encounter of the self with an other. In summary the decentring modifications of this encounter will also be accounted for. All descriptions consider both the perceptual and praxical aspects of the encounter and apply to all four levels of experience isolated earlier. Further analysis will be required to develop the specificity of each of these levels. What is here significant is the fundamental modalities persisting due to the foundation of each higher-level constituted meaning in the primordial perceptual–praxical encounter with the other in the sphere of ownness such that the essence–attribute distinction is instituted. There are three basic modalities of this encounter: 1) The other is "like" the self; the other is yet "other," which splits into two variations; 2) the other as "enemy;" 3) the other as "exotic." The other is appresented *as* a human psychophysical unity through the likeness of the other's body to mine. The *specific character* of continuous appresentations opens the contents of the other's psyche to me. There are two aspects of the presentation of the other's body which affect this transfer through "likeness." First, the presentation of my body to me is as a perceptual and praxical origin of a surrounding world. I am at the centre. Thus, I do not see my body as I see the body of an other. I cannot see the back of my head, for example. Perception is oriented and shades off, through fringes, to non-perceived areas. Such areas can be *brought into* my perceptual field through actional modifications. Nevertheless, I do not *in principle* perceive my own body as the body of an other which is, in this respect, like any physical object in that it can be turned around, seen as an object placed *in* space and time, and so forth. Second, the sense in which I perceive an other's body as "like" mine requires clarification. There are differences of race, sex and size in human bodies which must be overlooked, seen as "non-essential," for such a likeness to be perceived.[23] Moreover, the other is always an already encultured body which essentially displays itself through clothing, bodily attitudes, and so forth. In order for the other to be seen as *human* "like" me, such apparent differences in humanity must be overlooked. Thus, the first modality of self–other encounter shows that I never perceive the other's body strictly as I

do my own. I must overlook important differences, most fundamentally the "incompleteness" with which I perceive my body as
a physical object. Founded on this, to the extent that I view the
other as "like" me, I overlook the physical and cultural differences
of the other. We see here the basis for the failure to see the other as
another human psyche: Such differences may overpower the likeness, in which case we have the second modality of
encounter—the enemy. To the extent that differences are regarded
as essential, the other is not appresented as a properly human
psyche. Moreover, the contents of the psyche are not available at
all. The other is perceived merely as an animate creature whose
contents of consciousness, should there be any, are utterly strange
to me. Husserl remarks that the "harmonious confirmation of the
apperceptive constitution" is often preserved through a
normality–abnormality distinction and that the question of ani-
mals enters here: "Relative to the brute, man is, constitutionally
speaking, the normal case—just as I myself am the primal norm
constitutionally for all other men."[24] If differences overwhelm
likeness, the other is essentially strange and incomprehensible to
me. The enemy is the human whose projects are essentially anti-
thetical to mine, whose difference is essential and whose likeness is
merely an accidental attribute.

In discussing Marx above it was shown that capitalism is the
society in which one's activity as a means for a generalized other
comes to pervade and structure the experience of oneself. One
regards oneself as an other; self-identity is established as a reflection
of one's use-value for the other. In this sense, capitalism is a subset
of the self–other dialectic that, due to the lack of any positive self-
determination, seeks security by escalating the insecurity of the
other. Attributes of the self are legitimized to the extent that they

threaten the other, and, of course, the other responds in like manner. Through an escalating dialectic fuelled by insecurity, the self seeks identity through its enemy; recoil from the utterly unlike, the inhuman other, confirms the self in its humanity. This is an utterly unstable dialectic in which one false step can destroy the civilizing task altogether. Dialectical negation no longer offers an escape-hatch, but merely opens up a new round of affirmation. In this postmodern situation, in which the self is its own other and creates the enemy in a gamble for identity, the end of rational autonomy is infinitely delayed. The goal of modernity in the highest level of subjectivity as "end-in-itself" is thwarted by the earlier stages of natural insecurity and the self as a means to relieving it. If likeness prevails over difference, as pointed out in the first modality, differences are non-essential. But they may be recognized as attaching contingently to this essentially similar other. Thus, one perceives an "essential humanity" with characteristics that do not serve to attach content to it. The assimilation of races, sexes, classes and cultures to a "universal" human culture that does not question itself reflects this modality; also, when ethnic characteristics are regarded as commodities which are available to all, rather than as expressing a definite content of humanity. Often, differences regarded in such a way are attractive, since they are unlike but not threatening. Thus, the exotic other is a source of romantic attraction—a decorative attribute without effect. The consumer society thrives on such exotica. Purchase of non-essential tokens of otherness releases a pleasurable sensation of self. Ephemeral, due to the non-essentiality from which it is derived, such pleasures decay into the cynicism of indifference to otherness. Only to be revived by the tinsel of the latest token. These three modalities of the self–other encounter exhaust the possibilities within the essence–attribute distinction. With regard to the "otherness" of the other, the persisting differences, there are three responses: 1) overlooking and ignoring; 2) reduction to an animal or an enemy requiring incarceration or extermination; 3) exotic preservation. Due to the two-sided character of the self–other relation, each of these can be reversed. The above descriptions were from the viewpoint of a centred self. If the self expires, is decentred by the other, each of these modalities can occur in reverse image: 1) ignoring the self, or experiencing oneself as non-essential and marginal; 2) self-hatred, an extermination of the self; 3) exotic preservation of one's differences as if they were differences of "just anyone." These modalities also permeate the self–other relationship at the interpersonal, cultural, intercultural and civilizational levels.

The end of modern ethics consists in the infinite delay of autonomy and reconciliation since this very project redoubles the essence–attribute distinction from which it arises. It requires a geneaology of the most primordial constitution of otherness within the immanent sphere of ownness. From such a genealogy we can discern the origin of the three modes of otherness in postmodern culture and clear the way for a postmodern ethics that institutes cultural identities through "belonging." The metaphysical *telos* of reconciliation attempted to leap over modern displacement, to write over the experience of displacement the historical project of its cancelling. Thus, the framework of cancelling, or redeeming, displacement was inserted into the experience itself. It seems the individualized fear that instituted modernity could only be described in a language that promised its redemption. The framework for curing displacement has been deployed into two dimensions: Origin-*telos*—from which modernity elaborates the project of the recapture of self-identity, or authenticity; and identity-difference—from which it projects reconciliation with the other. But postmodern culture initiates an infinite delay of the *telos* of reconciliation.

The three modes of otherness constitute an infinite delay for the *telos* of reconciliation that is constitutive for modern ethics. Such a delay cannot, of course, in itself cancel a *telos*. But it has been shown that the *telos* and its delay are co-constituted within modernity; and here is a motive for a genealogy which shows the condition for the *telos*. Understanding modernity as a closed system that cannot satisfy the projects it generates is an entry into a questioning that exceeds modernity. In one sense, postmodern culture is the completion of modernity in its only possible mode— infinite delay. In another sense, it is an entry, not to a programme, but to a question: Where may we found modes of belonging? The historical condition for the essence–attribute distinction which underlies contemporary modes of otherness is displacement— schism and cut, displacement in time and space, that reveal an individualized pain and fear. In Sartre's sense, scarcity grounds the struggle not to be one of the expendables. But "scarcity" itself needs reformulation. The displacement that reveals individualized pain simultaneously constitutes a world in which the individual cannot belong. There can never be enough wealth to compensate such pain: Production multiplies in all directions; identities and differences are staged to simulate authenticity and reconciliation; without cure, pain simply stimulates another round; there cannot be "wealth;" and displacement is repeated.[25] The primordial constitution of self–other relations reveals two aspects which indicate an escape-hatch from this postmodern repetition: First, the "incompleteness" of the likeness of the other's body to my own, such that I am a *source* of empathic transfer while the other may decentre me as an occupant *in* space and time. Second, the "conditional access" to cultural groups, such that participation is founded on the performance of specific acts which define the *content* of the cultural consciousness in question. These two characteristics are revealed only by escaping the metaphysical *telos* of reconciliation and risking the asymmetrical constitution of the other within the sphere of ownness. From this, two correlative aspects of self–other relations emerge. First, the self, or the cultural identity in question, is the source of empathic understanding of *both* one's own and other identities. Second, *display* of the contents of the other's identity is essential to the actual performance of empathy. Thus, while access is conditional on display, it can only be actualized through a recovery of the self as source. This asymmetrical relation is the primordial phenomenon from which an ethics responding to the postmodern situation must be developed. Neither of these characteristics of empathy, or abjection, and display, nor both in tandem, should be understood as determinants from which social practice could be derived, as if they were external factors that could be opposed to social practice. Rather, they are constituents of social practice itself. In order to give the most universal expression of this asymmetrical phenomenon, it can be termed "expiration–inspiration," based on the breathing in and out that may stand for the body's prereflective living relation to the world. I have derived this usage from Emmanuel Levinas's use of the metaphor of inspiration to refer to the taking-in that characterizes ethics.[26] Empathy and display are the breathing in and breathing out by which the body lives the world. The double-sidedness of this phenomenon is often apparent due to the self–other separations and relations that set up social practices. Nevertheless, if we focus on the phenomenon itself, on the primordial encounter which allows of subsequent separations, it would have to be called *spiration*—the moment between breathing in and out, of the moment of silence that can occasionally overtake a worlded awareness. Spiration is the unity of the meeting-place in the meeting, but also the non-reciprocal relations which are constituted by the modes of this meeting. As breath passes from one pair of lungs to another, spiration is the invisible which inheres in the alterities of visibility. Such a formulation should be free from the misinterpretation that social ontology is being derived from individual consciousness here. By contrast, the procedure has been to effect a phenomenological reduction to the stream of consciousness in the midst of socio-historical life in order to clarify the constitutive acts that are operative in communicative intersubjectivity. These communications can be focused on at four levels of abstraction—interpersonal, cultural, intercultural, and civilizational levels. In each case, spiration devolves upon an expiration–inspiration nexus which is the asymmetrical constitution of differences and relations.

A central theme in modern versus postmodern ethics can be derived from a consideration of alternative ways of understanding the border, or boundary, inserted in spiration that constitutes the relation between self and other. The individualized pain of displacement has motivated the modern view of the border as an ending of the self, as an encircling wall with aliens outside the gates. Thus, the essence–attribute distinction arises to leap over the wall and proclaim the *telos* of reconciliation. To the extent that this experience remains within the postmodern condition, the *telos* of modern ethics is not simply abandoned. When self-identity is threatened by otherness, autonomy is its first line of defence. Such situations will continue to arise; the essence–attribute distinction will retain applicability in such cases. But these situations must be comprehended on the wider uncharted ground of spirations of otherness, on which autonomy can never be grounded nor finally accomplished. Modern ethics is now a circumscribed project, a moment of balance within the enfolding symmetry of postmodern ethics. For postmodernity, a border is also that which lets one's own territory appear: the display of the other is essential to one's own identity. A border is where the othering of the self begins. As Heidegger says, a boundary is "that from which something *begins* its presencing."[27] The beginning of presencing is what I have called spiration. Every presence involves the bifurcation into inspiration–expiration, an inside and outside, a self and other. Thus, one's own culture is a manifestation of humanity as such, a humanity which needs the other to appear, and suggests an "active curiosity" with respect to otherness (which does not thereby become a possession) as a condition for self-awareness. Postmodern ethics centres on belonging within the horizon of localized displays constructed through a border that is animated by an active love of diversity.

When spiration splits itself into expiration and inspiration by instituting a border, the two sides of *display* and *abjection* emerge. This asymmetry indicates an "involuntary" moment inherent in one's location. In history and geography one is located, now in the first place by a schism from origin, second by a cut from the other whose difference is displayed. This no longer founds a project of recovery. In postmodern culture, thought must move beyond, outside, the metaphysical frame. It must probe the schism and the cut to clarify our displacement. One can no longer flee this pain into a metaphysical cure. There may be no cure, but neither can one find cynical solace in a certainty that there can be no healing. Risk is still alive and the face of the other that demands my abjection.

For thought without guarantees, the probing of schism and cut is a discovery of the pain that displacement has etched on our bodies. Acceptance of the involuntary, of what we are made by our bodies and their response to others, motivates an empathic eagerness for displays of otherness. The central issues for postmodern ethics concern non-reciprocal relations, such as ethnicity, race, gender, and class. The modern focus on authenticity and reconciliation cannot formulate these relations properly since it will always tend to reduce the asymmetry of the double non-reciprocity to a self-certainty and autonomy. By focusing on the schism and cut whereby spiration constitutes modes of otherness, the non-reciprocal foundations of a postmodern ethics can be elaborated. It is precisely what is not shared that is now the central theme of ethics. Only from this starting-point can possibilities of belonging be instituted which recognize difference, separation from origin, and yet sustain possibilities of identity.

NOTES

1. Immanuel Kant, *Critique of Practical Reason*, trans. Lewis White Beck (Indianapolis: Bobbs-Merrill, 1956) p. 90.

2. G. W. F. Hegel, *The Philosophy of Right*, trans. T. M. Knox (Oxford: Oxford University Press, 1952) p. 110.

3. Ibid., p. 122.

4. Ibid., pp. 160ff.

5. Ibid.

6. Kant, *Critique of Practical Reason*, p. 123.

7. G. W. F. Hegel, *The Philosophy of Right*, p. 281.

8. See, for example, Marx's paean to the revolutionary spirit of capitalism in the first section of *The Communist Manifesto* in *The Marx-Engels Reader*, ed. Robert C. Tucker (New York: Norton, 1978) pp. 473–8.

9. See "The Sale and Purchase of Labour-Power" in *Capital*, Vol. 1, Ch. 6. Marx's work is discussed here solely as a diagnosis of capitalism and modernity.

However, one can see in this formulation the source of the failure of his "solution." Once the self is fully alienated as "other," there is no basis from which it can rebound to become the "subject" of history. Only the assumption of an "essence" of self can provide the basis for a rebound from alienation to subjectivity.

10. Friedrich Nietzsche, *On the Genealogy of Morals*, trans. W. Kaufmann and R. J. Hollingdale (New York: Vintage, 1969) p. 45; First Essay, section 13.

11. Edmund Husserl, *Cartesian Meditations*, trans. Dorion Cairns (The Hague: Martinus Nijhoff, 1969) p. 98.

12. Ibid., pp. 112–13. It can be noted here that Husserl overlooks the entire range of complex questions concerning "media of communication" and, specifically, the role of the body as such a medium. Consequently, a prejudice in favour of "face-to-face" communication in the "living present" is introduced without justification into phenomenological descriptions. The previous chapters of this book have opened this assumption to criticism and exploration. For a clear example of this prejudice, which is common in phenomenology, see also Alfred Schütz, "Symbol, Reality and Society" in *Collected Papers*, Vol. 1 (The Hague: Martinus Nijhoff, 1971) p. 318.

13. Edmund Husserl, *Cartesian Meditations*, p. 119.

14. René Toulemont, "The Specific Character of the Social According to Husserl" in *Apriori and World*, ed. and trans. W. McKenna, R. M. Harlan and L. E. Winters (The Hague: Martinus Nijhoff, 1981) p. 228. In this essay Toulemont summarizes Husserl's published and unpublished investigations.

15. Edmund Husserl, *Cartesian Meditations*, p. 132.

16. Ibid., pp. 134–5.

17. Ibid., pp. 110 and 119.

18. Ludwig Landgrebe, "The Phenomenology of Corporeality and the Problem of Matter" in *The Phenomenology of Edmund Husserl*, ed. Donn Welton, (Ithaca: Cornell University Press, 1981).

19. Jean-Paul Sartre, *Being and Nothingness*, trans. Hazel. E. Barnes (New York: Philosophical Library, 1956) p. 263.

20. Ibid., p. 364. Sartre would, of course, call this a "dialectic" and proceed to differentiate it from Hegel's. However, it is unclear in what sense there can be "dialectic" without "reconciliation." Since a critical history of dialectical thought is hardly possible here, the term "double non-reciprocity" is used to signify this fundamental difference.

21. Jean-Paul Sartre, *Critique of Dialectical Reason*, trans. Alan Sheridan-Smith (London: Verso, 1982) p. 130.

22. Alfred Schütz criticizes Sartre for taking over Hegel's "optimism" regarding

the interchangeability of self and other. "Sartre's Theory of the Alter Ego" in *Collected Papers*, Vol. 1, pp. 197ff. The present analysis focuses on the description of decentring, which is a valid phenomenological datum. However, the extent to which this implies "dialectic" was indeed overestimated by Sartre.

23. The case of gender was pointed out by Eugen Fink in the discussion of Alfred Schütz's "The Problem of Transcendental Intersubjectivity in Husserl" in *Collected Papers*, Vol. 3 (The Hague: Martinus Nijhoff, 1970) p. 84. Such considerations have not yet been systematically introduced into phenomenological descriptions, though they are a large part of what is at issue in contemporary postmodern social theory.

24. Edmund Husserl, *Cartesian Meditations*, pp. 125–6.

25. This, in short, is why the Marxist programme fails. There is a burgeoning literature on "need" in Marx as both "historically defined" and "capable of being overcome" in a generally wealthy society, a contradiction which is founded on this analysis of displacement. See, for example, William Leiss, *The Limits to Satisfaction* (Toronto: University of Toronto Press, 1976) pp. 75–8.

26. Emmanuel Levinas, *Otherwise than Being, or Beyond Essence*, trans. Alphonso Lingis (The Hague: Martinus Nijhoff, 1981) pp. 111, 140ff, 180ff.

27. Martin Heidegger, "Building Dwelling Thinking" in *Poetry, Language, Thought*, trans. Albert Hofstadter (New York: Harper and Row, 1975) p. 154.

7

BEYOND GNOSEOLOGY

In philosophy's ancient inception, the dual commitment to knowledge and action was held together by cosmological intuition such that human affairs were enfolded within world order. Action based on the love of knowledge conflicted with the present community in the name of a higher community based on knowledge and the good. The emblem of this conflict is the death of Socrates. With the modern removal of world order from the scientific concept of nature, a new question was raised for the direction of human affairs. Scientific inquiry was directed to humanity incorporating the implicit *telos* of reuniting knowledge with ethical action. Phenomenology took up the task of self-knowledge by focusing on the various themes in social and historical experience, on the modes of consciousness necessary for such thematizations to appear, and on the process of thematization as such. The *telos* of phenomenology is the fully explicit description of consciousness as engaged in acts which function anonymously in the course of ongoing life which is normally directed toward themes. This universal and infinite task of self-knowledge requires a critique of "European sciences" in so far as they fail to actualize this ideal. In short, phenomenology takes up the task of philosophy's inception and radicalizes the goal of self-knowledge in a postcosmological age. Husserl describes this *telos* in this way:

> Mankind understanding itself as rational, understanding that it is rational in seeking to be rational; . . . that reason allows for no differentiation into "theoretical," "practical," "aesthetic," or whatever; that being human is teleological being and an ought-to-be, and that this teleology holds sway in each and every activity and project of an ego.[1]

But the connection to action that is claimed here through the unity of philosophy requires exploration. Can knowledge really have a healing function in a postcosmological condition? It has been argued that the claim for an inherent connection of knowledge to action requires a cosmology that Husserl, along with most post-Renaissance thinkers, rejects due to the new conception of science that arose as a consequence of the mathematization of nature.[2] More importantly, one might claim that the ethics to which Husserl appeals here is solely an ethics of humanity as knower and therefore cannot be the foundation of human community as such. In short, one suspects that philosophy has been constituted within an emphasis on the predominance of the question of knowledge that has held it within a gnoseological horizon that necessarily distorts the practical and ethical dimension of human life.[3]

My argument is that ethics is central to the task of phenomenology as an imagination of higher community. Emmanuel Levinas has most thoroughly thought the meaning of the ethical call. As he says in the justly famous first sentence of *Totality and Infinity*, "Everyone will readily agree that it is of the highest importance to know whether we are not duped by morality."[4] The relation of this fundamental posing of ethics to the radicalization of self-knowledge by Husserl is central to a contemporary rethinking of the *telos* of philosophy. The human sciences as a distinct sphere of inquiry have developed in response to the loss of world order from the concept of nature. Thus they have become key in the constitution of meaning, both crisis and renewal, as a question of knowledge and ethics. The project of the human sciences is the self-knowledge of humanity as a community engaged in meaningful practical life. The manner in which the two thematics of self-knowledge and socio-historical praxis are interwoven determines the way in which the task of the human sciences is taken up. In this sense, the relation between Husserl and Levinas is central for the practice of the human sciences and their binding by the *telos* of philosophy.

In one sweep, the human sciences as self-knowledge represent the field of human activity, cut it up and assign the pieces to various departments, and attempt to construct a story that confers meaning on the conduct of human life from their results. This conferring of meaning reaches at its limit Nietzsche's statement: Humans would rather will nothing than not will at all.[5] Science, art, philosophy, as well as friendship, love, and enemies all answer our call for meaning. Then what does the search for meaning in each of these express? More fundamentally, what is the character of the historical praxis that searches for the meaning of humanity in the human sciences? Reflection upon the project of the human sciences quickly observes that the humanity understood by scientific inquiry is not simply the same as the one who inquires. There is a splitting within the human subject into knower and known— and therefore a constant tension between the surfacing and the repression of the question of the relation between these two. Humanity is doubled, as Nietzsche and, subsequently, Foucault put it,[6] and the project of our self-knowing is suspended in this double. As Husserl discovered, the epistemological quest requires the transcendental reduction, which then poses the question of the relation of the "transcendental ego" to concrete human subjectivity. Some such doubling is a necessary result of any project which represents humanity as an object of knowledge. There is another thematic alongside this first. In a second sweep, understanding humanity requires at a basic level the understanding of the *social* condition—the intersubjective meaning of human life. This is another double: To the doubling of the knower and the known is added the self and the other. However, this doubling is not simply a question of knowledge but also of the foundation of ethical community. These two doubles encapsulate the tensions inherent in the project of the human sciences. The practice of the human sciences *assumes* constituted intersubjectivity; thus, its actual researches reveal plurality, raise the question of relativism, and, if pursued thoroughly, provide a motive for the transcendental reduction.[7] Thus, the constitution of intersubjectivity is foundational for the human sciences. The constitution of the other is simultaneously a problem of the self-knowledge of the human community and of the ethical bond of the community. This interweaving of knowledge and ethics thematizes the question of the foundation of community as central to the task of the human sciences. In a preliminary reflection on the initial question raised above, we may now say: the search that looks for meaning in the human sciences has experienced a historical disruption of community such that it seeks to establish community on the ground of knowledge and/or ethics. This historical experience that motivates the human sciences I have called "displacement." Thus, knowledge community and ethical community can be distinguished from historico-ontological community.

Though Levinas said of his own researches that "Husserlian phenomenology has made possible this passage from ethics to metaphysical exteriority," nevertheless, the passage in his work displaces traditional philosophical emphases with the claim that "in the intelligibility of representation the distinction between me and the object, between interior and exterior is effaced."[8] Through opening representation to an exterior, Levinas proposes a philosophy in which ethics is more fundamental than knowledge and in which the Other eludes capture in the cycle of the Same. From this point on we must register Levinas's point by rendering a distinction between the other constituted by the ego and the Other in its Otherness that eludes such constitution. I follow the translator's convention of indicating the "personal Other, the you," Levinas's "l'autrui," by capitalizing it and refraining from doing so for Levinas's "autre." To the extent that one accepts Levinas's account here, the implication is that Husserl's "other" should be referred to without the capital letter, since it is constituted by the transcendental ego.[9] He regards this criticism as applying to Husserlian transcendental phenomenology due to its emphasis on "constitution" and "representation" which tie it to the gnoseological horizon of philosophy.[10] By finding a space for Levinas's basic move within transcendental phenomenology, the present argument develops a foundation for the human sciences and the renewal of philosophy in an axiological and performative reduction. Thus, it answers the postmodern critique of representation based in the thesis of the end of philosophy (where philosophy is understood, following Heidegger, as the theory of representation). The centrality of representation does indeed have to be dislodged, but everything depends on the manner in which this is done.

The question of the constitution of intersubjectivity is central to phenomenology, and its resolution fundamental to answering the criticism of solipsism—a criticism now usually put by contemporary critics in terms of a rejection of "constituting subjectivity."[11] I will defend the transcendental turn as essential to the constitution of the other through an account, derived from Ludwig Landgrebe's interpretation of Husserl's phenomenology, of the unfolding tendency of Husserl's work toward an ethical basis for knowledge. However, this constitution is within a gnoseological horizon that culminates in an ethic of communal self-knowledge. It is not capable of accounting for the exteriority of the personal Other in, as Levinas describes it, the ethical primordiality that the face of the Other institutes. The otherness of the Other, the Other that demands of me, looks at me, cannot be reduced to an alter ego constituted by likeness to me. Levinas regards this failure as a necessary constituent of the transcendental reduction. In contrast, I will suggest that the ethical primordiality of the face appears through an axiological transcendental reduction which is implicit in Levinas's descriptions. It opens the field of ethics and grounds a community of abjection. Thus, the transcendental reduction is described here as enveloping two components which comprise a double foundation of transcendental community—each of these in tension with the historico-ontological community which the transcendental turn irrupts.

Husserl gave his classical account of the constitution of the alter ego in the Fifth Cartesian Meditation, where it is seen as an appresentation of the psyche of the other through the presentation of the likeness of the other's body to mine. The self-animation of my body is transferred to the self-animation of the other. He regarded this solution, which is not an inference but a perceptual evidence, as in principle adequate throughout his work.[12] In the present context, the important point is that it occurs within the gnoseological horizon that Levinas criticizes. At the beginning of these meditations, Husserl stated that "We take the general idea of science, therefore, as a precursory presumption, which we allow ourselves tentatively, by which we tentatively allow ourselves to be guided in our meditations."[13] Husserl is guided here by the idea of science as presuppositionless, as an absolutely self-accounting enterprise, an idea which is not actualized in any existing science, but in which the historico-teleological essence of European philosophy inhers. Thus, this *telos* rests on experiences of thought to generate its ethics and praxis, not on any external motives. This gnoseological horizon of the inquiry is also central to the phenomenological view of the unity of philosophy. With regard to the "theoretical modification" that justifies the applicability of philosophy's knowledge-orientation to the whole of experience, Husserl remarks in *Formal and Transcendental Logic*:

We spoke of the possible turning of any evidence into a doxic evidence. With greater universality it may be said here that any extra-doxic sense can at any time become the theme of a doxic act and thus enter the doxic sphere—and, in particular, the apophantic sphere. It is similar to the manner in which any modalized judgment can take on the form of a judgment made with certainty—a judgment in the normal sense. When this happens, possible, probable, or the like, makes its appearance within the judgment-complex; and the situation is similar in the case of beautiful or good. Thus the formal logic of certainties can not only be enriched by taking in the forms of the <doxic> modalities, but can also absorb, in a certain manner, the modalities of emotion and volition.[14]

This is the basis for Husserl's claim that "reason allows for no differentiation into 'theoretical,' 'practical,' 'aesthetic,' or whatever. . ."[15] All experience can be regarded as a doxic positing evidence and thus one can expand "formal logic to include a formal axiology and a formal theory of practice."[16] All this, as Husserl says, "in a certain manner." But what manner? That all consciousness, in the end, can be regarded as modalities of judgment with degrees of evidence, and thus exhibit a teleology of reason, does not show that this is the only manner, or the only relevant manner, of regarding acts. Perhaps all acts could also be regarded as emotional or as volitional. The gnoseological horizon of Husserl's investigations uncovered an all-pervasive teleology of consciousness, but it did not raise the question of other teleologies, of other modalizations of the synthesis of experience. In what follows I suggest that it is quite sensible to speak of an axiological modification—itself pertaining to the whole of consciousness—therefore, of an ethical reduction, and, moreover, that such a modification of transcendental phenomenology is essential to a proper reckoning with the crisis of Western humanity. In the next chapter, I will suggest that this axiological reduction is completed in a further performative reduction which is manifested in the phenomenon of silence. It is here that I find the basis for a renewal of philosophy that doesn't deny the gnoseological sense in which it has come to an end.

Levinas has commented on this presumption of knowledge in Husserlian phenomenology in the following way:

The Husserlian thesis of the primacy of the objectifying act—
in which was seen Husserl's excessive attachment to theoretical
consciousness . . .—leads to transcendental philosophy, to the
affirmation . . . that the object of consciousness, while distinct
from consciousness, is as it were a product of consciousness,
being a "meaning" endowed by consciousness, the result of
Sinngebung.[17]

The presumption of the primacy of theoretical consciousness leads
to transcendentalism, with the further—and more fundamental,
for Levinas—result that the Other is regarded as "constituted,"
that is, as a modality of knowledge, not as a personal Other, but as
an alter ego. Commenting on Husserl's Fifth Cartesian
Meditation, he says,

the comprehension of this body of the Other as an *alter ego*—
this analysis dissimulates, in each of its stages which are taken as
a description of constitution, mutations of object constitution
into a relation with the Other—which is as primordial as the
constitution from which it is to be derived.[18]

In short, the primacy of theory, the transcendental reduction, and
the eclipse of the Other collude to obscure the primordial ethical
relation which is visible in the exteriority of the face of the Other.
Let me quote just one of Levinas's beautiful descriptions of the
encounter with the face of the Other:

A trace lost in a trace, less than nothing in the trace of an excessive, but always ambiguously, . . . the face of the neighbour
obsesses me with this destitution. "He is looking at me"—

everything in him looks at me; nothing is indifferent to me. Nothing is more imperative than this abandon in the emptiness of space, this trace of infinity which *passes* without being able to enter.[19]

In the encounter with the face, the looking of a subject at the world in which the project of knowledge arises is reversed. The face looks at me and demands a response, an answer. This answer institutes ethics, but the answer can never be equal to the demand. The ethical demand is such that it can never be satisfied in a response. Thus, "the more I answer the more I am responsible."[20]

I will argue in what follows that this view confuses two separate questions—that of the primacy of scientific objectifying acts (representation) and that of the transcendental reduction. Levinas regards the transcendental dimension as necessarily hooked to the project of knowledge, as entirely circumscribed by the gnoseological horizon of the philosophical tradition. This is what I deny. In consequence, Levinas fails to appreciate the extent to which, though taking scientific objectifying acts as the paradigmatic case of theoretical knowledge, transcendental phenomenology is actually more fundamentally directed to the *accomplishing* of objectifying acts with intersubjective validity within the stream of conscious experience. Thus, it is not stuck within the problematic of representation. Rather, the phenomenological critique problematizes representation by investigating the presuppositions of its accomplishment and, furthermore, turns philosophical interest to the preobjective, non-thematic origin of knowledge and ethics as a striving toward explicitness. Husserl emphasized the "difference and identity" of the concrete and transcendental egos.[21] An understanding of this point will allow the important distinction of

Husserl's concept of the transcendental ego from the notion of "constituting subjectivity" that is criticized by postmodern writers, and which is an effect of a Kantian rather than a phenomenological notion of the transcendental ego. The origin of this fundamental misunderstanding of Husserl is his earlier appropriation in French existentialism that accomplished the "mundanizing," or historicizing, of the transcendental ego that is later rejected by poststructuralism and postmodernism. Clarification: The transcendental ego is identical with the concrete ego in so far as it is *not in, or of, another world.* There "is" only the concrete world. The transcendental ego can perform no function of escape, or insulation, from this concrete world—as Sartre, for example, claimed that it did and who was followed in this regard by Merleau-Ponty.[22] The transcendental ego is, however, different from the concrete ego in so far as the concrete ego does not confer meaning on the events of the world. To say that the transcendental ego is concerned with the process of conferring meaning is a way of opening up an investigation of the world that is *thoroughly cultural* in the sense of not beginning from the modern distinction between nature and culture, or nature–history, but it is not the activity of a worldly concrete subject, which always occurs within the process of "always-already-conferred meaning," as does any worldly phenomenon. Thus Husserl says that "human subjectivity is not transcendental subjectivity"[23] in order to reject precisely such a conflation of meaning-giving to the concrete, individual subject —an error that he called "psychologism." Thus, phenomenology is, on this point, at one with the current "postmodern" tendency to view concrete, worldly subjectivity as "culturally" formed such that the individual subject is not his or her own origin. For phenomenology this implies that the striving for knowledge is a process of coming-to-know the always-already-constituted meanings that generate actual worldly subjectivities. It has nothing to do with the assumption of a worldly "constituting subjectivity" that is rejected by postmodernists. Some of these misunderstandings can be avoided by following Merleau-Ponty in preferring the term transcendental "field" rather than "ego," which does, it must be admitted, lend itself to an empirical misreading.[24]

By separating these two issues of gnoseology and transcendentality, it is possible to incorporate the encounter with the Other as described by Levinas within transcendental phenomenology. Due to its progress beyond the early standpoint of *Ideas I* that remained the basis for Levinas's critique throughout his work, Husserl's late philosophy opens to the ethical infinity described by Levinas. While the constitution of the other occurs within a presumption of the idea of science, and was regarded as in principle satisfactory throughout his work, Husserl's investigations of the idea of scientific knowledge took on an increasingly radical character. In order to understand the significance of the constitution of the other for transcendental phenomenology, it is necessary to place it within the formulation that culminates Husserl's investigations. Thus, the constitution of the other can only be properly understood within Husserl's analysis of the crisis of the Western sciences. There are two aspects to this crisis: The historical teleology of Western science, its entanglement with objectivism, and transcendental phenomenology as the overcoming of the crisis; and transcendental phenomenology itself, which as the comprehension of historical existence is not simply an aspect of historical life, but is a universally accessible philosophy. In short, there is historical exigency and philosophical comprehension; for phenomenology, these are related but not identical issues.[25] In this relation, the philosophical *telos* of rational, meaningful human community becomes known in a historical struggle with objectivism and relativism through the questions posed by human scientists and philosophers. Here, the question of how such questions are influenced by the actual historical situation of the questioners, including institutions, scientific paradigms, modes of life and other socio-historical factors, requires a theory of hegemony to pose adequately the historical side of the relationship between philosophy and history. It is this relation between concrete history and transcendental philosophy that is not posed adequately by Levinas. Consequently, he associates the scientific with the transcendental and turns from both toward an ethics beyond both being and knowledge. The following account of the development of Husserl's conception of philosophical teleology, based on the work of Ludwig Landgrebe, liberates the transcendental turn from its purely epistemological formulation—which can now be seen as a first aspect of the historical crisis—and allows its extension into a transcendental ethics, beginning from Levinas, which is a second aspect of the historical crisis.

There is a progressive radicalization in Husserl's work, in which the problem of knowledge gradually becomes a universal critique of lifeforms and a justification of the *striving for* knowledge. Ludwig Landgrebe distinguishes three stages of this radicalization.[26] First, the stage of *Ideas 1* (1913) where the interest in the revision of the theory of knowledge and science requires the introduction of the transcendental reduction. Second, the stage represented by the lectures entitled *First Philosophy* (1923–24) where the issue has become the *motive* for the passage from the natural attitude to the transcendental reduction. Consequently, the theory of knowledge cannot be an adequate foundation for the reduction and the question becomes that of the *beginning* of philosophy in an *act* of the philosopher. Third is the last stage represented by the *Crisis*, in which it is no longer a question of grounding the sciences on a presupposed foundation of their validity and efficacy, but of justifying the striving for knowledge as such and therefore raising the question of the use of results of knowledge in the lifeworld.[27] At this point the question of knowledge has become an ethical question about the justification of the striving for knowledge. This interpretation is one of Landgrebe's decisive contributions to phenomenology.[28] He concludes that the question of the motive for the reduction cannot find an answer; Husserl's answer is circular because the insight that all that is has meaning only in so far as it is posited by the philosopher emerges only as a *result* of the philosophical act of the reduction, and cannot thereby provide its *motive*. The "Heraclitean flux," which is the anonymous transcendental life prior to its project of self-knowing, simply refers back to sedimented history, nothing other than its own history, and its origin in the primal instituting of reflection. Landgrebe suggests that this circle leads back to the "primal instituting of Greek philosophy." However, he also states that "the reduction is nothing other than a meditation on reflection as a recursive relationship." This formulation adds that the "primal instituting" can occur originally within individual experience without reference to Greek philosophy. This remains historical, but in an unusual and precise sense: It is a factual occurrence within experience that cannot be derived from anything else—in this sense an "absolute fact." It is not a contingent occurrence, even though it cannot be predicted or explained and has no necessity of occurrence.[29] The radicalization of the question of knowledge in Husserl's work leads to the centrality of the transcendental reduction, in which the anonymity of transcendental life prior to the reduction becomes the self-explication of transcendental constitution subsequently. The transcendental field is nothing other than actual history looked at from another level of reflection. Landgrebe has phrased it as follows:

> Empirical history, as it can be described from within the empirical sciences, accepts the relativity of its becoming as final, which, in turn, leads to the skepticism of relativism. Transcendental history, which can only be disclosed through reflection upon the transcendental functions on the basis of which there is something like history for us, leads to the absolute in all relativities. It leads to the existence of the subject for whom it is history and for whom it forms its historic world.[30]

This transition from anonymity to self-explication is tied together by the "principle of individuation" whereby factual history is brought to the *telos* of rational, meaningful community through its explication within the lives of concrete individuals.

Husserl's analysis of the constitution of the other in *Cartesian Meditations*, which he regarded as in principle sufficient throughout his work, occurred within a reflection on knowledge that was progressively radicalized. Thus, we can distinguish three meanings of the account of the constitution of intersubjectivity as it is deepened through the radicalization. In the first stage, and as it is presented in *Cartesian Meditations*, it is a question of knowledge of the existence of the other; not knowledge in the sense of any special science, but in the sense of the guiding idea of science tending toward thematized objectifying acts: the thematization of the knowledge of the other operative in everyday life. In the second stage, where the question of the motive for the reduction has emerged, constitution of the other means asking why the question of the existence of the other becomes an issue at this historical juncture. Of course, this question has its own history throughout modern philosophy. However, from the present standpoint, the history of the question of "other minds" is a symptom of the loss of meaning in the crisis, of the displacement that undergirds the claims of modern ethics. Philosophical reflection must give an in principle answer to the question of the alter ego (the first stage), but the question arises because the *telos* of rational, meaningful community through individuated self-knowledge has been distorted and forgotten in historical life (the second stage). Only then does the radical epistemological question arise.[31] This claim parallels Husserl's *Crisis*, but is directed to the crisis of ethico-political thought in modern philosophy. In the third stage, which is now often investigated through the notion of postmodernity, it is a question of the self-knowledge of the historical human community through the principle of individuation. The meaning of the constitution of the Other is not merely as knowledge operative in everyday life, nor even the historical juncture that raises the question of knowledge of the other. It is a question of the will to base one's life on self-knowledge in which "self-knowledge" is understood as a point of individuated communal self-realization in relation to others. Since the final point of the radicalization of the question of knowledge is to establish the striving for knowledge as an *ethical act* which transforms the meaning of history through the principle of individuation, the meaning of the constitution of the other at this point is the social dimension of the striving for self-knowledge: To what extent is the other a constituent of the striving for self-knowledge? That is: First, to what extent does self-knowledge, being knowledge of a social being, require knowledge of the social dimension of the self? Second, to what extent does the principle of individuation transform social ethics?

As with all of Husserl's earlier researches, the constitution of the other is not abandoned by later more radical reflections, rather, its meaning is deepened and takes on wider historical significance. To this extent, the constitution of the other takes on the meaning, at the end of Husserl's work, of individuated historical self-consciousness in tension with the Other, and this is posed as an ethical question. The classical Cartesian description of the constitution of the other is placed within the steadily unfolding philosophical diagnosis of the crisis of the sciences. The apogee of this radicalization is that the gnoseological horizon is placed within an ethical dimension. In short, I am arguing that, at the final stage of Husserl's researches, the constitution of the other by the ego is superseded by an ethical call of the Other, of *l'autre* by *l'autrui*, in Levinas's terminology. Levinas's view of Husserl is arrested at an early stage and misses its progressive radicalization whereby the gnoseological horizon is itself understood as an ethical demand. But Husserl's conception of the ethical dimension that is revealed at the root of the historical *telos* is wholly described as an individuation of the *self-knowledge* of the community. We discover history as the coming to consciousness of human community in individuation and self-knowledge, but not yet history as love, desire, suffering, labour and joy. The opening to ethical experience has been broached by the way of life that is required to alert the striving for knowledge, but there is not yet the issue of the placing of the striving for knowledge in relation to other claims in human life. Alongside the *telos* of truth discovered in the crises of scientific civilization, there is also the motive to discover the primal ethical encounter enlivened by the historical disruption of human community. This transformation of the meaning of the constitution of the o/Other is ignored in Levinas's critique of Husserl due to his exclusive reliance on the formulations of *Ideas I*.[32] With this radicalization carefully in view, it is possible to extend and redirect phenomenological inquiry without a radical break toward the encounter with ethical experience as described by Levinas.

The transcendental reduction within the gnoseological horizon discloses the evidential correlations of the whole of consciousness by setting aside the natural belief in the world as actually existing independently of consciousness. The world is the unthematized horizon of horizons. Only the transcendental reduction reveals this presupposed belief and its inherence within all the thematizations of natural consciousness. There is a parallel transcendental reduction within an axiological horizon implicit in Levinas's work that is particularly relevant to the ethical *telos* of philosophy and the human sciences. The thematizations which occur in natural existence not only have a belief-structure pertaining to independent existence, but also a belief-structure pertaining to ethical action. There are two main natural interpretations of such ethical beliefs: They are viewed either objectivistically as normative claims on the acting subject rooted in historical communities, or subjectivistically as values posited by the will. In either case, ethical beliefs are taken as simply existing; normative action is enfolded within natural existence. The transcendental reduction within an axiological horizon suspends belief in the pervasive ethical dimension of natural existence, not in order to deny its claims, but to bring the axiological encounter as such to the fore for examination. The face of the Other, as investigated by Levinas, is the transcendental condition of axiology: The encounter with an Otherness that claims me before myself, that opens me to an exteriority that demands, is the experience of abjection through which all norms are articulated. This is not an abjection that can be contrasted with a Nietzschean willing of values. Rather, it is an encounter with a command that embraces both actual possibilities of natural interpretation of its origin in historical communities or subjective positing. Levinas finds the following words for this abjection:

> Vulnerability, exposure to outrage, to wounding, passivity more passive than all patience, passivity of the accusative form, trauma of accusation suffered by a hostage to the point of persecution, implicating the identity of the hostage who substitutes himself for all others.[33]

This description of the "origin" of ethics, an origin which can never be enfolded within a system of knowledge, is not empirical, but rather the "basis" for our empirical experiences of the ethical demand in the faces of Others. Theodore de Boer explains that Levinas's ethics is transcendental because "it is not based on experience or self-evidence but on a tracing back from every intuition or reason to an ethical condition that cannot be thematized."[34] The axiological reduction discloses the transcendental dimension as a claim on all concrete, human subjectivity to respond to the exterior origin of ethical action.

With this account of the axiological reduction as parallel to the gnoseological reduction, and as different ways into the transcendental field, we have accomplished the separation of the two issues confused by Levinas in his critique of Husserl: The primacy of objectifying acts (representation) and the transcendental reduction. Against Levinas, we suggest that transcendental phenomenology is not limited to the gnoseological horizon that pervades Husserl's works, nor to the ethic of self-knowledge in history in which this horizon culminates. Rather, the transcendental reduction is essential to the descriptions of the face, exteriority and infinity which Levinas performs; these are not empirical, but transcendental descriptions. This view requires far-reaching revisions and extensions of the theory of the transcendental reduction, reflections which bear on the meaning of philosophy and thereby on the question of whether, or in what sense, it has come to an end. While these revisions and extensions of transcendental phenomenology cannot be developed extensively here, it is significant that they overlap with the necessity for a historico-critical inquiry into the crisis of ethico-political thought in modern philosophy paralleling Husserl's *Crisis*. Such an inquiry would take the standpoint of the developing crisis of community in modern philosophy as an opening into the transcendental field through the ethical reduction. In very broad and schematic outline, we can discern three stages of this crisis, paralleling the three stages of the radicalization of the question of knowledge in Husserl's work as sketched above.

The first stage is represented by the work of Machiavelli and Hobbes. The breakdown of historico-ontological community revealed an individualized fear of violent death that could be taken to justify an unrestricted centre of power. The transcendental question evoked by this historical event is the understanding of human community as a hermeneutic project establishing continuity through time and space. It begins from a basic distinction between nature and history, between the unchangeable and the products of human action whose method of understanding is inaugurated by

Vico. The second stage emerges in the Enlightenment problem of the social contract: How do self-interested individuals come together to establish social life? How is the communal good derived from the interest of each? This transcendental question emerges from the revolutionary eighteenth-century founding of constitutional states in order to overcome institutionally the recently unleashed self-interest inherent in market exchanges. It requires a distinction between theoretical and practical reason, necessity and freedom, and poses, but does not solve, the problem of their unity. The third stage of this critical history characterizes the twentieth century, where the historical situation is the destructive use of European science and technology—the crisis of civilization. The modern nation-state and the Enlightenment individual are enfolded within this crisis. The transcendental question is the "Other"—is there any relation to an "outside" that is not a merely solipsistic imperialism? The products and practice of knowledge and theory necessarily come under suspicion due to their key role in this process. These three stages of historico-critical inquiry serve to illustrate that it is the breaks, or ruptures, in empirical history that serve to set problems for transcendental inquiry. In this sense, transcendental inquiry is rooted in history but against history. It brushes against the grain of history, as it were, to aid us in readying ourselves for the next encounter, though it can never quite be enfolded within this practical intention. The interweaving of transcendental inquiry as gnoseological and as axiological in this inquiry require much further elaboration. Nevertheless, it is evident that Levinas's axiological reduction to the ethical demand of the face matches Husserl's radicalization of knowledge in posing the most fundamental questions for a contemporary transcendental phenomenology of community. In the present context, I will confine the concluding discussion to the notion of pluralism that emerges in Levinas's work, and its connection to the theme of community.

The face of the Other presents infinity, and thus an asymmetry between self and Other which is an ultimate situation. It is a claim on me, before me, in which the Other is placed above me, and commands. While this asymmetrical duality of the self–Other institutes ethics, it is through the "third" that it is translated into social life and can influence institutions toward furthering equality.

> The contemporaneousness of the multiple is tied about the diachrony of two; justice remains justice only, in a society where there is no distinction between those close and those far off, but in which there also remains the impossibility of passing by the closest. The equality of all is borne by my inequality.[35]

Thus, justice requires a pluralism, but this is neither a merely numerical plurality nor a genus that unites individuals by subsuming them.[36] We may translate this by saying that it is neither a liberal individualist pluralism, that counts each as one and perpetually dissolves claims on justice back into one's opinion, nor a bureaucratic socialism, that refers claims straight to the genus and passes over the closest. Levinas's pluralism is profoundly radical. It disturbs both individualism and collectivism: Infinities can be neither added nor subsumed. The transcendental *telos* of abjection is the closest act that beckons me, that challenges me and constitutes me as an ethical subject in beckoning. It is this identity of the closest beckoning and the turning toward justice that describes the ethical encounter as a transcendental one.

The o/Other essentially displays itself, and it is this phenomenon of display that is at issue here, rather than investigating the many modes in which display occurs. When the other displays itself as Other, that is, displays itself in a manner that manifests its worth, it makes an ethical demand. Levinas showed this for the human face, which is the manifestation of the necessity of ethics. Levinas's intention was to open up the radicality of the ethical demand as against the gnoseological horizon of the history of philosophy, but, one may ask, why is this ethical infinity limited to the human face? Is the face the only experience of ethical infinity? The radicality of the experience of the Other in the face, for Levinas, is that this is an experience of *who?* not *what?* such that "the answerer and the answered coincide."[37] It opens a dimension for explication which is thoroughly constituted by the ethical demand through an orientation to the "who-ness" or personality, that is the core of the experience of the face: "The face, preeminently expression, formulates the first word: the signifier arising at the thrust of his sign, as eyes that look at you."[38] It is the first word because it is not inscribed in an ongoing discourse, which would enclose it within a given horizon that is ultimately gnoseological, but is an origin, although an origin in which that which is presented can never be fully present (which would again return the issue to one of knowledge). The face is the welling-up of the ethical demand in a sign that cannot do justice to what it shows. Perhaps one may say that the face is a *condensation of personality*. It is that through which the ethical demand uprises, but the ethical demand is not confined to the face as seen. Why, then, only the human face? Does not an ethnic group have a "face," that implies that its distinctive way of life is worthy of retention? Doesn't a social movement propose an identity that manifests its worth, also? It is not possible that a deer, or a squirrel, can be such a condensation? Perhaps a tree can be the condensation of the personality of a place. Any identity of an Other, and one should no longer say *social* identity, if this were to be opposed to nature in the terms of modern philosophy, is displayed. Through its display it manifests its worth. Thus, I want to accept Levinas's shifting of the thrust of philosophy from knowledge to ethics, but to differ from Levinas on two points. First, as shown above, the radicalization of Husserl's investigations led him to the realization that knowledge is ultimately an ethical enterprise that individualizes the self-knowledge of the community. By Husserl, the gnoseological horizon is placed within an ethical dimension. This overcomes the error produced by Levinas's exclusive reading of the early Husserl, that ethics is *opposed* to knowledge by Levinas. It seems to be another domain entirely, whereas what is really at issue is the *partiality of the ethic of individuation*. Second, once the shift to ethics is accomplished, it cannot be confined to the phenomenon of the face. Every Other has a "face" which is its characteristic manner of displaying its worth. Display is the shining-forth of others that may be encountered as Others; abjection is the prostration before such an Other in which ethics arises.

Husserl's reduction within a gnoseological horizon discloses a transcendental community of historical self-knowledge bound by the principle of individuation. Levinas's axiological reduction discloses a transcendental community of abjection bound by the opening to infinity through the face of the Other. Communities in empirical history have suffered a displacement in space and time from their origins such that the constitution of community has become an issue for knowledge and ethics. Both of these are in tension with empirical history—whose major feature is the disruption of communities of belonging. Establishing new community requires a transcendental reduction of worldly involvements, both positings of existence and positings of value, to uncover a dual transcendental irruption in history—individuation and abjection, as the two poles of the transcendental *telos* of community. We are perhaps familiar with history as the story of self-consciousness, as the shouldering of responsibility for ever-wider domains of experience. This cannot be an empirical story, for it is just the tragedies of history—the lost and nearly forgotten brush against the trend— that motivate reflection on history's meaning. No more can ethical abjection be empirical—its encounter is founded on a historical effacement, a turning away from the Other's face. Here emerges a praxical beckoning that addresses the places of the Others. Such community is not based on a shared essence, but on an asymmetrical encounter *against history*. Opening to this beckoning is not within the *telos* of self-knowledge, but neither does it require a denial of this *telos*. Without this abjection, this incursion of exteriority, it would not be worth thinking, but the experience of thought cannot rest on this incursion. If we cannot find a single source for community, it is because such a single source could only be the unity of historical events, and this option is now closed to us by the historical displacement from which the project of the human sciences emerges. It is history itself that opens the transcendental plurification of communal life, which is articulated against the grain of history. A genuine plurality can only be encountered through philosophy, even though this has not been substantiated by modern ethics.

We have encountered two transcendental reductions. One, from knowledge to the striving for knowledge as an ethic of individuation (Husserl). Here the gnoseological horizon is crossed. Two, an axiological reduction to the face, from which the ethical demand arises (Levinas). These two reductions followed from a description of the end of modern ethics and the basis (spiration) from which a postmodern ethics might emerge in the twin phenomena of abjection and display. In the next chapter a third reduction will be proposed. Gnoseology is based on the "theoretical modification" whereby all experience is transformed into a mode of positing evidence. The axiological reduction depends on what one might call an "ethical modification." The discursive turn in philosophy and the human sciences presupposes a parallel "performative modification," whereby the whole of experience is regarded as a form of action. In order to locate spiration, the basis of postmodern ethics, we must discover a third transcendental reduction in, and from, discourse. In so doing, it will be shown that, without this performative reduction, social identities are stuck within a general agonistics—a kind of mutual cannibalism of discourses. The only way out of this mutual devouring to which contemporary culture tends is the discovery of silence from within discourse, which is the entry of the transcendental reduction into language. This reduction parallels Levinas's ethical reduction to the face, and is the basis for a recovery of philosophy as both ethical and discursive after the end of philosophy within the gnoseological horizon. The discovery of silence is the need for Otherness, a purgative for generalized solipsism, that does not exist in the general rhetoric that a non-reduced discursive turn generates.

NOTES

1. Edmund Husserl, "Philosophy as Mankind's Self-Reflection; the Self-Realization of Reason," Appendix IV in *The Crisis of European Sciences and Transcendental Phenomenology*, trans. David Carr (Evanston: Northwestern University Press, 1970) pp. 340–1.

2. Werner Marx and Jürgen Habermas, for example, both attribute incompatible intentions to this key aspect of Husserl's work. Habermas claims that Husserl's traditional (Greek) concept of theory involves a cosmological intuition that translates disinterested inquiry into practical efficacy. In contrast, Marx regards the absence of such a cosmological intuition in Husserl's work as implying the failure of his practical intention and suggests a cosmological turn based on Heidegger. See Jürgen Habermas, *Knowledge and Human Interests*, trans. Jeremy J. Shapiro (Boston: Beacon Press, 1971) pp. 304–6 and Werner Marx, *Reason and World*, trans. Thomas V. Yates and R. Guess (The Hague: Martinus Nijhoff, 1971) p. 46.

3. This notion of a "gnoseological horizon" is based on the work of Emmanuel Levinas and Jan Patočka. See Emmanuel Levinas, *Totality and Infinity*, trans. Alfonso Lingis (Pittsburgh: Dusquesne University Press, 1969) p. 295 and Jan Patočka, *Philosophy and Selected Writings* (Chicago: University of Chicago Press, 1989) pp. 333ff.

4. Emmanuel Levinas, *Totality and Infinity*, p. 21.

5. Friedrich Nietzsche, *On the Genealogy of Morals*, trans. W. Kaufmann and R. J. Hollingdale (New York: Vintage, 1969), Third Essay, especially Sections 1 and 28.

6. Friedrich Nietzsche, *On the Genealogy of Morals*, First Essay, section 13 and Michel Foucault, *The Order of Things* (New York: Random House, 1973) Chapter 9.

7. See Thomas M. Seebohm, "The New Hermeneutics, Other Trends, and the Human Sciences from the Standpoint of Transcendental Phenomenology" in *Continental Philosophy in America*, ed. Hugh J. Silverman, John Sallis and Thomas M. Seebohm (Pittsburgh: Dusquesne University Press, 1983) pp. 64–89.

8. Emmanuel Levinas, *Totality and Infinity*, pp. 29, 124.

9. See Emmanuel Levinas, *Totality and Infinity*, p. 26, footnote.

10. Ibid., pp. 67, 95, 123f., 127, 130; Emmanuel Levinas, *Otherwise Than Being, or Beyond Essence*, trans. Alphonso Lingis (The Hague: Martinus Nijhoff, 1981) pp. 46, 65ff., 71, 96, 104, 179.

11. Both Jean-François Lyotard and Jacques Derrida have been influenced by Levinas in so far as they regard the establishment of ethics and justice as necessarily entailing a rejection of transcendentality. I believe that it is from these two writers, as well as Foucault's later unsuccessful attempt to avoid the problem of doubling through the notion of praxis, that has formed the common sense of "postmodernists" in this regard. See also Ernesto Laclau and Chantal Mouffe, *Hegemony and Socialist Strategy* (London: Verso, 1985) p. 105. In this context, my

current attempt to reconcile, in a certain sense, Husserl and Levinas has implications for the contemporary philosophical scene beyond interpretations of these authors themselves.

12. See Edmund Husserl, *The Crisis of European Sciences and Transcendental Phenomenology*, pp. 216–19 and *Phenomenological Psychology*, trans. John Scanlon (The Hague: Martinus Nijhoff, 1977) pp. 81–2.

13. Edmund Husserl, *Cartesian Meditations*, trans. Dorion Cairns (The Hague: Martinus Nijhoff, 1969) pp. 8–9.

14. Edmund Husserl, *Formal and Transcendental Logic*, trans. Dorion Cairns (The Hague: Martinus Nijhoff, 1969) p. 136, see p. 160.

15. Edmund Husserl, *The Crisis of the European Sciences and Transcendental Phenomenology*, p. 341.

16. Edmund Husserl, *Formal and Transcendental Logic*, p. 136.

17. Emmanuel Levinas, *Totality and Infinity*, p. 123.

18. Ibid., p. 67. This and the previous quote illustrate the extent to which Levinas still construes the paradigm of knowledge in Cartesian terms. The abandonment of Cartesianism by Husserl is clearly documented by Ludwig Landgrebe in "Husserl's Departure from Cartesianism" in Ludwig Landgrebe, *The Phenomenology of Edmund Husserl*, ed. Donn Welton (Ithaca: Cornell University Press, 1981).

19. Emmanuel Levinas, *Otherwise Than Being, or Beyond Essence*, p. 93.

20. Ibid.

21. Edmund Husserl, *The Crisis of the European Sciences and Transcendental Phenomenology*, p. 202.

22. Jean-Paul Sartre, *The Transcendence of the Ego*, trans. Forrest Williams and Robert Kirkpatrick (New York: Farrar, Straus and Giroux, 1969) especially p. 105; Maurice Merleau-Ponty, *Phenomenology of Perception*, trans. Colin Smith (London: Routledge and Kegan Paul, 1962) p. xiv.

23. Edmund Husserl, *The Crisis of European Sciences and Transcendental Phenomenology*, p. 201.

24. See Maurice Merleau-Ponty, *Phenomenology of Perception*, p. 61. Husserl refers to the "necessary equivocation" involved in calling the transcendental an "I" and cautions in many places against misunderstandings at this point. See Ludwig Landgrebe, "A Meditation on Husserl's Statement: 'History is the grand fact of absolute Being'," *Southwestern Journal of Philosophy*, Vol. V, No. 3, 1974, p. 113 and "The Life-World and the Historicity of Human Existence," *Research in Phenomenology*, Vol. XI, 1981, pp. 133–4. See also Edmund Husserl, *The Crisis of the European Sciences and Transcendental Phenomenology*, p. 184. My use of the

term transcendental "field," is an attempt to avoid some of these misunder-standings. One of the major misunderstandings would be to view the egos as instances of an eidos, species of a genus, and so forth. Landgrebe notes this with respect to lifeworlds as a misunderstanding of Husserl in "The Life-World," p. 138. However, see Appendix 22 to *Zur Phaenomenologie der Intersubjectivitat, Dritter Teil*, Husserliana, Band XV (The Hague: Martinus Nijhoff, 1973) the text entitled "Teleology. The implication of the eidos transcendental intersubjectivity in the eidos transcendental ego," written 5 November 1931. Here Husserl speaks in just this way of the alteri as "included from the first in my fact as a free play of possibilities" ("in meinem Faktum von vornheit beschlossen gewesen als Speilraum von Moeglichkeiten" p. 382). This manner of speaking, as if the other is simply a modification of the I, occludes precisely the otherness of the Other that Levinas focuses on.

25. See José Huertas-Jourda, "On the Two Foundations of Knowledge accord-ing to Husserl" in *Essays in Memory of Aron Gurwitsch*, ed. Lester Embree (Washington: Center for Advanced Research in Phenomenology and University Press of America, 1983).

26. Ludwig Landgrebe, "The Problem of the Beginning of Philosophy in Husserl's Phenomenology" in *Life-World and Consciousness: Essays for Aron Gurwitsch*, ed. Lester E. Embree (Evanston: Northwestern University Press, 1972) especially pp. 42–4.

27. In the essay cited in the previous footnote, Landgrebe does not succeed in distinguishing clearly between stages two and three, and thereby capturing ade-quately the final radicalization of the question of knowledge by Husserl. Nevertheless, in his essay "A Meditation" he states the third stage more straight-forwardly and in a manner that definitively sets it beyond stage two. Of course, this periodization of Husserl's work allows for a certain unevenness in the gesta-tion of the issue, and in the clarification of its theme. The statement quoted by Landgrebe appears in an appendix to the second volume of *First Philosophy*.

28. Ludwig Landgrebe, "The Problem of the Beginning," p. 44; cf. "Husserl's Departure from Cartesianism" in Ludwig Landgrebe, *The Phenomenology of Edmund Husserl*, p. 117.

29. "The Problem of the Beginning . . .," p. 52; "The Life-World," p. 134.

30. Landgrebe claims in "A Meditation," p. 124, that "Husserl did not per-form the reflection on the motive by which his turn to history was led. It is because of this omission that his concept of teleology is inconsistent." This motive was the "present" between the two world wars in which "universal inter-dependence" and "threatening dangers" co-exist. Thus, the *telos* of history is not

such as to have been discoverable at any of its moments. Rather, it is the moment of danger, in which the question is asked on what basis there can be history for us, that teleology as practical action emerges.

31. All interpretations of the Fifth Meditation which do not take into account the radicalization of the question of knowledge past the formulation in the *Cartesian Meditations* will therefore fall into an insoluble dilemma: Either the "sphere of ownness," the reduction to which is essential to pose the question of constitution of the other, is seen as an actual level of experience or a conceptual abstraction. The first is an absurdity; how could intersubjective experience be founded upon an absolute solitude? This is neither genetically or essentially possible; it amounts to conceding to its critics that phenomenology is solipsistic. The second reduces phenomenological description to conceptual theory-building, with disastrous consequences for its validity. Robert Welsh Jordan, "Not Living in the Primordial World: Husserl's Correction of his Fifth Cartesian Meditation," *Proceedings of the 19th Annual Husserl Circle Meeting*, pp. 272–91, takes the former view; presumably, "postmodern" and other critics of phenomenology would take the latter.

32. See Levinas's early study of Husserl, *The Theory of Intuition in Husserl's Phenomenology*, trans. Andre Orianne (Evanston: Northwestern University Press, 1973). This study is primarily a commentary on *Ideas I*, as the translator notes on p. xi. On pp. 62–3 Levinas states that, "For him [Husserl], representation will always be the foundation of all acts. Even if the objects of complex acts, such as will, desire, etc., exist in another manner than do the objects of simple representation, they still must have to some extent the mode of existence of theoretical objects." Levinas never abandoned or developed this view of Husserl's phenomenology.

33. Emmanuel Levinas, *Otherwise Than Being, or Beyond Essence*, p. 15.

34. Theodore de Boer, "An Ethical Transcendental Philosophy" in *Face to Face with Levinas*, ed. Richard Cohen (Albany: State University of New York Press, 1986), p. 108.

35. Emmanuel Levinas, *Otherwise Than Being, or Beyond Essence*, p. 159.

36. Emmanuel Levinas, *Totality and Infinity*, pp. 121, 213.

37. Ibid., p. 178.

38. Ibid.

8

CRITIQUE OF GENERAL RHETORIC

Philosophy, especially for the last hundred years, has meditated on its own end, and has perhaps even turned this meditation into its constitutive feature. While it is in one sense a specific genre, philosophy also initiated delimited scientific domains and attempted to enclose science, art and ethics within a unity. This unity shaped a rational cultural form opposed to mythic, religious, or irrational forms. Such components, if not eradicable, were rigorously subordinated to philosophical unity. In this sense, philosophy is not simply a genre, but a universality encompassing and giving form to the plurality of genres. In large part, this unity conferred a cultural unity on European civilization, the "West." It is by no means an accident that when Edmund Husserl rearticulated this cultural unity in the face of fascist barbarism in Vienna in 1935, he pointed out that it did not include Papuans or gypsies.[1] Within the very formation of the idea of philosophy as the emergence to self-consciousness of "essential human capacities" is the tension between such universality and the particular cultural–historical formation within which it emerged. Though such universal capacities can, in principle, be awakened in anyone, such awakening involves a fundamental transformation of other cultural forms along lines first illuminated by the European one. Essential insight into the possibilities of humanity as such remains interwoven with a factual cultural unity that encounters other cultural forms, its "Outside," with a certain privilege. This privilege is not that of a specific genre, but is transferred from the universality of that genre to the cultural form as a whole. The end of philosophy is thereby an episode of the end of the West in the epoch of emergence of a planetary culture, but it is more than an episode in that the end of philosophy seems to plunge into an abyss the categories through which this emergence might be comprehended.

Philosophy may end in at least three ways. Through neglect, it may be forgotten or buried under the greater effectivity of other genres and traditions. Or, it may announce itself as completed, as having finished its task. Hegel is the great figure of the reconciliation whereby the task of philosophy claimed to be completed in the synthesis of reason with world history. As he put it in *The Philosophy of History*, "that this 'idea' or 'reason' is the *true*, the *eternal*, the absolutely *powerful* essence; that it reveals itself in the world, and that in the world nothing else is revealed but this and its honor and glory—is the thesis which . . . has been proved in philosophy. . . .".[2] Philosophy, when it is understood as both the completion of world history and the inner principle that directs it, announces its own end. But further, the end of philosophy may be announced simultaneously from inside and outside—or, to be more exact, the location of the announcement is undecidable. This must be distinguished from an announcement simply from outside by the genres historically co-existing with philosophy— such as rhetoric, religion, hedonism, and so forth—that competed with philosophy for political or theoretical hegemony and under which it might come to be buried in a given period. Such competitions presuppose the ongoing vitality of the competitors in the assertion of their different tasks. But it must also be distinguished from an announcement directly from inside, such as Hegel's, which suggests that philosophy has ended because its task has been completed. The end of philosophy is announced simultaneously from inside and outside when it is argued that philosophy is inadequate to the task that philosophy set for itself. The location of this announcement is undecidable because, while it must be philosophical in so far as it inhabits the task of philosophy sufficiently to know it and appreciate its value, it cannot be entirely philosophical because the task of philosophy is announced to have ended, not because it is completed, but because it is uncompletable. Thus "philosophy" is circumscribed as an unselfconscious task within world history that must be comprehended by a thinking which goes beyond philosophy but nevertheless is possible only because of philosophy.

This announcement was made in the nineteenth century by both Marx and Nietzsche. To select just one of many formulations, Nietzsche's diagnosis was

> that if a philosopher *had* been conscious of what he was, he would have been compelled to feel himself the embodiment of "*nitimur in vetitum*" [we strive for the forbidden]—and consequently *guarded* against "feeling himself," against becoming conscious of himself.[3]

The basis of this announcement was the experience of history, not simply of events within history, but of "history" itself as the origin of the themes and horizons of an epoch, an epoch which could not be comprehended by philosophy since it is the presupposed origin from which the task of philosophy is articulated. Thus, philosophical thought is announced to be traversed by an "unthought" such that its own task is unfulfilable "in principle"—whether this unthought is called will, praxis, or libido. This announcement, with an undecidable location that is neither inside nor outside, does not found a competing genre to philosophy—in which case it would be simply outside—but, since it is an outside made possible by philosophy itself, is a continuation of the genre of philosophy by other means. The experience of history as the origin of epochal determinations is not only a radicalization of the attempt of "first philosophy" to determine the fundamental principles upon which reason rests, but also depends upon the announcement of the end of philosophy in the second (Hegelian) sense: Only after the reconciliation of reason with world history can the experience of history as origin encompass philosophy also. The entwinement of philosophy with historical events posits a unity of thought and being that can subsequently be determined as an epoch when combined with the radicalized experience of history as origin, rather than events. Thus, the sense in which the announcement is made from outside is made possible by a reaching-outside by philosophy. Subsequent thought has had to appeal to this outside, but is unable to determine it since determinations are formulated within the philosophy circumscribed by an epoch. The end of philosophy is caught in the announcement of a certain closure and the inability definitively to step outside the closure. It confronts an other that it cannot name.

Philosophy, then, comes to an end through a philosophical (Hegelian) reconciliation of the relation between reason and the world that, subsequently, can be radicalized into a critique of philosophy itself (Marx and Nietzsche). One of the conditions for the

Hegelian reconciliation is that philosophy is fundamentally concerned with knowledge and reason. It is characteristic of philosophy to treat the various modalities of human experience as variations of theoretical positing of states of affairs that can then be determined with respect to their adequacy. In a move emblematic of the philosophical tradition, Edmund Husserl asserted that it is possible to transform any experiential modality into a "doxic positing" and that, in consequence, logic includes the modalities of emotion and volition.[4] This may be called a "theoretical modification" of the entire range of experience, which expresses the commitment of philosophy to reason and indicates that philosophy operates within a presupposed "gnoseological horizon," even though its universality is not restricted in *scope*. Nevertheless, while philosophy was centred gnoseologically, the question of knowledge did not encompass the whole of philosophy. Moreover, the primacy of the ethical and practical over theoretical reason was maintained throughout both ancient and modern philosophy. Questioning the gnoseological horizon of philosophy does not mean abandoning philosophy—no more than it means abandoning reason—but rather bringing the heretofore neglected and marginal components of philosophy to the foreground to be rethought in a postmodern context. The death of philosophy is the possibility of its renewal through what has been necessary but marginalized throughout its history, especially the face-to-face encounter through which philosophy has been taught. The circumscription of a gnoseological horizon constitutive of the philosophical tradition does not imply that the striving for knowledge can be neatly separated from philosophy. Nevertheless, this horizon has not defined the whole of philosophical practice and, at the present time, its circumscription is necessary to reveal marginalized dimensions of philosophy that are central to its renewal in the contemporary turning-point of the West—which may be defined through the end of philosophy. Indeed, the possibility of such a circumscription is both indicative and constitutive of the turning itself.

In contrast to the theoretical modification characteristic of philosophical tradition, after the announcement of the end of philosophy a "performative modification" of experience has appeared in various forms. Language, especially, can be considered primarily as an action, that is, as historically effective rather than descriptive of anterior events. For this reason, the theoretical situation after the end of philosophy is constitutively opened toward rhetoric—since viewing language as action is characteristic of the rhetorical tradition. However, because traditional rhetoric was a competing genre to philosophy it was concerned with historical effectivity as distinct from, or opposed to, the philosophical concern with truth. In contrast, the present opening toward a performative modification of experience occurs after a breakdown of this separation into genres. Consequently, rhetoric is itself expanded in its range, function and self-conception to what may be called general rhetoric. What is at issue is now the production of truth, or truth-effects, by the historical effectivity of language. The new set of questions that this puts on the intellectual agenda is indicative of the end of the classical separation of philosophy and rhetoric that is a consequence of the undecidable location of the critique of philosophy. More widely, it is indicative of a practical historical situation that has been called the postmodern condition. In order to address the intellectual issues of this postmodern condition, it is necessary to follow through the performative modification thoroughly and consistently. The core of the philosophical tradition is summed up and given a radical formulation in Edmund Husserl's discovery of the transcendental reduction—the suspension of belief in a world subsisting independently of anyone's perception of it. Such belief is not denied, but is simply suspended, in order that it may be held up for inspection and its pervasive influence described.[5] This is the contemporary, radicalized, form of the Greek "wonder" that was taken to be the origin of philosophy and which motivated the inquiry into truth that came to be constitutive of the philosophical tradition. Thus, the explication and development of the theory of the transcendental reduction is a central theme for a contemporary defence of philosophy. In the present context, characterized, in part, by the development of a general rhetoric, this core philosophical experience must be reformulated and rediscovered in relation to the active productions of discourse. I argue here that the end of philosophy pertains specifically to its gnoseological dimension. Thus, while it develops the notion of a general rhetoric, it does so in order to cirumscribe the limitations of even the widest conception of rhetoric and rediscover the origin of philosophy. It charts a deeper terrain though discovery of a practical *ascesis*—a transcendental reduction in language—that is attuned to a transformation, rather than an abandonment, of philosophy. This transformation shifts the locus of the origin of philosophy from a universality required to unify particular discourses toward a practical ethics of translation situated at the moment of encounter between discourses. In order to accomplish this task, I consider successively the conception of general rhetoric, the postmodern condition as a translation between discourses, and silence as a constitutive moment of philosophy.

As long as language is considered in relation to knowledge its task appears to be reporting on states of affairs to which it corresponds and which it represents with greater or lesser accuracy. Every language-use implies a dual task of clarification and critique directed, in the first place, at the specific fusing of theoretical statement and state of affairs and, in the second place, at the general conditions under which representation can occur. Within this gnoseological horizon, philosophy is thus concerned with the representation of representation; that is, the formulation of the general conditions of knowledge such that specific researches find their place and ongoing justification within this ground plan. Philosophy is both the prior laying out of the possibility of representation and the posterior ordering of representations within an actualized architectonic of forms of knowledge.

Language can also be considered, apart from its ability to represent events, as an event itself. Language-events perform actions that intervene in worldly events. Commenting on someone's appearance, for example, is not only (or even primarily) a description of a state of affairs, but the setting up of a certain relation between the speaker, that which is spoken about, and the one spoken to. An organized set, or system, of these language-events is generally called a discourse. A discourse is a finite group of utterances which together constitute a set of social relations which are brought into play whenever the discourse is invoked. The positions that one may occupy in these social relations are thus not brought by pre-existing subjects into the discourse, but constituted within the discourse by the ongoing system of utterances. Thus, if these utterances shift in their systemic role, the relations between subject-positions, or identities, shift. Consequently, an important question for analysis of a discourse is the internal social relations which come into being, mutate, and pass away with it. From this point of view, a science is itself a system of utterances. One is less concerned with the laws of physics, for example, than the system of knowledge development and exchange, relations between physicists, the process of education that inducts a new scientist, relations between physicists and non-physicists, and effects of the discourse of physical science—the nuclear bomb, for example. In this sense, the laws of physics are simply formalizations of discursive practice. The entire edifice of scientific representation that refers to states of affairs is a product of a more fundamental discursive formation that constitutes both social relations and states of affairs.

A discursive formation such as this must, therefore, have an "outside." The world does not, and cannot, consist of one discursive formation. First of all, a discursive formation does not consist of all possible utterances, or even of all meaningful utterances, but of all actual utterances, though of course embedded in these utterances are conditions under which it is appropriate to make new utterances. Nevertheless, it is often the case that new utterances are provoked by developments within other discourses—such as a different set of social identities or a formalization that can be given an analogous role in a different discourse. The distinction of internal from external sources of innovation and, especially, the interaction between them is significant for analysis of continuity and change in a given discursive formation. But, more fundamentally, a discourse cannot, in principle, extend to the totality of given discourses because, in order to do so, self-referential statements would need to be entirely enclosed within the discourse. Such internal coherence can only be an attribute of a very simple system. Any system of at least the complexity of elementary arithmetic is necessarily incomplete and its consistency cannot be proven within the system. The idea of a discursive formation without an outside is based upon the ideal of formalization within the gnoseological horizon of representation. But the formalization of a system through isolating a conceptual structure and exhaustively defining its properties through axiomatization and rules of transformation has come upon internal limitations.[6] In the case of systems difficult to formalize, pertaining to social life, historical events, emotions, and so forth—in short, the rhetorical subject-matter of the human sciences—limitations to the project of isolation upon which the theoretical ideal of self-enclosure through coherence and completeness rests are even more central for the theoretical system. Thus, even within a representational model the requisite enclosure of self-reference is impossible.[7] It is even less justified within a discursive model of language because the move to actual language-events undermines the formalization required for axiomatization. Self-reference always overflows the boundaries of a given discursive formation.

The postmodern condition can be characterized as a shift from language as representation to discourse as action, which entails the loss of a unifying foundation and architectonic—or, as Jean-François Lyotard says, "grand narrative"—for the plurality of discourses. Since the attempt to recuperate discursive plurality through grand narratives of knowledge or emancipation is characteristic of modernity, Lyotard has defined postmodernity as "incredulity toward metanarratives."[8] Consequently, subjects and social relations cannot be guaranteed through a prior meta-narrative, or recuperated within a subsequent totalization, but are positions constituted within discursive formations. This condition generalizes the critical task of rhetoric and undermines its subservience to philosophy. While the history of rhetoric has at many times contested this subservience, the contemporary shift to language as performance and the consequent expansion of rhetoric's terms of reference makes such subservience even more difficult to maintain. A contemporary debate between rhetoric and philosophy cannot, therefore, rest on the terms established in the philosophical tradition by Plato and Aristotle. It is analogous to the debate engendered by the appearance of Socrates among the Sophists prior to the fixing of philosophy into representation. A post-representational debate encounters a new open field in which rhetoric and philosophy seem to merge. The postmodern condition thus requires a transition from a restricted to a general rhetoric due to the key role that productive discourses take in defining the postmodern condition. Rather than being confined to the exterior transmission of a previously discovered truth, rhetoric penetrates to the centre of all discursive formations. The generality of general rhetoric pertains to the key figural-persuasive dimension of all discursive formations combined with their centrality to the social formation as a whole.[9] As Aristotle defined it, rhetoric is "the faculty of observing in any given case the available means of persuasion." While special arts such as medicine and geometry instruct and persuade solely with respect to their own subject-matter, rhetoric pertains to any subject-matter whatever. Moreover, rhetoric deals with judgments in which we deliberate without arts or systems to guide us. "Individual cases are so infinitely various that no systematic knowledge of them is possible."[10] In this classic formulation, rhetoric undermines neither the expertise nor the independence of special arts or sciences. Rather, it is concerned simply with the means of persuasion independent of subject-matter and the application to individual cases. This may be called a *restricted rhetoric* because, despite a certain universality of range and application, it is neatly distinguished from both delimited scientific truth and the universality of philosophy, or dialectic. In this classic formulation, rhetoric has the universality of ethico-political life. While any art, or *techne*, aims toward an end, the end is beyond the activity itself. Making shoes, for example, is not for the shoemaker, but for the comfort of the one who wears the shoes. It is characteristic of politics and ethics, by contrast, that the end toward which they are oriented is the activity itself. The good life is its own goal.[11]

The shift from restricted to general rhetoric occurs with the postmodern plurality of discourses due to the inability to stabilize a grand narrative that could perform the integrative, theoretical, universal and rational role assumed within the representational tradition by philosophy. The most spontaneous move of philosophical criticism is to ask the reflexive question of "within what discourse is this plurality of discourses comprehended?" In other words, to try to totalize the open field through a discourse of knowledge, and then to justify and explicate the rules of this discourse as epistemology. This reflexive move doubles, or repeats, the performative dimension of discourse with a claim to knowledge that is embedded in performance. It reinscribes the turn to language as performance within language as representation and will consequently have little difficulty in restricting rhetoric and subordinating it to philosophy, as action to truth, in quite classical fashion. This spontaneous philosophical move expresses the deep-rooted commitment of philosophy to reason, to a way of life centred on knowing, but this is, at bottom, simply a refusal to go all the way with the intellectual transition toward language considered as action which transforms rhetoric from restricted to general. Such a reflexive move is not wrong, but it is a failure of philosophy to enter the debate with rhetoric on the grounds constitutive of the postmodern condition. The new open field revealed in the postmodern condition is populated by a plurality of discourses and the absence of a grand narrative that could unify them. Within this field, the distinctness of philosophy as representational truth and rhetoric as situational enactment is replaced by a convergence on the utterance. The contemporary debate between rhetoric and philosophy centres on their respective ability to produce utterances in the new open field and the type and role of criticism of discourse that is possible and desirable within it. Here I develop the idea of an expanded general rhetoric in order to argue that, despite this convergence, philosophy cannot be collapsed into rhetoric. It finds in the production of a specific type of utterance—those that prepare for the silence initiated by their own ending—the philosophical nodal point which cannot be inscribed within rhetoric. By being synthesized with the philosophical moment of silence, general rhetoric can perform its discursive criticism without succumbing to the endless proliferation of discourses that it produces.

The postmodern situation is characterized by the recognition of a plurality of discourses, the internality of considerations of legitimation or justification (in the epistemological, ethical and aesthetic senses) to a given discourse, and, therefore, the confrontation of a new open field which cannot be subsumed under any definitive organization. This new open field has been characterized from several different angles. Indeed, it is a central feature of the postmodern situation that any attempt to characterize this open field will begin from specific discourses but will encounter different discourses in the very description of the postmodern situation itself. Richard Rorty uses the term "hermeneutics" to describe his response to the new open field revealed by the critique of representation:

Hermeneutics is an expression of hope that the cultural space left by the demise of epistemology will not be filled—that our culture should become one in which the demand for constraint and confrontation is no longer felt. The notion that there is a permanent neutral framework whose "structure" philosophy can display is the notion that the objects to be confronted by the mind, or the rules which constrain inquiry, are common to all discourse, or at least to every discourse on a given topic. Thus epistemology proceeds on the assumption that all contributions to a given discourse are commensurable. Hermeneutics is largely a struggle against this assumption.[12]

This hermeneutic hope wants to continue "the conversation of the West" in which philosophy becomes "useful kibitzing," without its traditional ambition to become the regulator, synthesizer, and provider of foundations for the various contributions to culture. Philosophy is reduced to professional inhabitors of philosophy departments in universities who have read a certain canon of received texts and, it is hoped, can say something useful in various cultural discourses as a result.[13] The positivist reduction of this view of philosophy is an emblematic, though ideological, response to the new open discursive field: Once one cannot claim to totalize and provide foundations for the plurality of discourses, it may seem that the only option is to keep existing discourses going. Legitimation of discursive practice tends toward the criterion of continuing the conversation. This discursive legitimation converges with the technocratic legitimation "If we can do it, it should be done" in so far as the claim to provide an evaluation of a discourse (tied to a representational idea of knowledge) shrinks into an "evaluation," or legitimation, of utterances solely within a given

discourse. The tendency toward purely internal discursive legitimation by performance replaces the grand narratives, such as
knowledge or emancipation, developed within the philosophical
tradition, and seems to throw out the idea of critical reflexion
upon practices central to philosophy (except in so far as local critical reflexion is already part of an ongoing conversation). Thus, the
tendency to internal legitimation within existing discourses is characteristic of the postmodern condition though, if it were the whole
story, it would make impossible the characterization of this condition as a plurality of discourses.

The emergence of a moment of universality within postmodernity is also expressed in the introduction to *Dialectic of
Enlightenment*: "We had set ourselves nothing less than the discovery of why mankind, instead of entering into a truly human
condition, is sinking into a new kind of barbarism. We underesti-
mated the difficulties of interpretation, because we still trusted
too much in the modern consciousness."[14] Horkheimer and
Adorno were concerned to diagnose the contribution to increased
domination by exactly those scientific and technical potentials
that were previously expected to contribute to enlightenment. In
so doing, their perspective took leave of the assumptions of modernity and became a critique of civilization as a whole. Thus, the
framework within which the possibilities of "enlightenment or
domination" could be articulated could no longer be left uninvestigated. The key assumption of modernity—that there was a
universal meta-discourse (philosophy) that was both internal and
external to "specialized" discourses and could thereby encompass
and harmonize them—was dropped. The most characteristic
modern philosophy, from this perspective, is that of Hegel, who
defined the movement of speculative philosophy as follows: "The

self-moving concrete shape makes itself into a simple determinateness; in so doing it raises itself to logical form, and exists in its essentiality; its concrete existence is just this movement, and is directly a logical existence. It is for this reason unnecessary to clothe the content in an external [logical] formalism; the content is in its very nature the transition into such formalism, but a formalism which ceases to be external, since the form is the innate development of the concrete content itself."[15] Speculative philosophy is thus a complete speech, encompassing all other discourses—which may then be called "specialized" because their limits have been determined. Such complete speech is equivalent to silence in the sense that any articulation, properly understood, represents and leads to the totality and is therefore not distinct "in truth," but only "accidentally," from any other articulation.[16] Modernity thus consists in a recognition of the plurality of discourses integrated with a simultaneous grand narrative of totalization. The turning in critical theory emerges from the realization that such a grand narrative both permeating and transcending specific discourses in such a manner that it can decide whether utterances within specific discourses are contributions to enlightenment or mystification is unsustainable. The development of the plurality of discourses undermines the claim to totality. The tensions of modernity have ushered in the postmodern condition—which appears, at least initially, to be a condition of pure plurality. Thus, the tendency to purely internal legitimation of discourses must be reckoned a key component of postmodernity. None the less, there is another tendency that is no less key: The postmodern condition also involves the attempt to universalize legitimation by performativity into an attempted steering of the whole social system. This nightmare of the "totally administered society," in Adorno's phrase, haunts all attempts to respond to the new open field which characterizes the postmodern condition. This is not to say that such a possibility can become an actual state of society, but by articulating itself as a principle for society as a whole, performative legitimation encounters a contradiction that can be unmasked as ideological. As John Keane puts it,

> corporate organizations seeking to administer their environments by means of scientific-technical rules are obliged continually to solicit the active participation of their members and clients, whose initiative and autonomy these organizations must nevertheless forbid. . . . The end of ideology thesis is evidently contradicted by the intense controversies over the limits of state action and the future of state-administered socialism. These controversies indicate a *renewal* of ideological forms of discourse. They signal the return of types of vindicative discourse within social conditions which have become problematic for the dominant power groups, who defend themselves through justificatory arguments.[17]

Such a contradiction emerges only to the extent that the criterion of performativity is articulated as a principle for the social system as a whole, that is, to the extent that it is proposed as a meta-narrative spanning discourses. By making such a universalizing claim, it becomes subject to a critique that reveals its functioning as furthering specific particular interests, as ideological. It is not the reduction of legitimation to performativity alone that is at issue here, but the combination of this reduction with its articulation as a system-principle.

While ideology-critique of the reduction to performativity

within a discourse, and a technocracy of cybernetic system-engineers, is both possible and important, if it remains satisfied with unmasking their non-universality, then one is thrown back into the plurality of discourses. The particularity of the performance criterion may well be matched by the particularity of the critical standpoint that is doing the unmasking. In order to oppose the reduction to performance and to provide a justification for critical reflexion, Habermas has argued that every discourse incorporates the counterfactual assumption that discursive practice is oriented to the reduction of systematically distorted communication: "[C]ommunicative action has nothing to do with propositional truth; but it has everything to do with the truthfulness of intentional expressions and with the rightness of norms."[18] Thus, a given case of systematically distorted communication motivates reflection on the truthfulness of utterances considered as actions in a language game—do the utterances obscure the goals which they tend to bring about?—and the validity of the intersubjective norms to which the participants in the discourse accede—are the subject-positions produced by coercion? These counterfactual assumptions enable a reflexive critique of communicative distortions that seeks to reorient discourse towards consensus. Now, there are three possibilities here: The resources that enable reflexion may either stand outside and above the given discourse (such as the meta-narrative of modernity), or they may be within it (as in hermeneutic continuation of the conversation), or they may emerge in the process of translation between discourses. In the first case, the discursive resources enabling binding reflexion are rooted in the meta-narrative of knowledge or emancipation that has become incredible in the postmodern condition. Such an approach fundamentally disputes the description of the postmodern

condition as a "plurality of discourses" and seeks to reinvigorate the
analysis of modernity as a conflict between specialized systems
and the socio-historical totality. In Habermas's words, "it is a question of building up restraining barriers for the exchanges between
system and lifeworld and of building in sensors for the exchanges
between lifeworld and system."[19] In the second case, the discourse
is assumed to possess exactly the universal characteristics of reflexion that the theory is designed to establish. There is a hermeneutic
circle implied between the characterization of a specific communicative interaction as "distorted," the appeal to universal norms
with which to criticize the distortion as systemic, and the enactment of critical intersubjective reflexion in a reorientation of
discursive practice toward consensus. The circle of interpretation
requires the context of tradition in order to proceed. That is, the
subjects engaging in a given discourse must all have access to
common discursive resources which enable the reflexive move and
imply its universal bindingness. If not, the hermeneutic alternative
of "continuing the conversation" amounts simply to convention-
alism, or, worse, a positivist elevation of what exists into a norm.
Thus, in the case of this alternative, one must either place critique
hermeneutically within an existing tradition or appeal to the first
alternative of a meta-narrative of emancipation "above" a given discourse. The third possibility is not explored by Habermas. In his
review of Hans-Georg Gadamer's *Truth and Method*, he followed
Gadamer's emphasis on translation in order to overcome the
Wittgensteinian view of self-enclosed language games as modes of
life—which leads to a view of purely internal legitimation that we
have seen in Rorty's notion of "continuing the conversation"—and
to legitimate hermeneutic interpretation as a "fusing of horizons"
in which the "unity of language, submerged in the plurality of

language games, is reestablished dialectically in the context of tradition."[20] However, when Habermas argued against Gadamer that
tradition is interwoven with domination, he did not employ or
develop the notion of translation to legitimate critical reflexion,
but instead argued that language is an incomplete model for social
theory because of the legacy of non-normative, non-communica-
tive components, "not of deceptions within a language but of
deception with language as such."[21] From this Habermas developed his own synthesis of interpretive and explanatory sociology,
which are held together by a higher legitimation of critical reason.
But, here, the same problem re-emerges: Either the context of tradition supersedes the unmasking of domination, in which case
language is assumed to possess sufficient resources to enable the
possibility of critique—which is Gadamer's hermeneutic alternative—or the inability of tradition to legitimate a sufficiently
independent concept of critique leads to a standpoint outside language. In short, when the question of translation did arise in the
context of a confrontation between critical theory and hermeneutics, it was relegated to subsidiary status and, consequently, the
earlier alternative of situating critical reason either in a meta-
narrative or as presupposed within language games was reasserted.
Though, this interchange did have the merit of establishing that
the relationship of discourse and critical reason must be
approached through the notion of a plurality of discourses that are
not external to each other.

In contrast, Lyotard, by virtue of his diagnosis of the postmodern condition, must definitively avoid the recourse to
meta-narrative legitimation of critical reflexion. But the difficulty
is that, since not all existing discourses provide sufficient resources
for binding critical reflexion, in the postmodern condition the

utilization of these resources outside of their legitimation within specific language games appears to be as arbitrary as existing practices (which may well incorporate forms of domination). In response to this situation, in which he can appeal to neither of the two alternatives, Lyotard proposes a local form of criticism that he terms "paralogy," which he claims is characteristic of contemporary science. Whereas innovation is a move within the language game as constituted—or, a continuing of the conversation in Rorty's sense—paralogy is the proposal of new norms for understanding, an utterance that shifts the rules whereby new utterances are produced. The production of paralogy is always in response to a local situation and disturbs the existing consensus. Paralogical interventions may call forth a response from the existing consensus that seeks to remove one of the players from the game—a countermove that Lyotard calls "terrorist." From this point of view, the consensus on binding reflexion on norms embedded in language games, to which Habermas appeals, appears as coercive rather than emancipatory, as enforcing the rules of a given discursive formation rather than disturbing them. In short, if reflexive resources exist they are too local to address the postmodern condition as a whole and, in many discursive formations, they do not exist at all. This paralogical strategy for addressing the new postmodern open field suggests that recognizing the plurality of heteromorphous language games requires recognizing any consensus as local, a temporary contract that can be criticized by a "multiplicity of finite meta-arguments" limited in space and time. Moreover, Lyotard suggests that, despite the tendency to universalization of the criterion of performativity, the present postmodern condition also contains a tendency to such locally oriented meta-critiques and, we may add, that it is to the extension of this tendency that criticism should aim.[22] Paralogy is the local disruption of consensus. One may immediately ask whether Lyotard's justification of paralogy is itself a local intervention in a discourse. When he identifies paralogy with contemporary science, he seems to imply a general legitimation of the strategy.[23] This would be simply a new form of scientism—the normative imposition of the rules of one discourse that is unaccountably elevated to meta-narrative legitimation—but his diagnosis of the postmodern condition rules out this implication. Also, in order not to fall into the classical sceptical or relativist self-contradiction of proposing a universal theory that denies the validity of universal theories, one must interpret paralogy as locally justified. The justification of paralogy is itself paralogical. In this sense Lyotard's logic is akin to the Sophistic logic that would negate the applicability of a universal logic *only in this case* and remain agnostic about its universality "as such." But, in this case, what entitles us to distinguish paralogical interventions from terrorist countermoves? Either intervention will simply modify the positions of the subjects—which is simply continuing the conversation and doesn't need paralogical justification—or, by disturbing consensus, paralogy will disrupt, reverse, and perhaps eliminate them. If terrorist and paralogical interventions are indistinguishable "in principle," doesn't all of this amount to saying that one can always overturn the board if the game doesn't come out well? This seems a rather thin justification of critical reason. The unsatisfactoriness of this alternative as a standpoint of critical reason does not rule out its exemplariness with regard to the dilemmas of the postmodern condition. A genuine philosophical theory of postmodernity needs to overcome this false alternative as well as to show why this unsatisfactory alternative continually reappears. Because what used to be called

critical reason has been reduced to a move within a general agonistics, its "justification" is no different than any other—it is one's
desire. Only with the transformation of this agonistic field by
silence can the false alternative be overcome. It is in response to
this concern that Keane suggests that "democracy cannot be interpreted as merely one language game among others" and that
institutional procedures to prevent a hegemony of one discourse
over others and safeguard a plurality of public spheres are a necessary component of a postmodern recognition of plurality of
discourses.[24] But here we come back to the alternative we found in
Habermas: Either we must resurrect a meta-narrative to justify
the emancipatory component of reflexion or, because every language game does not distribute the possibility of reflexion
throughout its subject-positions, must appeal to the special privilege of those factual discourses within our tradition that do so to
get the hermeneutic process going.

The legitimation of critical reflexion in the postmodern condition thus seems to be forced toward one of two alternatives: The
existing discourses that contain resources allowing subjects within
the discourse to appeal to binding norms of reflexion, or the
(attempted) meta-narratives of reflexion and emancipation. But
the logic of this appeal to hermeneutic and/or meta-narrative
resources must be to deny that the new open field of discursivity
presents an unprecedented problem—in short, to argue that the
postmodern condition is, in principle, similar to that of modernity.
Critical reflexion seems to be hung on a dilemma: Its universality
can only be guaranteed by denying the loss of meta-narrative that
constitutes the postmodern condition, whereas its practical effectivity relies on existing discourses which harbour reflexive resources
but whose universality is denied. But there was another logical

possibility—that the activity of translation itself is the locus of critical reflexion.

There is a reflexive component in the activity of characterization of the postmodern condition. The response to the situation is also a characterization of the situation, and this reflexivity invokes a universality that can be considered as an action apart from claims to truth or representation. The characterization of a plurality of discourses *as* a plurality requires a conception of a field, or space, within which these discourses encounter one another. Without some such concept, each discourse would be an entire and self-enclosed mode of life, unable to characterize other discourses. But our contemporary, postmodern culture is defined by just such cross-characterizations, transcodings, or, as we will say, translations of discourses: Community activists have ways of talking about the actions and language of scientific experts. Workers, blacks and women have discourses that respond to and characterize the difference and defects of the discourses that attempt to pin them down. And, of course, these examples could be reversed. This is a central difference between the situation analysed in *Dialectic of Enlightenment* and the present debates concerning postmodernity: The discourses of opposition to performativity, technocracy and system-maintenance are now an integral part of the culture to be analysed, though this cannot (as is sometimes imagined) relieve critique of the necessity of reflexive justification. Moreover, the new open field uncovered in the postmodern condition has been characterized from an array of intellectual discourses with mutually antagonistic presuppositions and methods. It is in this ability to characterize the postmodern condition within a plurality of discourses, which is also the origin of the cross-characterizations of discourses and of ideologies attempting to define the totality, that we may find an emergent universality that can justify reflexive critique. The postmodern condition is neither a simple plurality of discourses (as Lyotard claims), nor adequately addressed by continuing the conversation between subject-positions within a discourse (as Rorty claims), but also an open field of discursivity constituted by a mutual and continuous process of translation of discourses. The plurality of discourses can be characterized within a single discourse precisely because other discourses are not eternally, in principle, exterior to it. A contingent exteriority can always be reduced by translation into an interiority. This is not, it must be recalled, a claim that through translation a discourse appropriates all that is true or enlightening in another discourse, which would be to return to a representational theory of truth. Here, we remain firmly within the performative modification. The notion of postmodernity as the inability to totalize a plurality of discourses must therefore be understood as a dynamic relation. It is best formulated as a *continuous process* of failure to establish a discourse totalizing discourses, or a meta-discourse of the whole, within an open field in which there is continuous translation between discourses. For example, the discourses of "free trade" and "fiscal responsibility, restraint" continually attempt to become the meta-narrative of contemporary society by cannibalizing all others and claiming that they are dependent on it for their possibility, but this attempted elevation of a single narrative is never fully successful and only suceeds to the extent that it repels continual assaults by competing discourses. We may characterize this dynamism in the open field as a "general agonistics" between discourses. I use Lyotard's term here, since it is a good one. But, as far as I can see, he applies the term solely within a discourse, though, of course, this includes paralogical moves.[25] This is to be expected since, if the implications of the "general agonistics between discourses to hegemonize the activity of translation" were to be followed out, his characterization of the postmodern condition would be revealed as insufficient.

It is this dynamism which general rhetoric responds to and intervenes in. Whenever a given discourse attempts to translate the others into itself in such a manner as to produce a grand narrative of the whole, it calls forth its own deconstruction. To the extent that a totalizing translation begins to succeed, it is besieged by the countermove of rhetorical criticism which re-establishes the untranslated residue through recourse to the instituting components of the discourse in question. That is, the prospective grand narrative is retranslated into the various given discourses through which it attempted to establish its totalization. Thus, the loss of meta-narrative is not a single event, but *an event continuously reproduced by the very attempt to establish a meta-narrative.* The postmodern condition is thus not a simple plurality of discourses, but also the unstable process of their attempted totalization and deconstruction. A focus on simply the legitimation of a diversity of discourses by modernity will thus undermine the concept of postmodernity, since the present plurality will seem, in principle, to be the same as the plurality legitimated by de Tocqueville and other early modern theorists. John Keane has criticized Lyotard in this manner.[26] When a given discourse translates another discourse into a theme within itself, it aims at totalization; the outside of this totalization is recovered through deconstruction with reference to its own instituting moment. Therefore, deconstruction is not just a theory or a strategy, but a world-event.[27]

Within this open field constituted by a general agonistics between discourses, the role of rhetorical criticism of a given discourse is generalized from the persuasive component within - discourse to the criticism of discourses as a whole in the new open field. Every discursive formation embodies a set of procedures, that can be formalized as rules, which express the rationality practised in the performance of utterances. The giving of reasons thus assumes a discourse within which certain statements function as reasons in given circumstances. This exchange of reasons within a discourse can be traced back to a primal image which becomes the foundation, or *arche*, for the discourse in question. A discourse is thus instituted through the metaphorical extension of an image, a figurative showing, on the basis of which a discourse takes on theoretical, universal and rational dimensions. Such a primal metaphor is practical, particular, and imaginative. In this situation the range of rhetorical criticism is expanded from its restricted character in which it is oriented primarily to persuasive language-events within a given discourse (though this included also the general characteristics of such persuasion). General rhetorical criticism becomes the uncovering of primal images that found and regulate discourses, the study of the metaphorical, or tropological, origination of the plurality of discourses. Rhetorical criticism either sustains or undermines discourses as a whole in this type of intervention in the general agonistics. This critical and reflexive move is therefore in a complementary relationship with the instituting speech that is poetry. Therefore, the institution of a discourse must be understood as poetically enacted and rhetorically sustained, rather than as founded in philosophical universality. Without a grand narrative, it seems that philosophy can no longer restrict the scope of rhetoric. The discourse of truth gives way to a plurality of regimes of truth, and rhetorical criticism consists in interventions which undermine the insupportable—but nevertheless continually arising—claim of a single discourse to fix meaning within itself and thereby to substitute itself for the lost grand narrative. From this perspective, any claim by philosophy to fix meaning in a "privileged" discourse that monopolizes the activity of translation is no less an unwarranted attempt at domination of the field of discursivity than any other attempt at totalization.

The loss of grand narrative characteristic of the postmodern condition, then, is not adequately conceived as the loss of a universalizing dimension to discourse, as Lyotard's characterization suggests. If we simply had ceased to be able to totalize discourses at a given moment, we might attempt to create, or perhaps simply wait for a higher power to dispense (as Heidegger suggests), a substitute. The situation is more complex because there is a universalizing and reflexive component within every sufficiently complex discourse that, in principle, can translate every other discourse, though it cannot achieve a fully universal status under which it might subsume particular cases.[28] Recognition of the plurality of discourses therefore does not imply, as is often imagined, that each discourse is an enclosed vessel, that there can be no discourse spanning discourses. In fact, it implies the opposite—that each discourse spans all other discourses, that there is no pure externality. Consequently, the move to purely internal legitimation of a discourse through "continuing the conversation" is not an adequate response to the postmodern condition. Neither is the reassertion of a meta-narrative. From the viewpoint of postmodernity, these two alternatives can be seen as mirror opposites: The alternative of internal or external legitimation appears when the modern conception of "sublation" (*Aufhebung*), whereby speculative reason is both internal and external to a given discourse, has been torn into two halves. Initially, and it is here that many discussions of postmodernity are stuck, this appears as a necessity to decide between the two sides of this alternative. But in the present formulation, we can see that the postmodern condition is not merely an episode of scepticism, a defence of the many as against the one, or of the particular as against the universal. It is rather a new configuration of unity and plurality, particularity and universality, and cannot be countered by simply asserting the traditional arguments concerning the self-cancellation of relativism and scepticism, the necessity of unity to the definition of plurality, or claims to universality in the perception of particulars, and so forth.

The new open field of the postmodern condition simply means that a discourse spanning, or translating, different discourses cannot be given an independent legitimation—that there is no one discourse that can monopolize the locus of translation. Modernity, by way of contrast, consists in an unprecedented recognition of the plurality of discourses integrated with a simultaneous grand narrative of totalization. Premodern, traditional societies consist in the regulation of discourses by a grand narrative. The grand narrative does not have to be legitimated by recuperating the plurality of discourses, as in modernity, but penetrates them from the outset: A given discourse can only be legitimated in reference to the grand narrative. This, thereby, generates the illusion of traditional society as consisting of a single discourse which, if it were not an illusion, would make impossible the emergence of modernity.

Continuous translation of discourses embodies a universalizing component which simultaneously falls back into a particular discourse. Universality fails to stand above and order the discourses, while particularity asserts itself as capable of incorporating other discourses. It is this general translatability that makes general rhetoric possible and it is the tendency of particular discourses to attempt to hegemonize the field of discursivity that makes it necessary. Loss of boundaries between discourses inaugurates a new open horizon for the field of discursivity. The postmodern condition can thus be defined as the continuous interplay between totalizing translation and rhetorical criticism of aspiring meta-narratives in an open field of discursivity. The effect of translation is to undermine the fixity of meaning within a discourse. Aspiring meta-narratives attempt to fix meaning within a higher totalization. In destabilizing attempted meta-narratives rhetorical criticism re-establishes unfixity of meaning. This continuous dynamism generates a radical unfixity of meaning within the field of discursivity as a whole. Proliferation of temporary senses continuously undermined injects madness into general agonistics. Since translation reduces boundaries, other discourses, and the discursive field itself, enter every discursive formation. Madness, which is this unfixity of meaning, invades each utterance within a discourse from its outside. General rhetoric is thus haunted by madness. Rhetorical criticism re-establishes plurality of discourses and therefore unfixity of meaning within a discourse. Unfixity pervades the field of discourse and therefore the practice of rhetorical criticism itself. Madness appears as both product and practice of rhetoric. Of course, there are many strategic compromises that serve to keep madness at bay. Only by timidly holding back, by ceasing to follow the performative modification to its end, can a semblance of fixity, of saying what we mean and meaning what we say, be preserved. But the encounter with madness is fundamental to discursive interventions due to the new relation between universal and particular in the postmodern field of discursivity.

The madness of the field of discourse is constituted by the

inability of philosophy, or indeed any other discourse (including rhetoric), to monopolize the activity of translation. General rhetoric engages the continuous translation that defines postmodernity, but, in the same moment, succumbs to the dynamism of postmodernity. This cannot be avoided, because of the tension encapsulated in this general applicability of rhetoric combined with its inability to master the open field (an inability shared with every other discourse). General rhetoric is at once a particular critical discourse and a theory of discursive interventions in general—a particular discourse that speaks about discourse uni-versally—though it is not unique in this respect since every utterance now overflows its borders into other discourses and into the open field. Nevertheless, rhetoric focuses specifically on the characteristics of discourses and, in this sense, is not just another discourse. Its overflowing consists in a certain absence of subject-matter. Traditionally, rhetoric centred on the manner of presentation, of persuasion, but its generalized function implies that it is now situated at precisely the moment of overflowing in translation. Its specific character consists in not being a delimited discourse and thereby being able to thematize the procedures of delimitation. When a discourse translates other discourses it assumes a rhetorical function. Rhetoric "itself," as it were, is this rhetorical capacity in all discourses. Consequently, it is not simply translating, as are other discourses now, but without a delimited domain *into which* translation can occur. This absence means that rhetoric, even though it is of universal application, cannot itself become a totalizing discourse. Because it operates at the moment of translation, it always recovers plurality. Thus, in its universal aspect rhetoric dissolves through translation (or, we might say, by rhetorical criticism of itself) into the particular discourses it criticizes. In its particular aspect, as a specific discourse, rhetoric is characterized by a certain absence of content such that its critical activity—for example, uncovering the tropological origin of a discourse and engaging in a discussion of the "general" characteristics of tropes—cannot be sufficiently delimited to claim totalizing status. It has been argued that in the postmodern condition every (delimited) discourse involves an interplay of particular and universal—translating out and translating in. The uniqueness of rhetoric is that its universality, rather than aiming at totalization, recovers plurality; its particularity, rather than standing distinct from delimited discourses, clarifies their procedures of formation. Since criticism recovers a plurality *every time*, it thereby engages in an activity with pervasive characteristics that seems to call for a universal theory of discourse, but does not enjoy the delimitation necessary to develop a theory that could master the domain. We may call this dynamism a general agonistics, or an anti-dialectic in which each side both requires and repels its other without reconciliation. It pervades every critical practice within the open field of discourse: Particular critical practices overflow themselves toward a theory of discourse; a theory of discourse that attempts the justification of critical practices is never sufficiently universal—it seeps back toward a particular local intervention. It is this complex interplay in general rhetoric that describes the postmodern condition. A characterization that begins solely from the plurality of delimited discourses will fail to thematize the activity of translation that calls forth general rhetoric and, thereby, this new description of the difference between rhetoric and delimited discourses. The madness of general rhetoric is none other than the madness of the postmodern condition itself.

One may ask: Is there any alternative to "succumbing" to the postmodern condition at this point? We have disqualified rhetoric, despite its strategic position, from monopolizing the activity of translation. If madness could be stemmed only by a monopolization of translation, this amounts to an admission that philosophy consists solely in a meta-narrative of representation. The postmodern condition would be co-extensive with the range of contemporary general rhetoric. And, in a certain sense, this is so, but unless we are to simply put aside the perennial debate between rhetoric and philosophy, we must inquire whether there is a moment in the general agonistics of the field of discourse from which the philosophical life may take its departure—a moment in discourse that transforms the entire field of discursivity. A contemporary defence of philosophy centres on whether rhetoric can adequately understand, in its performance, the condition of translatability in the new open field with which it operates. If not, there is an opening to philosophy from within the performative modification of language. Let us seek to escape inherited notions of philosophy as a meta-narrative guaranteeing an architectonic of knowledge and seek its transformation, alongside that of rhetoric, in the discursive field. Whatever we may discover here, it could not entail a domination of uncertainty that would end the madness generated by the plurality of the field. To put it in a slightly elliptical way: Now that we have discovered the Sophists as our contemporaries, may we not discover Socrates also?

For the plurality of discourses to be characterized as a plurality requires an encounter with the postmodern field of discourse through a specific discourse. This is the moment of its totalization, when it translates the others into itself. In this moment, a discourse *names the site* from which it emerges. The postmodern condition is named from a discourse that emerges within it. As this totalization deconstructs, the discourse is translated into others. It ceases to name the site as they begin to do so and becomes the *site of naming*—when what is said within a discourse can only be understood through a larger context in which it is placed. The dynamic switching between the naming of site and the site of naming constitutes the postmodern madness. These are not alternatives between which one might choose, or which might choose oneself. They are two mutually exclusive, but co-extensive, descriptions of the same territory between which it is impossible to decide. Translation is the border that switches the naming of site into the site of naming. It does not separate two distinct spaces, but describes an ineradicable tension between them.

The madness can also be read back through the border where translation occurs, and this is the point of emergence of a philosophical critique of general rhetoric. General rhetoric both navigates and succumbs to the field by proliferating discourses. At the border between discourses, general rhetoric encounters both silence and babble—uncontrollable proliferation of speech and a residue that will not cross. With every utterance haunted by madness, the performative feat is to design an utterance that ends itself, that calls for the silence beyond itself. This silence is not the same as that which is *silenced* within a given discourse in a Foucauldian sense, that which cannot be expressed within it. Nor is it the same as refraining from speaking, which is a speech act like any other since it is a move within an established language game. Since philosophy can no longer style itself as the master discourse, in the postmodern condition it seems to yield to rhetoric as does any particular discourse to discursive criticism. Only if philosophy is not a discourse but a distinctive and radical type of move within discourse, a move which nevertheless modifies discourse in its entirety, can it navigate the rhetorical tide without stemming it. Thoroughly imbued with particularity, within the horizon of determinations that surround every utterance, it is a unique move to orient discourse toward its end. The practical intervention of philosophy is to design utterances, and, through them, perhaps shape discourses themselves, which are not oriented to proliferation but to an explicit termination. Preparing for the end of speech modifies the entire field of discourse. Philosophy is not itself silence, but the preparation for a silence that opens to the Other. After representation, we are before Plato. Philosophy is not a rule but a way of life. One among many. The one that does not seek to dominate the many, that proposes abjection within the field of display.

In its Platonic origin, philosophy imagined temporarily leaving the world of discourse to encounter cosmos, world-order, with a penitent awe expressed in silence.[29] Armed with a cosmological order from beyond language, it could enter the world of discourse and rediscover order. From here emerged the possibility of philosophy as meta-narrative, as the ordering of the plurality of discourses. In ancient philosophy, the permeation of particular discourses was such that they could achieve no independent legitimation. Later, without cosmos, this world-order became divine, historical, artistic, technological—each *arche* defining an epoch, in its turn. Modernity repudiated this permeation and thus released the potential of separated discourses to develop their internal resources. Nevertheless, this repudiation itself, as well as the continuing legitimation of modernity, unleashed discourses precisely because they could be expected to contribute to a general knowledge and enlightenment. The technical term for this expectation is *Aufhebung*; without it, there is no modernity. The complete discourse achieved through sublation was equivalent to the silence of absolute knowledge. Here again, the fortune of philosophy is entwined in silence. But in the postmodern condition, at the border, there is neither leave-taking from discourse nor a completion of discourse—only a moment of switching from silence to babble. In pausing with this silence from within discourse we recover philosophy as a moment in the field of discourse that will infiltrate its other moments. This is a performative rediscovery of the Platonic claim that rhetoric cannot know itself, but is known by philosophy.[30] Rhetoric cannot perform itself, since its own performances multiply into babble. Only the moment of stopping constructed by philosophy can fix, and therefore perform, meaning. Silence is no longer simply encountered, but constructed. This silent, still point is the moment in translation where the residue asserts itself through the origin of a certain fixity that cannot stem the madness, but can let it be seen as madness, opening an utterance that will close itself. This pinpointing of this moment of silence was the constitutive feature of Samuel Beckett's late writing. As he said in *The Unnamable*, "One starts things moving without a thought of how to stop them. In order to speak. One starts speaking as if it were possible to stop at will. It is better so. The search for the means to put an end to things, an end to speech, is what enables the discourse to continue."[31] Unless speech can stop, it is only the proliferation of sounds, or madness; meaning is parasitic on silence.

This is a discovery of a moment beyond language, though the beyond of language cannot be discovered outside language, but is that within language that allows its outside to appear. Silence is the outside of discourse, of all discourse. It surrounds discourse as the emptiness enclosing the earth, rendering a place in the here and now to every utterance. This place will later be undone by the unfixity of the general proliferation, but it can be designed anew.

Always anew, without hegemony, an utterance may design its own silence. Only with respect to this place, this siting, can the question of the relation between discourse and the world be properly posed, because only at this point would it no longer be a question of relating discourses to a world conceived as existing before discourse, positivistically. Siting is the worlding of discourse, the world-founding of utterance, the coming-to-be of the world as a world within a cultural praxis that overflows language through the infiltration of silence.

This outside of discourse also appears within discourse. In this taming of silence it appears in the pauses between utterances, and the spaces between words,[32] to make meaning from the babble and in this way holds the madness at bay for a while. In this way philosophy comes to the aid of rhetoric and releases its legitimate and necessary field of operation. Stalling unfixity allows temporary meaning within specific discourses, which is, in turn, undermined by the madness of general rhetoric. Within discourse, silence reverts behind pen to paper, slowing the undermining of meaning enough to allow the operation of general rhetoric. Outside discourse, through the moment of translation that peers outside, silence surrounds and lies behind, all speech. Before and after the utterance, silence supports discourse with all that which cannot be said, since saying is always underway but must both begin and end. Beginning is eruption, not only a starting but a closing off of the silence that reigned before. In this closing, discourse achieves a specificity. The totality of what is closed off isolates a determinate discourse from other discourses by resisting translation. Practising translation interrupts the eruption, reintroducing silence into discourse. Without silence, discourse would be without birth and death. It would have no meaning for those of us who speak because we could not be present at its occasion. But with the incorporation of philosophical silence, rhetoric can operate with and upon the many births and deaths in and of discourses in the political world we share with others.

Philosophy, unlike religion or myth, requires a relation to something that is not itself, say tradition, religion, rhetoric, hedonism, science, technology—in short, non-philosophy—and is constituted through this relation. Thus, philosophy can end from two opposite directions: it can simply historically cease as the "discourse about discourse" since the gnoseological horizon which enabled this representational totalization has been circumscribed. Or, it can cease through the incorporation of its outside; in cannibalizing everything philosophy is finished. It becomes general rhetoric. Yet, if this new general rhetoric can be circumscribed, it can become the other to a performative rediscovery of philosophy. An utterance that does not simply terminate, but makes its own ending, opens general rhetoric to a new performative philosophical turn that originates an ethics within the postmodern agonistic field. The life without silence is not worth living. This is not every speech, but a desire born within language, given form within language, that reaches beyond language, in the moment of calm when one finds the courage to end.

NOTES

1. Edmund Husserl, "Philosophy and the Crisis of European Humanity," Appendix 1 of *The Crisis of the European Sciences and Transcendental Phenomenology*, trans. David Carr (Evanston: Northwestern University Press, 1970) pp. 273, 290.

2. G. W. F. Hegel, *The Philosophy of History*, trans. J. Sibree (New York: Dover, 1956) pp. 9–10.

3. Friedrich Nietzsche, *On the Genealogy of Morals*, trans. W. Kaufmann and R. J. Hollingdale (New York: Vintage, 1969) pp. 112–13.

4. Edmund Husserl, *Formal and Transcendental Logic*, trans. Dorion Cairns (The Hague: Martinus Nijhoff, 1969) p. 136.

5. Edmund Husserl, *Ideas Pertaining to a Pure Phenomenology and to a Phenomenological Philosophy, First Book: General Introduction to a Pure Phenomenology*, trans. F. Kersten (The Hague: Martinus Nijhoff, 1982) pp. 51–62.

6. Kurt Gödel, "Über formal unentscheidbare Satze der 'Principia mathematica' und verwandter Systeme," *Monatschrift fur Mathematik und Physik*, 38, 1931; B. Rosser, "An Informal Exposition of Proofs of Gödel's Theorem and Church's Theorem," *Journal of Symbolic Logic*, Vol. 4, No. 2, 1939; and J. N. Findlay, "Goedelian Sentences: A Non-Numerical Approach," *Mind*, Vol. 51, No. 202, 1942.

7. See the discussion in Ian Angus, *Technique and Enlightenment: Limits of Instrumental Reason* (Washington: Center for Advanced Research in Phenomenology and University Press of America, 1984) pp. 19–40.

8. Jean-François Lyotard, *The Postmodern Condition: A Report on Knowledge*, trans. G. Bennington and B. Massumi (Minneapolis: University of Minnesota Press, 1984) p. xxiv.

9. The term "general rhetoric" has been used previously by others but not with this meaning. J. Dubois and his colleagues used the term to refer to a rhetoric "meant to be applicable to all modes of expression" though they have acknowledged (in a subsequently written Afterword included in the English translation) that the term was too ambitious and "theory of the figures of discourse" would be more accurate. J. Dubois, F. Edeline, J.-M. Klinkenberg, P. Minguet, F. Pire, and H. Trinon, *A General Rhetoric*, trans. P. Burell and E. Slotkin (Baltimore: Johns Hopkins University Press, 1981) pp. 167, 215. The generality in question in this case was that of the available theory of rhetoric, not that of the expansion of its field of applicability. Roland Barthes used the term to indicate the expansion of rhetorical methods and concerns from language to images; see "Rhetoric of the Image" in *Image-Music-Text*, trans. S. Heath (New York: Hill and Wang, 1977) p. 49. This concern has been taken up by Jacques Durand in "Rhetoric of the Advertising Image," *Australian Journal of Cultural Studies*, Vol. 1, No. 2, 1983. In this usage, it is an issue of the expansion of the field of rhetoric's applicability in a manner such as Saussure's expansion of linguistic concerns toward a general theory of signs. This usage is closer to my own, though still in this case it is a question of developing a suitable theory for analysing an expanded field of cultural phenomena. My use of this term is directed more toward the

field of applicability of rhetorical methods and concerns rather than toward a theory of rhetoric as such—though, no doubt, such an expansion of applicability is accompanied by an flowering of rhetorical methods themselves. Even further, I am concerned to emphasize that this expanded applicability is not simply a matter of theoretical development but is based in a new postmodern intellectual situation. In particular, the thematic of knowledge as a production through discourse breaks down the traditional division of labour between rhetoric and philosophy and institutes the necessity for renewed thinking about their relation. It is this that is especially important for the generality in question here. This usage is is implicated in the contemporary debates concerning the end of metaphysics since the separation of the two genres was settled by the metaphysical distinction between truth and persuasion.

10. Aristotle, *Rhetoric*, trans. W. R. Roberts (New York: The Modern Library, 1984) 1355b, 1356b–7a.

11. Aristotle, *Rhetoric*, 1356a; *Nichomachean Ethics*, trans. Martin Ostwald (Indianapolis and New York: Bobbs-Merrill, 1962) 1094a. Aristotle also suggested the compatibility and complementary character of rhetorico-political universality and philosophical universality (see, for example, *Rhetoric*, 1354a, 1355b, 1356a, 1358a). But this is highly questionable, even within the terms of Greek thought. For Plato, there is a fundamental distinction between good (scientific, philosophical) and bad (merely empirical, political) rhetoric; see *Phaedrus*, trans. R. Hackforth in *The Collected Dialogues of Plato*, ed. Edith Hamilton and Huntington Cairns (New York: Pantheon, 1966) 269–74. Also important here is Hannah Arendt's claim that the philosophers "turned away from the polis" and refashioned the concept of the political from their anti-political, philosophical stance; see Hannah Arendt, *The Human Condition* (Chicago: University of Chicago Press, 1973) pp. 17–21. Her attempt to regain a properly "political" concept of politics is very important after the end of philosophy and is congruent with what is attempted here under the term general rhetoric.

12. Richard Rorty, *Philosophy and the Mirror of Nature* (Princeton: Princeton University Press, 1979) pp. 315–16.

13. Ibid., pp. 393–4.

14. Max Horkheimer and Theodor Adorno, *Dialectic of Enlightenment*, trans. John Cumming (New York: Herder and Herder, 1972) p. xi.

15. G. W. F. Hegel, *Phenomenology of Spirit*, trans. A. V. Miller (Oxford: Oxford University Press, 1979) pp. 34–5.

16. Bernard P. Dauernhauer, *Silence: The Phenomenon and its Ontological Significance* (Bloomington: Indiana University Press, 1980) pp. 86–92.

17. John Keane, *Democracy and Civil Society* (London and New York: Verso, 1988) pp. 227–8.

18. Jürgen Habermas, *Communication and the Evolution of Society*, trans. T. McCarthy (Boston: Beacon Press, 1979) p. 119.

19. Jürgen Habermas, *The Philosophical Discourse of Modernity*, trans. Frederick Lawrence (Cambridge: MIT Press, 1987) p. 364.

20. Jürgen Habermas, "A Review of Gadamer's *Truth and Method*" in *Understanding and Social Inquiry*, ed. Fred R. Dallmayr and Thomas A. McCarthy (Notre Dame: University of Notre Dame Press, 1977) p. 340.

21. Ibid., p. 360.

22. Jean-François Lyotard, *The Postmodern Condition*, pp. 60–7.

23. Ibid., pp. 53–60.

24. John Keane, *Democracy and Civil Society*, pp. 239–40. Though Keane also says that such institutions could never be accepted "fully" because a "universal metalanguage" could never be adopted once and for all. This does not resolve the issue; it simply restates it on a "higher" level. Perhaps it is a sufficient practical stand for political intervention. If I extrapolate correctly, this implies regarding democratic institutions as a metalanguage with respect to political debates, but not as "finally" indisputable and, in special circumstances, liable to become the subject of debate themselves—in which case we enter into some further metalanguage (whose identity Keane does not discuss). Theoretically, this requires an argument for a "hierarchy of (meta)languages" applied in the political realm that could gain support from some types of systems theory.

25. Jean-François Lyotard, *The Postmodern Condition*, pp. 10, 16, 15, 57, 59.

26. John Keane, *Democracy and Civil Society*, pp. 213–45.

27. The work of Jacques Derrida is significant in expressing this moment of deconstructive rhetorical criticism; see especially "Differance" in *Margins of Philosophy*, trans. Alan Bass (Chicago: University of Chicago Press, 1982) pp. 1–27. The significance of the "outside" in this moment is elaborated by Ernesto Laclau and Chantal Mouffe; see *Hegemony and Socialist Strategy* (London: Verso, 1985) pp. 122–45.

28. This distinction of a universalizing from a universal judgment is developed originally in Kant's *Critique of Judgment*. Hannah Arendt has utilized it in developing the idea of politics as a singular judgment not subsumable under a rule. Max Horkheimer and Hans-Georg Gadamer have also focused on Kant's Third Critique in developing the traditions of critical theory and hermeneutics respectively. If we keep in mind that it was Kant's Third Critique that led to the development of Hegel's notion of history, we can see in this convergence of

interest in twentieth-century thought a return to, and rethinking of, the point of self-consciousness of modern philosophy in Hegel's notion of *Aufhebung*. See Max Horkheimer, *Kants kritik der urteilskraft als bindeglied zwischen theoretischer und praktischer philosophie* (Stuttgart: Verlag von W. Kohlhammer, 1925); Hans-Georg Gadamer, *Truth and Method* (New York: Crossroad, 1975); and Ian Angus, *Technique and Enlightenment: Limits of Instrumental Reason*, pp. 99–118.

29. Plato, *Republic*, trans. Paul Shorey, 518c, 540a, 585a–6a, 611a–12d; *Phaedo*, trans. Hugh Trendennick, 79d, 81a, 83b; *Timaeus*, trans. Benjamin Jowett, 90a–d; *Seventh Letter*, trans. L. A. Post, 344b; in *The Collected Dialogues of Plato*.

30. Plato, *Phaedrus*, 269.

31. Samuel Beckett, *The Unnamable* (New York: Grove Press, 1978) p. 15.

32. Bernard Dauernhauer notes these two forms of silence—within discourse and framing discourse—whereas Jacques Derrida describes only the former, which he calls "spacing," since he has writing in mind. Derrida's collapsing of these two forms of silence is the basis for his rhetorical critique of philosophy which cannot design an ethics that transforms the general agonistics. See Dauernhauer, *Silence*, and Jacques Derrida, *Of Grammatology*, trans. Gayatri Chakravorty Spivak (Baltimore: Johns Hopkins University Press, 1976) pp. 39, 68, 70, 139, 200, 203.

9

THE EPOCH OF DISEMBODIED SIGNS

Any object in the human world has meaning and thus can been seen as a sign. One can view food, clothing, or anything else as a sign and, as such, its meaning emerges by being situated within the context of other signs. The primary reference of a sign is to the complex of signs, whereas the primary reference of food or clothing is to the practical activities of eating or wearing. There is no need to choose between these two references, since every object is both a sign and is used in practical activities. Indeed, discussing an object as a sign is a way of elucidating its practical use, not another use tacked on to the first. The discursive turn in philosophy and the human sciences is proposed as a way of clarifying human practice. None the less, this way of understanding the meaning inherent in human practice has preconditions and assumptions that tie it to a specific historical epoch. The disembodiment of signs is character-istic of modernity. It is based on the standing back from the world and doubling it in thought that occurs in representation. When the world is represented in thought it appears as a plurality of objects that stand over against the thinking subject. The doubling of the world in thought allows objects to be regarded from the point of view of the relation between them established by their representation in thought. Here emerges the idea of a self-enclosed system of signs where each sign derives its meaning from its relation to other signs within the system. Thus the modern age is permeated by the development of self-referring sign-systems in all fields of scientific endeavour. Cybernetics, information theory, semiotics, as well as similar systems in the fields of mathematics and computer science, are characteristic products of the modern epoch which is defined by the representation of the world as standing over as against a subject. These systems are then used to reorder the practical world on their pattern. The world is thus technologically known, altered and arranged to conform to systems of representation. I have attempted to make some headway with the theme of doubling by investigating it as a constitutive paradox.

Since sign-systems refer to the world (understood as a plurality of objects) and alter the world (understood as a field for the application of technologies) they cannot be simply opposed to, or distinguished from, human practical activities. There is nothing left out of the net of representation. However, one can begin to define what is obscured, altered or missed by representation by beginning from the sense in which human practical activities can be regarded as signs. Food and clothing are signs, but are they *only* signs? That is to say, is there nothing about eating or wearing clothes that is not captured sufficiently by their sign-function? It is difficult to formulate this lack because any formulation can be interpreted as part of the system of representation and thus as confirming the sign-system rather than pointing to its limitation. Moreover, this interpretation is not definitively wrong; it will always resurface, since the process of representation has no limit of extension in the sense of leaving something out, but only a prior limit in the sense of presupposing without incorporating. Food is a sign whose meaning refers to the complex of foods and the social identities established through their relations. Food also nourishes, but to give this "also" a positive formulation risks at every moment that the meaning of "nourishment" be turned back into the sign-system of food. Indeed, whenever nourishment is understood, or formulated positively, it cannot escape such a reference. It is the practical activity of eating that is altered when it is viewed as a representation. In their critique of philosophy (understood as representation through the Idea) both Marx and Nietzsche turned to the realm of praxis as that which underlies and subtends representation—whether it be in the terminology of metaphysics or the system of generalized exchange. I have used the term "embodied history" to refer to the practical activities that generate representation but escape it, that is the source of unsettling, or dis-figuring, the identities established within the system of representation. It is this (re)discovery of the practical origin of sign-systems that is a turn away from the modern epoch of disembodied representation. It may then be called a postmodern turn. The postmodern impulse gains effectiveness to the extent that it turns signs and discourse away from representation toward understanding them as a figuration of praxis. In order to clarify these figurations as they operate within praxis, the activity of philosophy must be a move against the grain, a regressive dis-figuration.

But no general return to concrete praxis, no outright bypassing of representation, is possible. Every utterance contains a *said*, a content, which orients it toward a truth-claim that attains its apogee in representation. The *saying*, the uttering of the utterance, brings one face-to-face with an other. It is a practical moment of encounter which is oriented toward ethics, not mainly about knowledge. Mimicry and gesture indicate the ethical dimension of language as embodied praxis. Signs in their historical sense are not defined by the intention of an inscriber as Husserl claimed, but as the meaningful face of the world.[1] Furthermore, every saying occurs at a *site*, a historical location whose institution as a primal communicative scene sets up social relations. The saying and the site take discourse beyond representation. As a consequence, every communication act is an "institution" in a double sense. It is a rhetoric within a given communication medium through which it is a saying within the cultural complex of institutions that defines a world and as such defines a politics that takes place within an already-instituted primal scene. It is also an *instituting act*, whereby a given form of expression is brought into being and sustained as such, as a formation of the site. In this sense, it implies a rhetoric of media forms in which a historical epoch appears with a certain perceptual, social and cognitive emphasis. Every communication act occurs within a given cultural complex but also alters or sustains that complex, and is thus a "choice" to promote a certain view of expression, which involves a manifestation of expression as such. This manifestation I have called a "spiration," in so far as it is from this instituting that a border between different positions emerges such that a politics can take place. These three components of said, saying and site apply not just to the spoken word, but throughout media of communication.

The (re)discovery of praxis in the postmodern turn occurred not through an abandonment of thought but through an intensification of reflexion. The critique of philosophy by Marx and Nietzsche, which showed that its ideal of internal development as the unfolding of the Idea occluded the praxis from which it

emerged, was possible through an intensification of the philosophical notion of critique. This is apparent in Marx's recalling of
his debt to Hegel in the 1873 Afterword to the second German
edition of *Capital* and also in Nietzsche's admission of the piety of
his work: "We godless anti-metaphysicians still take our fire, too,
from the flame lit by a faith that is thousands of years old, that
Christian faith that was also the faith of Plato, that God is the
truth, that truth is divine."[2] This intensification of reflexion leads
to a constitutive paradox for the enunciating subject. It is continued by Husserl, whose transcendental–phenomenological
reduction consists in putting aside (but not denying) any belief in
the existence of the world apart from its perception. This radicalization of philosophical doubt has a double consequence. It opens
up new investigations of the constitution of the world (since presuppositions about its being have been dropped) but, even more
important, it demonstrates the irreducibility of reflexion to any
given state of the world and allows a radical investigation of the
nature of reflexion itself—the wonder of a relation between living-
in and "seeing" the living-in that can never coincide. Reflexion and
embodied history are opposites without mediation, though each is
manifested in every communication which, therefore, has a constitutively paradoxical character.

Several aspects of the concept of media of communication
derive from its character as reflexivity within embodied history, a
tension between philosophy and situation. A medium of communication initially appears to be simply the manifest form in which
a communication content occurs, from which derives the conventional lineage of media forms—orality, writing, print, photograph,
gramophone, etc. But, in the version developed here, a medium is
also understood as that which makes the communication possible.

That is to say, while there is an immanent history of media forms, there is also a transcendental history of the constitution of media forms themselves. Put another way, every speech act occurs *within* a medium of communication but also *through* its medium of communication, amplifies the notion of expression that is constitutive of human Being itself. This notion of expression, though it is manifested within the immanent history of media of communication, is, in a certain sense, the *presupposition* of the immanent history. Every determinate history of media forms is expressible due to the phenomenon of expression itself. Thus, while every immanent history tends toward systematic formulation, it also presupposes a transcendental history that undoes its systematicity. Through this doubling, or constitutive paradox, immanent history is turned "outside" toward a wonder at the phenomenon of expression itself. A theory of media of communication as human science is concerned with the immanent history of media forms, but it presupposes a philosophy of media forms in which the transcendental possibility of expression itself is manifested. This possibility is manifested in the phenomenon of silence, which gives expression an ethical twist, and transforms the general agonistics of embodied history.

What possibility of expression is manifested in disembodied sign-systems? If every sign overflows its system as praxis, how is it possible that the idea of a sign-system as a system of self-reference can arise? The supposedly disembodied sign has to be understood more exactly as a certain historical form of embodiment. It consists in a doubling within the human body that is the origin of the phenomenon of expression and the medium of communication manifested in orality which provides the basis for humanism. The body, in the same double sense of institution, is both an origin of expression and is enfolded within an immanent cultural complex. Within the latter it may be disciplined (in Foucault's sense), but it always contains the possibility of an original perspective from which to view the world (in Husserl's sense). The expressive body is thus a "folding-in," whereby an expressive origin is folded within immanence to produce an exhaustive set of self-references that constitute a system. The modern epoch is constituted by such a folding-within of its origin, a making-systematic of what originates every system. This immanent closure is achieved through inscribing within the immanent of the manifestation of immanence itself. Such a turning-inward constitutes a certain epochal form as a closure of the unboundedness of the manifestation of expression itself. Modernity achieved this closure by figuring the transcendental manifestation of immanence as a moment witin the internal self-development of immanence. Dis-figuring this closure allows the instituting of epochal forms to become visible as such.

The embodied history and reflexivity of the theory of media of communication is the point at which the discursive turn in the human sciences and philosophy may turn from being an expression of modernity into its critique. Uncovering sites of inscription shifts the concern with signs toward the materiality of expressive forms themselves. This materiality constitutes a "form of life" (Wittgenstein) "in its characteristic style" (Husserl) such that "as men produce their life, so they are" (Marx). It also opens on to the manifestation of expression itself, which is not closed within a given form of life. An immanent history of expressive forms is the mirror-image, as it were, of the transcendental manifestation that is the philosophical constitution of the phenomenon of expression. Manifestation enters into immanent history only in glimpses. It is these glimpses that institute historical epochs, and which philosophy must dis-figure when it rediscovers the unbounded. When social movements confront existing institutions with their incipient forms of instituting anew, they assert the practical dis-figurations with which the reflexive allegiance of philosophy finds its embodied solidarity.

NOTES

1. Husserl claimed that signs are defined by intention and are thus distinguishable in principle from hoof-prints and other "natural" signs. Husserl's analysis is correct from the viewpoint of the scientific language that concerns him, but it is not a general theory of signs. As a consequence, neither can it properly demarcate the scientific use of signs. The present argument orients the origin of signs toward the question of the face of the Other described by Levinas. All signs orignate in an ethical beckoning. See Edmund Husserl, *Logical Investigations*, trans. J. N. Findley (London: Routledge and Kegan Paul, 1970) p. 280.

2. Friedrich Nietzsche, *The Gay Science*, trans. Walter Kaufmann (New York: Random House, 1974) p. 283; Book Five, aphorism 344.

INDEX

Adorno, Theodor 32, 36, 37,
   228, 230
alienation 73–4, 160
Althusser, Louis 53, 63, 64, 75
Aristotle 104–8, 224
articulation 52, 57, 62–87

Bakhtin, Mikhail 39
Beauvoir, Simone de 54
Beckett, Samuel 249
border 150–52, 155, 179, 247,
   249, 259
Burke, Kenneth 108

Canada 60, 115
capitalism 1, 159, 174
common sense 22, 28–32,
   47–8, 61, 98, 124
communication xii, 7, 13, 18,
   23, 36, 99, 102–26,
   130–52, 167
   medium of 18–19, 97,

99–101, 104, 114–16,
   120–26, 134, 138–41,
   146–9, 182 n12
contingency 52, 61–2, 67–9,
   75–87, 92, 197
critique 4, 5–6, 7, 14, 15, 22,
   23, 28, 30, 33–49, 126,
   129–30, 232, 235–6, 245
   epochal 92–3, 96, 99, 126,
      151
   restricted 22–3, 92
   totalizing 33–40

deconstruction 57, 62, 65,
   83–4, 239
democracy 103–4, 129–52
   radical xi, 31, 129, 131, 141,
      147, 150–51
Derrida, Jacques 36, 37, 136,
   147, 210 n11
Descartes, René 51, 73, 100,
   156

dialectic 63–4, 105–6, 135,
    164, 168, 170, 174–5, 182
    n20
discourse xi, 4–5, 7, 8–12,
    16–18, 19, 23, 24, 26 n11,
    33, 97–9, 116, 220, 221–3,
    226, 232
    field of 65, 71, 75, 85,
        226–30, 236–51

enlightenment xi, 32–4, 45,
    228
epoch 14, 16, 23, 28, 30, 31–2,
    35, 47–8, 70, 75, 99,
    115–26, 216–17, 256,
    262
ethics 19, 22, 24, 56, 155–81,
    185–209, 251

Foucault, Michel 36, 51, 187,
    262
foundationalism 60, 66, 106,
    116, 126
Frankfurt School xi, 32, 34, 35,
    39, 42, 43
Frege, Gottlob 105
Freud, Sigmund 15

Gadamer, Hans-Georg 6,
    109–11, 232–3
Gergen, Kenneth 5
gnoseology 21, 185, 188–91,
    193, 195, 200, 203, 206–9,
    218, 251
Goody, Jack 113

Gramsci, Antonio xi, 15, 18,
    58–9
Grant, George 31, 77–8, 84

Habermas, Jürgen 6, 36–8, 43,
    46, 210 n2, 231–3, 234,
    236
Havelock, Eric 117–18
Hegel, G.W.F. xii, 16, 20, 22,
    28, 32, 33, 54–7, 63, 65,
    71, 73, 74, 87, 148, 157–8,
    215–16, 228–9
hegemony 58, 61–2, 65–6, 68,
    77, 78, 85, 98, 196, 243,
    250
Heidegger, Martin xi, 15, 18,
    52, 77, 118, 152, 180,
    241
hermeneutics 6, 46, 101,
    109–13, 203, 226–8, 231,
    232, 236
horizon 21, 24, 31–2, 38, 47,
    56, 58, 61–2, 66–70, 88 n8,
    93–6, 123, 146–52, 201
Horkheimer, Max 32, 35, 36,
    228
Husserl, Edmund 7, 20, 21, 29,
    51, 54, 55, 61, 67–8, 72,
    95–6, 100, 152, 163,
    165–8, 171, 174, 185–6,
    188–203, 214, 218, 259,
    262

ideology 12, 32–3, 48
    critique of 7–11, 32, 35, 92

immediacy 28, 54–7, 67–8
Innis, Harold 114–15
institution 29–31, 99–100, 115–26, 144
institutions 43–6, 97–8, 103, 104

Jakobson, Roman 18–19
Jay, Martin 36

Kant, Immanuel 74, 87, 156–8
Keane, John 142–3, 230, 236, 239
Kierkegaard, Søren 56

Laclau, Ernesto 26 n11, 52, 57–87
Landgrebe, Ludwig 189, 196–8
language xii, 6, 16–18, 20, 23, 26 n11, 51, 105, 219–23, 233, 249
Lefort, Claude 29, 30
Lévi-Strauss, Claude 114
Levinas, Emmanuel 22, 178, 185, 188–9, 191–3, 195, 200–203, 205–9
Luhmann, Niklas 43–6
Lukács, Georg 76
Lyotard, Jean-François 36, 39, 210 n11, 223, 233–5, 238, 241

McLuhan, Marshall 135
Macpherson, C.B. 131

madness 243, 245, 246–7
Marx, Karl 2, 7–13, 14, 21, 28, 54, 57, 120, 159–61, 260, 262
Marxism 10, 11, 14, 15, 52–3, 57, 63, 64
Merleau-Ponty, Maurice 29, 54, 194, 195
metaphor 17–18, 26 n11
metaphysics 52–4, 62, 65, 76, 96, 101, 106–8, 112–13, 158–9, 170, 176
end, closure, of 57, 93–5, 116, 135, 139, 162
modernity 1, 56, 62, 70–75, 148, 154, 162, 177, 179–81, 228–9, 236, 256–8, 262
Mouffe, Chantal 26 n11, 52, 57–87

Nietzsche, Friedrich 2, 13–15, 21, 32, 36, 37, 38, 47, 93–5, 122, 161–2, 186, 187, 216, 260

paradox 22, 28, 33, 36–49, 51–2, 92, 120, 124–6, 260, 261
particular(ity) 14, 15, 30, 47–8, 52, 58, 61–2, 76–87, 129, 242, 245
phenomenology xi, 21, 53–7, 62, 66–75, 184, 189–209

philosophy xii, 2–4, 10–11, 14,
    15, 17, 19–24, 28–31, 39,
    43, 44, 45–9, 51–2, 78–82,
    188, 196–7, 203, 208,
    214–21, 225–6, 240, 251,
    263
    ancient 21, 72, 106, 117–18,
        184, 220, 248
    modern xi, 15, 20–21, 43,
        63, 184, 199, 207, 248
Plato 14, 20, 72, 94, 118, 224,
    249
poetry 23–4, 77, 128 n26, 240
postmodernity 1, 4, 16, 28, 30,
    48, 70, 95, 113, 116, 126,
    129, 145, 152, 163–4,
    175–7, 179–81, 188, 199,
    219, 223–51
post-structuralism 62, 194
praxis 12–13, 21, 51, 53, 162,
    171, 186, 258, 261

reduction
    axiological 202–3, 207–9
    transcendental 22, 24, 89 n26,
        164, 187, 189, 196–8,
        201–3, 207–9, 220
representation 7, 12, 23, 73,
    146, 162, 188, 222–3, 225,
    238, 246, 257
rhetoric 23–4, 40, 42, 43, 64,
    76, 80–82, 83, 84, 101–2,
    104–9, 118, 121, 135–6,
    219, 223–51
    general 85, 220, 224

restricted 224–5
Ricoeur, Paul 109–11, 137
Rorty, Richard 6, 226–7, 232,
    234, 238

Sartre, Jean-Paul 54, 79–80, 81,
    83, 134–5, 168–9, 171–2,
    177
Scheler, Max 72
Schütz, Alfred 66
Searle, John 105
silence 150–51, 179, 191, 209,
    226, 229, 247–9
social constructionism 5, 46
social movements 58, 60–61,
    143, 206, 263
society 19, 24, 33
speech 19, 24, 26 n11, 109–10,
    137, 229
step back 61, 84–5
structuralism 52–4

totality 16, 28, 29, 30–49,
    52–4, 57–87, 93–5, 145–6,
    161
transcendental ego 193–5,
    211–12 n24
translation 70, 124, 138–9,
    145, 148–52, 220, 231,
    233, 237–51

universal(ity) 22, 50 n11, 52,
    58, 61, 70, 72, 77–87, 129,
    156, 214, 228, 235, 242,
    245, 237–51

universalization 26 n11, 62, 77,
86–7

Watt, Ian 113
Weber, Max 76

Wittgenstein, Ludwig 5, 6, 26
n11, 46, 262
writing 109–11, 137–8, 147

Žižek, Slavoj 86

DATE DUE

			Printed in USA

HIGHSMITH #45230